THEY CALL ME
BIG HOUSE

JOHN F. BLAIR, PUBLISHER
WINSTON-SALEM, NORTH CAROLINA

THEY CALL ME BIG HOUSE

Clarence E. Gaines
with Clint Johnson

The paper in this book meets the guidelines
for permanence and durability of the Committee on
Production Guidelines for Book Longevity
of the Council on Library Resources

Design by Debra Long Hampton
Cover photo coutesy of Naismith Memorial Basketball Hall of Fame

Library of Congress Cataloging-in-Publication Data

Gaines, Clarence E.
They call me Big House / by Clarence E. Gaines with Clint
Johnson.
p.   cm.
Includes index.
ISBN 0-89587-303-6 (alk. paper)
1. Gaines, Clarence E. 2. Basketball coaches—United States—
Biography. 3. Winston-Salem State University Rams (Basketball
team) I. Johnson, Clint, 1953- II. Title.
GV884.G25A3 2004
796.323'092—dc22
2004011450

I want to dedicate this book to my mother, Olivia; my father, Lester; my grandparents; and all those aunts and uncles who helped raise me back in Paducah, Kentucky. All of us might have been dirt poor in the Depression, but I was made rich by the love and confidence they showed in me.

I also want to thank my wife, Clara, for sticking with me through thick and thin for more than 50 years.

If I am "somebody" today, I owe it all to my relatives and my bride.

Contents

Foreword

Eight hundred twenty-eight wins. Division II national champion. Twelve CIAA crowns. The coach of Cleo Hill and Earl "the Pearl" Monroe. All are records and achievements of the man known as Big House. His records are now known to all, but to me he is so much more than records. To me, Clarence "Big House" Gaines is one of the truly great individuals I have ever known.

I will never forget our first meeting, when as a cocky sophomore at Wake Forest I went across town to see Winston-Salem State play and to check out their so-called superstar, Cleo Hill. As I entered the gym, it never crossed my mind that I was a white man on a black man's campus. I was there to watch a game, and to see for myself whether this hotshot could play, and probably also to see if the man called House could coach or just roll out the ball. I don't know how House saw me, but within minutes I heard a voice: "Son, why don't you come over here and sit on our bench?" He was always the gentleman, always a person who opened up to others, and always a man who thought way ahead of the rest.

It wasn't long before I developed a great relationship with Cleo and his teammates. And as I look back on those great days when we scrimmaged against each other, we were probably under the watchful eye of House. Yes, oh, yes, Cleo could really play, and House could really coach.

My respect for House grew as each year went by, for as an assistant coach at Wake Forest I often went over to State to observe his training methods and stern discipline, but also his great ability to communicate with his players.

When John Thompson led Georgetown to the NCAA championship in 1984, he commented, "If I am a pioneer as the first black coach to win the national championship, it is only because men more qualified than I were wrongly denied the opportunity." Great wisdom from a Hall of Famer, who certainly was referring to men like John McLendon and Coach Gaines.

When I moved on to a career in broadcasting, I could always count on Coach for constructive comments—comments that I cherish to this day, comments with as much insight as any TV executive has ever given me. He has always possessed the ability to provide an honest appraisal, and even if it was less than positive, you always came away better prepared to face future challenges.

House has given so much to so many. He was a solid force in the days of racial tension in Winston-Salem, a great leader for the Boy Scouts, an accomplished administrator, a father figure for so many young men in need of guidance, a devoted partner to his beautiful wife, Clara. This book is about a true Hall of Famer in every respect of his life. The man called Big House is someone whose friendship I will always treasure. Thanks, Coach, for your help and guidance to all of us.

Billy Packer

They Call Me
Big House

CHAPTER 1

Crossing Over to the White Side

I first noticed the same questions being asked when the basketball team I coached, the Winston-Salem State University Rams, racked up a few victories that brought me closer to the 500th win in my college coaching career. Hard-core fans and sports reporters all agreed that this "milestone" was supposed to mean something to me.

"What is it going to feel like when you win that 500th game?"

"How many do you expect to win in your career?"

"Do you think you will ever break Kentucky coach Adolph Rupp's record?"

"What's your secret to winning all these games?"

I must have heard these questions dozens of times, and I answered them in some fashion as best I could. Still, the best answer was one I finally gave to a reporter who looked puzzled when he wrote it down.

"When you start driving to California from North Carolina, eventually you will get there."

That answer really is self-explanatory. I coached basketball at Winston-Salem Teachers College, which later grew into Winston-Salem State

University, from 1946 through the 1992-93 season. That's 47 years, made up of 47 teams of young men playing at least 20 games.

Winning each game was like driving another 10 miles down the road toward California. If my teams won enough games, and I stayed on as their coach long enough, eventually I would get to whatever coaching record I would have.

As it turned out, my personal record is 828 wins. When I left coaching in 1993, that was good enough to rank first among black coaches and second on the all-time collegiate wins list to Rupp's 876. In the 11 years since I retired, three other coaches—Dean Smith, now retired from the University of North Carolina in Chapel Hill; Bobby Knight, still the coach at Texas Tech University in Lubbock; and Jim Phelan, now retired from Mount Saint Mary's College in Emmitsburg, Maryland— passed me on the total number of wins. At the time of this writing in the spring of 2004, I am now fifth on the all-time list but still the top black coach.

I am proud to have stayed around long enough to reach that "destination" of 828 wins, but there were a few blown tires along the way. I also have a record of 447 losses.

Rupp virtually created the whole concept of basketball as a serious collegiate sport. Smith produced two national champions and 13 ACC championships in NCAA Division I, and Bobby Knight has three national championships and one of the highest graduation rates in college history. But I am also proud that Jim Phelan joined me on the winning-coaches list. Coach Phelan and Mount Saint Mary's College helped me demonstrate that small colleges in Division II can play basketball that is just as exciting as that played by the Division I schools.

But to repeat a cliché, winning isn't everything. There are other more important aspects of my career of which I am also proud.

I graduated players with real college degrees who left school armed with the knowledge they could do something more important than sinking a three-point basket.

While many schools concentrate on producing basketball championships that generate money to run their multimillion-dollar programs, I concentrated on producing young men who could earn their way in

*I don't remember what year this was taken, but I appreciate the young
fan's sentiment that WSSU was number one.*

(PHOTO COURTESY OF CENTRAL INTERCOLLEGIATE ATHLETIC ASSOCIATION)

the world long after their playing days were over. The latest NCAA graduation-rate data, if you believe it—and I am not sure I do—says about 45 percent of male college basketball players graduate. I think the actual number is much lower. At any rate, I estimate that at least 80 percent of my players graduated from college to become teachers, principals, school administrators, recreation directors, doctors, lawyers, and all types of professionals. There were even a few who strayed really far afield and became college coaches. I don't know how that happened, but I know they were—and are—successful at it. One of them, Monte Ross, is an assistant coach at Saint Joseph's University, which was the nation's only undefeated Division I team at the end of the regular season in 2004.

I know what happened to almost every player who played for me over those 47 years. I "fired" some—sent them home because they simply were not college material. Of that group, I sent a few to the only professional team then accepting black players, the Harlem Globetrotters. They became stars at playing ball when they couldn't become stars in the classroom.

I came along at just the right time in history to witness and to play a small part in the crossing over of black sports talent from segregated black colleges into the professional basketball ranks. Later, I would be there to watch the mainstream universities that had once been reserved for white people accept their first black players.

What I experienced starting in the early 1950s and continuing through the early 1970s was an awakening on the part of white people that the time had come to let black people compete on equal terms on the baseball diamonds, the basketball courts, and the football fields.

Young athletes who today play for scholarships at Division I universities and who then leave school early to sign multimillion-dollar professional basketball and football contracts have no sense of how black athletes in earlier decades paved the way. Today's sports stars believe being welcomed into expensive restaurants and high-class hotels is just part of the benefits of being a good ballplayer. They believe being interviewed on national television comes as part of the contracts they sign. They think of endorsement contracts as their birthright because

In this photograph, two historically black colleges face off. Winston-Salem State's Stenson Conley (#32) jumps center against Elizabeth City State University. Also facing the camera are Tom Paulin (#14) and Carlos Terry (#42).

(WINSTON-SALEM STATE UNIVERSITY ARCHIVES)

they can handle a basketball or a football a little better than anyone else on the playground.

The young men I coached in the '40s, '50s, and '60s knew better.

The basketball pioneers I coached knew that even integrated Northern and Midwestern colleges sometimes barred black athletes from living on campus because no one wanted to room with black kids. The kids I coached knew I could not take them in the front door of a restaurant before a game and order food as a coach would for any team of white athletes. We could go to the back door and be served the same meal the white folks were eating out front, but sitting with those white folks was forbidden. The young men who played for me knew they could use only the "colored" bathrooms when we stopped on the road for gasoline. If the gas stations were too small to have separate facilities, we had to walk into the woods and "hide our waists," as the saying went.

Segregation went to extreme lengths. Some cities banned interracial athletic competition by issuing written regulations barring two different races from playing against each other. White high schools and colleges did not play black high schools and colleges, so there were no natural cross-town rivalries. Even pickup basketball games between white and black players were literally illegal.

It was in this sort of environment that I began coaching in 1945.

I will tell my story, but I don't think I can properly relate my small contribution toward breaking down racial barriers between whites and blacks without telling the story of a much more famous, much more important man in the history of sports. It was really his sacrifice that laid the groundwork for me and thousands of other black athletes and coaches to be successful. I never knew him personally. I saw him play, and I still remember how talented he was. He was one of the best athletes—white or black—ever to put on a professional sports team's uniform.

The man's name was Jackie Robinson.

For several years starting in the early 1940s, the white president of the Brooklyn Dodgers, Branch Rickey, had been thinking about integrating Major League Baseball, as much to tap the black market for more ticket sales as to end an obvious inequality between black and white athletes. The source for those players would be the Negro Leagues, an entirely separate league of black professionals who played among themselves, just as the white National and American Leagues played each other.

Rickey believed that the first black man to try to break into white professional baseball would have it rough both from the fans and other players.

He decided to stack the deck in his favor by looking for the perfect black man for the job. He sent scouts to the Negro Leagues to find a young, black player who seemed most like a white man, or at least one black man whom white baseball fans would find least objectionable.

Jackie Robinson fit that bill. He was a college graduate who had lettered in four sports at the University of California at Los Angeles. He had served in the United States Army as a lieutenant. Most importantly, Robinson was married and devoted to his wife, so the racists lurking on the fringes of baseball would not be able to label him as an opportunist who would use his fame to date white women.

Robinson, who was playing for the Negro League Kansas City Monarchs, knew nothing of what Rickey really wanted him to do. When Robinson and Rickey met face to face for the first time, Robinson thought he was signing to play for the Brown Dodgers, a Negro Leagues team that Rickey had been spreading the rumor he would be starting. That was a lie, a cover story Rickey created so no one would suspect why he really was scouting black ballplayers.

Robinson was shocked when Rickey told him that if he did well playing for the Brooklyn Dodgers' farm team, the Montreal Royals, he would be moved up the next year to the "bigs," the Brooklyn Dodgers.

Rickey asked only one thing of Robinson, that he ignore any insults, slurs, and taunts that might be shouted at him. Robinson bristled at that and asked Rickey if he wanted a player who would not fight back. Rickey replied he wanted a player who had the guts not to fight back.

All of this drama of integrating white sports was being played out in 1946 when I was in my first year of coaching football and basketball at Winston-Salem Teachers College in North Carolina. Following

Robinson's career was easy because a black reporter for the *Baltimore AFRO-American* named Sam Lacy traveled with Robinson all during spring training. Lacy's articles about what happened to Robinson were picked up by black newspapers around the country.

Black coaches and players on the college level had more than a passing interest in what was happening to Robinson. We, too, wanted to play with the white folks because we knew that was where the money was. It was at the white colleges. If Robinson could break into professional baseball and be accepted by white fans, we hoped the effect would trickle down to us.

We knew Robinson's quest would not be easy. For instance, Lacy wrote that, while traveling to spring training camp in Florida, Robinson and his wife were refused service at restaurants. When they stayed overnight in New Orleans, they were turned away from the white hotels and sent to dingy colored hotels. When bumped from a flight to Jacksonville, Florida, they were forced to ride in the back of a cross-country bus. At rest stops, they were directed to colored waiting rooms. The man was a former army officer and an active professional baseball player, but he was treated as if he were some lower form of life.

When Robinson suited up for his first day game with the Royals— the first time in history a black man had ever dressed out for a AAA ball club—he and another black player, Johnny Wright, were met by a delegation of white citizens led by the mayor of Sanford, Florida. The group told Rickey that the town would not stand by while black and white baseball players mixed on the playing field.

Today, that sounds outrageous, but black coaches of any high-school or college sport played in the South could have warned Rickey and Robinson about that rule in 1946. At that period of history, none of us would have dared to suggest an intrasquad game with a white school in our own town.

On March 17, 1946, the farm-team Royals played an exhibition game against their parent team, the Dodgers. Robinson went hitless that day and the Royals lost 7-2, as might be expected when a AAA team faced a major-league team.

But a barrier had been broken. A black man had played in a major-league baseball game. According to the newspaper reports, something surprising happened. The few boos heard from the predominately white crowd were more than drowned by the cheers of the other fans, who included more than 1,000 black fans who sat in a segregated section along the first-base line.

That the whites gave only a few boos was astounding to the other owners of major-league baseball teams. They had convinced themselves that white people would not only reject black players but might even turn violent if they saw a black player on the field.

That did not happen. White people just watched the game! It was a simple fact, but a welcome revelation among us black coaches and players who recognized what had just happened. White people had enjoyed a baseball game with a black man on the team, and nothing serious had happened. This groundbreaking game had turned out to be just another game. The big news was that there was no big news— no riot by white fans, no walkout by white fans, no nothing by white fans.

Still, some Southern cities went overboard in their reaction to Robinson's presence on the team. Nothing was too ridiculous. We read in Lacy's articles of how the city of Jacksonville padlocked a stadium rather than hold an exhibition game in which two black players would participate. The cities of Savannah and Richmond sent word to the Dodgers and Royals that they wanted nothing to do with the two black players. Scheduled games in those cities were also canceled.

The next year, 1947, Robinson officially integrated the big leagues. Just as he had promised Rickey, Robinson did not argue with the umpires. He did not yell insults back into the crowd. He just ignored what slurs he heard and let his playing skills silence his critics.

In 1949, with the permission of Rickey, the real Jackie Robinson burst forth. He became more open with his teammates. He argued with umpires. He jabbed back at the opposing players. He stopped being a black ballplayer and fully joined the team as just another ballplayer. That year, he won the Most Valuable Player award.

Like most black people, and maybe because I was a college coach, I was pleased with Robinson's success. I read everything I could about his games. He really was not new to me or many other black baseball fans. I had seen him play several times when he was with the Negro Leagues, and I went to see him play with the Royals and the Dodgers. He was living history to any black person interested in sports, as I was.

Robinson was a good ballplayer, though I have to agree with the critics that he was not the best black ballplayer in the sport, just one of the best players on the field when he was on a white team. That is not meant as a knock against the white players. It is just that there were many better players in the Negro Leagues who did not meet Rickey's strict requirements.

I was pleased with Robinson's crossing over into white sports, but I was not pleased with what I saw and heard in the stands. I am not talking about the occasional catcalls from the white people. Those were to be expected.

I was more disturbed with what I heard from the black fans.

What I heard when Robinson was on the field were loud cheers and clapping. I saw standing ovations. What I saw irritated me as a baseball fan.

Whenever Robinson would catch a pop fly, the blacks in the crowd would cheer. When he would snag an easy grounder hit to him at first base, they would cheer. When he would hit a single and run to first base, the black people in our segregated bleachers would roar as loudly as if he had hit a home run.

I expect Robinson was as embarrassed to hear those cheers as I was.

Robinson was doing what he was supposed to be doing as a professional baseball player. Yet his fans were stamping their feet, clapping their hands, and shouting their praise as if he were hitting grand slams and making impossible catches.

Those black people were so starved for the sight of a black man competing successfully with whites that they cheered simple actions.

I wanted those black fans to act like white fans. The white fans ignored the white players until they did something worthwhile. They held their applause, giving it only when their favorite players deserved it. They cheered when a hustling runner made it to second on a hit that should have been a single, not when a batter sauntered to first base on a single to the outfield.

That is what all sports fans—black or white—should do. You cheer excellence. You accept the merely competent.

My father loved baseball. One weekend when I was home visiting, he drove my uncle and me 175 miles from our home in Paducah, Kentucky, to St. Louis just to see Jackie Robinson play against the St. Louis Cardinals. It meant a day without pay for my father, plus the cost of tickets, gasoline, and food on the road, but he wanted us to witness the history that was being made for black people in sports.

From my seat in the stands, I could see the whites' reactions to all that black cheering. They were amused. In 1946 and 1947, before Jackie proved that he was the very best player of any color on the field, the white baseball fans believed that he was there as a marketing ploy. The whites thought Robinson's presence was all about separating the black fans from their money, rather than giving a black man the chance he deserved.

By applauding Robinson's every move, those black fans were degrading not only him and the talent he possessed, they were also degrading themselves. They were forgetting what was really important about Robinson's place on the field at shortstop and first base.

He belonged there! He was the best ballplayer, whether at shortstop or first base!

It was time in 1947 to recognize that talent—athletic or otherwise—knows no color boundaries. That is why Rickey demanded that Robinson not respond to any of the taunts that would be thrown at him from the stands. Rickey understood that Robinson's talent for playing the sport was much bigger and better than anyone's prejudice against skin color. If Robinson could prove on the baseball diamond that he had the talent to play for the Dodgers and was not just there as some kind of social experiment, then the white "boo birds" in the bleachers would look foolish.

It took only two years for that to happen. Robinson's breaking into the major leagues in 1947 was important, but I think that his winning

Most photographers liked to shoot me from a low angle, so I would look even bigger than I really was.

(PHOTO COURTESY OF CENTRAL COLLEGIATE ATHLETIC ASSOCIATION)

the Most Valuable Player award in 1949 was even more important. It proved beyond a doubt that he belonged on the diamond, and that the rest of us black people should have our chance to prove ourselves equal to the white race.

Today, not even 60 years after Jackie Robinson blazed the trail on the professional level, sports—professional, college, high school, junior high, and club—are one of the most color-blind of all aspects of society. If a player has the talent to make any team in any sport, he or she does. If the talent is lacking at any level, the player is dropped without any consideration that race had anything to do with it. Athletic ability, not the color of one's skin, determines the roster of the teams from junior high right through the professional ranks.

And that is the way it should be in our society. We should reward talent and strive to be so valuable in our careers that employers need us in order to be successful. In particular, black people should not do less than we are capable of doing just to get along in society. If we blacks don't take every opportunity to prove what we can do, we run the risk of being jeered as Jackie Robinson was by people who think we are being given something just because we are black.

But even when we break through to equal treatment, we have to remember that using our talent is still much more important than overcoming common prejudice. That is what those cheering black folks at those games forgot. The blacks accepted Robinson's mediocre play, while Rickey knew Robinson had to be the best at his position in order to be accepted by the white players and fans.

This desire of black people to be accepted in white society is evident in all kinds of ways. I remember walking into the Wachovia Bank in Winston-Salem not long after its managers had made the decision to integrate its teller staff in the late 1960s. Behind the teller windows was a young, light-skinned black woman I knew had just graduated from Winston-Salem Teachers College. Apparently, the bank's managers had hired her thinking that her light skin would be more acceptable to their white customers than if she had been blacker.

I knew her to be a very bright, articulate young woman who had not only a college degree but also the brain power to make it at anything she wanted to do. She could have gone on to graduate school and qualified to become a professor. At the very least, she would have been one of the best, most confident schoolteachers any system would have been proud to have.

Instead, she was satisfied with a teller's job that likely paid her the same amount of money as she would have made flipping burgers. Like those early Jackie Robinson supporters in the stands cheering him for gloving grounders, she was happy just to be behind the previously all-white teller cage. She had been accepted. Instead of applying to the bank's corporate management training programs, the equivalent of what Robinson had done, she had settled for a teller's job.

If I have a message for young people of any color reading this book, it is this: Don't settle. Don't go to school just to be accepted, or without a purpose in mind. Use the opportunity given to you, just as Jackie Robinson used the opportunity given to him. Cross over into whatever field interests you—education, law, medicine, science, or sports.

The following chapters will detail my life in sports and education. This may be my autobiography, but I want readers to note how many young men used the opportunity given them to become successful in life. That is what my most important contribution has been—not in coaching basketball games but in coaching young men to leave their mark on our society.

CHAPTER 2

The Best Raising a Boy Could Have

No one in my family knows how both of my parents' ancestors came to Paducah, Kentucky, a small city of 26,000 in the far western tip of Kentucky, where Illinois and Missouri meet along the Ohio River. They could have come from anywhere. Southern Illinois is across the river. Eastern Missouri is 30 miles to the west. Western Tennessee is 60 miles south. Southern Indiana is 60 miles to the east.

I know a little bit about my mother's people. In her recorded oral history, she said her grandfather, Ambrose Bolen, was a slave, probably born on one of Kentucky's plantations, which held 30 percent of the black population of the state until the Civil War. Ambrose somehow made his way to Paducah and opened a blacksmith shop on land he purchased, so he must have been a resourceful and successful business-man. Years later, the city took his land by eminent domain to put up a water treatment plant.

I've never seen any photos of Ambrose, but I wonder if it is his genes that I inherited that led to my eventual size of six-foot-five and

Here I am at age three in my backyard in Paducah, Kentucky. Notice the outhouse and the doghouse? I still have most of that curly hair.

(Clarence E. Gaines Collection at Winston-Salem State University)

265 pounds. Blacksmiths were usually the strongest and biggest men in a community, made even more fit from constantly swinging heavy hammers against their anvils to form steel and iron tools.

If Ambrose was the source of my size, I thank him. Being large always came in handy when it came to impressing—and frightening—new college basketball and football players I would have to coach. All of them claim to remember seeing me for the first time and resolving right then never to give me any trouble. Few of them ever did.

I never asked my father about his people, and he never told me about the origins of the Gaines family and how we came to Kentucky. My father was a quiet man who may not have known about his ancestry and never asked his father. If my father did know his history, he might not have considered it as important as caring for his family in a poor neighborhood of 1920s Kentucky.

By the time I came along as Clarence Edward Gaines on May 21, 1923, the only child of Lester Gaines and Olivia Bolen Gaines, black people were somewhat rare in western Kentucky. After the Civil War, most of them started moving across the river into the North, where they could find industrial jobs in the big cities. There certainly was not much future in rural Kentucky, where sharecropping remained the standard way many black people made their living well into the 20th century. Whatever the reason, I know there were not many black folks in my neck of the woods when I came along. Kentucky's black population had dropped to 7 percent in the decade in which I was born, down from 30 percent in the old slavery days.

I think it is safe to say that being born black in 1920s Kentucky was challenging. My family was part of a small minority in a small city in a small state in the sparsely settled rural South, where mixing of the races in any social setting was frowned upon, if not outright forbidden, by local and state laws.

Still, I don't remember any outright racial discrimination or violence of the Ku Klux Klan variety against the black population of Paducah. To my knowledge, the white power structure in town didn't try to do anything to us. Black people in Paducah were kind of like the Ohio River. We were just there, part of the landscape of the city. Maybe it was because we black people were such a small minority that the white people never worried that we would try to become part of their power structure. We represented no threat to the white folks, so they left us alone.

That doesn't mean that black people were ignored. We were needed to fill the lower-paying jobs in the few, small factories in town. We were a necessary part of the labor force, and in that capacity we were welcomed and appreciated—as long as we knew our place. That is not an indictment of Paducah then or now. It was just the way it was in most areas of the country, North and South, in the 1920s. White people held most of the good jobs, and the black people filled the lower jobs.

While many think the two-income family is something new that came along when the baby-boom generation wanted bigger houses, it was quite common in the poor communities of the South for both father and mother to work.

This photo was my mother's gift to my father in 1955.
Born as Olivia, people called her Ola.

I am not quite sure how Lester and Olivia—called "Ola" by most people in Paducah—met, but I suspect it must have either been in our segregated grade school or in the neighborhood. The black community was just a couple thousand people. They very likely would have known each other since they were children.

I know that they must have met each other early in life because they were married as teenagers. Marrying that young was not uncommon in those days, particularly in the South, in Kentucky, and in the black community.

My father did anything and everything to put food on the table for his family. He dropped out of school after the sixth grade to take his first full-time job. He was a cowboy—not the kind you see in the John Wayne movies roping longhorns on the open range, but the kind who took care of dairy cows by moving them from pasture to barn by walking along behind them and waving his hat.

He became best known in our town as a cook in two of the local white hotels, the Ritz and Boswell's Hotel. My father was a good cook by all accounts, as he was always in demand. He must have been a lucky man, too. One morning when he arrived at work to begin the day's cooking at Boswell's, the gas stove exploded when he struck a match. Speculation was that a slow gas leak allowed the gas to accumulate in the bottom of the stove. According to the stories told to me, the explosion literally blew my father through a wall in the hotel. He ended up outside the building with the stove. I remember when they brought him home he was covered in bandages—so much gauze we couldn't recognize him.

After a few days, he got up out of bed, stripped off the bandages, and left for work. Somehow, an explosion that should have killed my father and left my mother a young widow with a young child left him only slightly injured but with a determination that he had to return to work to provide for his family.

I sometimes wonder about that incident, which happened when I was very young. Perhaps God, knowing a little boy needs a father, had sent a guardian angel to save my own father so I could grow up knowing the role a father provides for his family. In my career as a coach,

21

My father Lester cooked at two different hotels in Paducah.
Unfortunately, I don't know the name of his buddy on the car.

(CLARENCE E. GAINES COLLECTION AT WINSTON-SALEM STATE UNIVERSITY)

when I was dealing with athletes who often spent their youth without a man around their house, I would usually employ the same quiet, firm manner my own father used to raise me.

When my father was not cooking, he became what I call a jackleg carpenter, a man who could hire on at any job site that would take black people and fill any role that construction site needed. As I recall, he sometimes found work building dams and levees on the Ohio. He often had to cross the river to get work in Illinois and Indiana because he could join the carpenters' union in the Northern states. In those days, a black man could not compete with white union carpenters in Southern states such as Kentucky. All of his carpentry and building skills were self-taught.

I don't think I could have asked for a better daddy than Lester

Gaines. His number-one goal in his married life was taking care of his wife and his son. Though it seemed as if he worked most of the time to earn a living for his family, he also found the time to take me fishing and hunting. He also taught me how to hit a baseball and toss a football, but I think it was my basketball-playing mother who must have taught me how to dribble a basketball.

My father also liked professional sports, and he would split gas money with his brother Raymond to drive us to St. Louis to watch professional baseball. Sometimes, it would be to watch the white professional team, the St. Louis Cardinals, play. In those days, St. Louis was a powerhouse in the National League. I saw white players like Dizzy Dean, Leo "the Lip" Durocher, and other members of the Gas House Gang beat just about every team that came to St. Louis.

Later, when Jackie Robinson joined the Dodgers, my father would naturally pull for Jackie's team even when they faced his Cardinals.

Of course, my father, my uncle, and I had to watch the games from the bleachers segregated for black fans. Baseball's owners wanted the money from black folks, but they didn't want us sitting next to the white folks.

We also had teams to root for who looked like us. Sometimes, we would go up and watch a Negro League game with the St. Louis Stars playing the New York Black Yankees, the Birmingham Black Barons, or the New York Cubans. When we went to those games, we could sit anywhere we wanted.

I still remember those days sitting in the baseball stands with my father and uncle watching the action on the field and sharing hot dogs, popcorn, and soft drinks. If I had a wish for any child, any boy or girl of any color, it would be that they would have the opportunity to enjoy that sort of experience with one or both of their parents. I knew what it meant for my father to take a day off from work to spend time with me. I treasure those memories. I wish every father would take that sort of time to show his children how much he loves spending time with them.

My mother contributed as much to the family income as my father. It was the job she held most of my youth that helped shape my future experience with race relations.

Here I am at age 13. Judging from the coat, it appears winter is coming. Notice how my mother bought my coats several sizes too large so I could wear them as I grew.

(Clarence E. Gaines Collection at Winston-Salem State University)

Not long after I was born, my mother got a job stacking staves at a cooperage. With that description of my mother's occupation and the puzzled looks that must be on the faces of some readers, I think I have proven just how old I am.

When I was born 81 years ago, cooperages were a common type of factory in many small towns. They were not only common, they were thriving. A cooperage is a factory that makes wooden barrels. Staves are the wooden slats that are arranged in a tongue-and-groove fashion vertically and then bound by an iron ring to form the shape of the barrel.

Making barrels was a more complicated business than it might sound. My mother had to sort the staves into three barrel grades—"slack," for common storage and shipping of dry products such as crackers and apples; "oil," for shipping liquids such as vinegar and wine; and "bourbon," for the highest-grade barrels, which were used to store and age whiskey for the distilleries that operated in that part of the South.

Life in our part of the world in those days was not the bright lights of the big-city flappers like you see in those old newsreels describing the Roaring 20s in New York City and Chicago. Most of the lower classes in Paducah were more than just poor. We were dirt poor, with little hope of ever getting out of that class. Our only chance to get out of that poverty was to use an elementary and high-school education and the all-but-unthinkable dream of a college degree.

What some people might find surprising is that our poor community was not separated by race. Lacking money is not a black-and-white concept. It is a green concept—the color of dollar bills. At our level in the society of Paducah, in the Mechanicsburg neighborhood along Jackson Street, there was no such thing as legally enforced segregation. Poor whites lived side by side with poor blacks. We black folks didn't think it odd, and those white folks didn't think it odd. We were all poor together.

This shared situation forced the poor blacks and whites to get along with each other, to help each other, to appreciate each other. While the wealthy whites in Paducah might have thought of our community as black with some "poor white trash" living in it, the people who lived in Mechanicsburg never thought of it that way at all. It was just our community. It was where we lived among our neighbors of all colors.

That common, shared experience in my first neighborhood taught me something as a child that has stayed with me for the rest of my life. What divides people racially is often not the color of one's skin and the expectations the races have about each other based on that pigment color. What divides people is more likely based on the education or talent people have and the manner in which those people use that education or talent to succeed.

It is not always race that divides us, but economic and social class. While I might not have understood the sophisticated versions of that concept as a child, I must have recognized it on a simple basis.

In Mechanicsburg, if someone slaughtered a hog for a barbecue, everyone on the street was invited. And yes, in the 1920s, it was not uncommon for families in town neighborhoods to keep livestock. Our family had livestock, as did most everyone else. If you traded garden greens with your white neighbor for a few chickens, you always sent over a chicken pot pie. If your white neighbor had more collard greens, turnips, onions, or carrots than he needed, and he owed his black neighbor a favor, he dropped off the produce on the neighbor's front step. You never worried the gift might be stolen from those steps. Neighbors didn't steal from neighbors.

Being neighbors went beyond just sharing extra food. It meant life and death.

No one in our community had the money to go to the hospital in those days for something routine, such as having babies. We had midwives, self-trained women who knew how to help other women deliver their children. We had white and black midwives in our neighborhood, and it did not matter to them the color of the expectant mother. If the white pregnant mother needed help from a black midwife, she got it. If a white midwife knew how to properly set a broken arm, the black man thought nothing of asking her help.

When someone died in our neighborhood, they received a decent burial, taken to their resting place by white and black pallbearers. The preacher might have had a black or white face, and in the congregation would be a mixture of skin colors to send the departed to a better world.

My family also shaped my lifetime experiences. When my mother could not be at home because she was working, my mother's mother, Ida Bolen, kept me. My grandmother was a deeply religious person who had a habit of going into a corner of a room to pray. In the morning, she would start off praying very softly in a whisper. As she went on asking the Lord's blessing on her family, she would get louder and louder, until she would wake up my mother and father and me—and maybe the neighbors. My mother remembered that my grandmother

Somewhere in that crowd is me being baptized. Look in the background. My baptism stopped barge traffic on the Ohio River!

(Clarence E. Gaines Collection at Winston-Salem State University)

would sometimes go into the corner of a hayloft or sometimes a store to pray when the need to ask the Lord's help came over her. We weren't embarrassed by her beliefs. Shoot, if Grandmother Bolen could get the Lord's attention by praying in the corner of a store, more power to her.

I know Grandmother Bolen loved me, but one time I must have disappointed her. When I was baptized, it was done by full immersion in the Ohio River. As the preacher was leading me up out of the river, my grandmother called down, asking me how I felt. She was expecting me to answer with some sort of religious awakening.

I answered, "That water's c-c-c-c-c-cold."

I've always been a realist.

Grandmother Bolen had one major belief that passed down through my mother to me: "If you lose your character, you have lost everything. All the money in the world will not make up for ever losing your character."

My mother passed that belief in character down to me, and I instilled it in my own children as well as the boys I coached in football and basketball.

My mother and father also passed on a sense of thriftiness that I tried to instill in my family and my surrogate family of athletes. I remember my parents always were careful about saving their money—at least a nickel out of every dollar they earned. They practiced what modern-day financial advisers preach: Pay yourself first.

The Depression was very cruel to everyone, including my parents. I know our family lost around $1,000 in a savings account when the local bank failed early in the Depression. That sum may not sound like much today, but in the 1930s it was a significant nest egg and a testament to what good savers my parents were.

Being good with finances ran in my family. Across the street from my house was my uncle Manuel Bolen, one of my mother's brothers. Uncle Manuel was the entrepreneur in the family. Every weekend, he held a barbecue in his backyard, selling sandwiches right off the grill to customers. He alternated the menu between pork and goat.

My uncle knew how to cater to the marketplace. Most of his customers were white people who heard by word of mouth in Paducah that Uncle Manuel was a great cook who understood controlling the heat of a fire made the difference in the taste of the meat.

And like all good cooks, Uncle Manuel had a secret recipe for his barbecue sauce. He gave it to me before he died. I've since lost it somewhere around my house in Winston-Salem. If my friends and acquaintances ever hear that I have become suddenly wealthy, it will not be because of anything coming from Winston-Salem State University. It will mean I have found that piece of paper with the barbecue sauce recipe. I remember the sauce being very tasty and bringing out the best flavor in my uncle's particular method of slow-cooking that meat.

Uncle Manuel was a very persuasive individual. When he was still a teenager, he convinced his mother, my maternal grandmother, Ida Conner Bolen, to mortgage the house to give him the operating capital to open The Crystal Creamery, an ice-cream factory. That made Uncle Manuel the first black man to operate a business on Paducah's Main Street. The factory made good ice cream. He had to change locations at least once to move to bigger quarters. It was such a success that when the draft board thought about drafting Uncle Manuel to go to Europe in World War I, they decided it was more important that he stay at home and make ice cream so it could be shipped overseas.

I know I have some Bolen genes in me that would make Uncle Manuel proud. I have a weakness for eating good ice cream. I've been known to pull off the highway in any number of towns in any number of states and drive directly to the best ice-cream parlor in that town. If your town has the best peach ice cream in the country and I don't already know about it, drop me a line with directions to the ice-cream parlor.

Uncle Manuel did not stop with ice-cream factories. Later, he operated Paducah's first black-owned taxi, and somehow he thought there was a market for mirror replating in Paducah. I know the taxi business was successful, and I've been told that even the mirror replating was one of those ideas that Uncle Manuel had that was ahead of its time.

My life changed for the better while I was still a baby, long before I was old enough to know that it was changing. It was a change that would help me understand white people and learn how to deal with them for my entire career.

One day in 1924, Hollis Johnson, owner of the Paducah Cooperage Company, was given an ultimatum by his wife, Florence Anne Johnson. He had two choices. Either Mr. Johnson could ask his two brothers and his wife's brother to move out of the Johnson house, or Mr. Johnson could find someone to do the laundry and house chores. Besides the three extra adults living in the house with Mr. and Mrs. Johnson were three children—Hollis Jr., Mary Anne, and one-year-old Dick, who was just a few months older than I.

Mr. Johnson rarely ignored the wishes of his wife. She was tough and demanding, but never without reason. He knew if he tried to ignore her demands, his brothers and brother-in-law would soon find themselves out on the street looking for a boardinghouse.

After hanging up the phone, Mr. Johnson walked outside of his office. He saw a teenage black girl he had hired to stack wooden staves.

"Ola, would you rather stack staves here at the factory or go to my house and help my wife with the household chores?" he called.

Within minutes of the phone call from Mrs. Johnson, Ola Gaines, my mother, was in Mr. Johnson's car on the way to his house.

I think it says something about the character of both women—Ola Gaines and Florence Johnson—that they immediately took to each other.

My mother was a poor black teenager with a baby—me—who was being taken care of by her mother while she worked in a barrel factory. She knew very little about housework in general, much less what might be expected of a domestic worker in a white household.

Florence was a color-blind woman who knew immediately that she would have to teach this inexperienced girl everything she needed to know about running a household.

This working relationship between the black Gaines family and the white Johnson family would last for more than 25 years, outliving Mrs. Johnson and continuing until Mr. Johnson remarried in the late 1940s. Dick and I, both in our 80s, are still telephone friends. His brother and sister have passed, but to demonstrate how close that family remained to mine beyond the time my mother worked for them, it was Mary Anne, the Johnsons' daughter, who took care of my mother when she became ill. Later, Mary Anne would make all of the funeral arrangements when my mother passed away.

My mother did everything the "domestics" did in those days, six days a week, counting a half day on Saturday. When Mrs. Johnson entered a long illness in the late 1930s, my mother took on even more chores, such as ordering the groceries and running family errands. It was a job that required that she sometimes drive the Johnson family car, something that did not sit well with all of the upper-class whites in Paducah.

To their credit, the Johnsons did not care what their white peers thought about the way they treated their black employee, my mother. Over time, she became more than a domestic servant. She became a trusted employee, then a friend, and then somewhat of a family member. As Mrs. Johnson grew more sickly, my mother took on the role of a surrogate mother to the three children.

According to my friend Dick, one of Mr. Johnson's brothers learned soon enough that my mother held a valued role in the Johnson household. When he made some kind of disparaging comment to my mother that must have related to their separation by class or race, Mrs. Johnson made it clear to him that there would be changes made in that kind of behavior on his part.

"You will apologize to Ola this instant, or you will pack your bags and leave my house," came the icy command from an unwavering Mrs. Johnson.

The brother-in-law stammered an apology to my mother. Never again would my mother hear a derogatory comment from any member of the Johnson household. Whatever the white people of Paducah might have been saying under their breath and behind the Johnsons' backs about my mother's standing in their household, they never dared to say it out loud to Mr. and Mrs. Johnson. Those white folks knew that the Johnsons' loyalty lay with my mother, and it always would.

My personal relationship with the Johnsons went beyond my mother's employment with them. Often, she would take me along when she went to work. As a baby, I would share a playpen with Dick. As the three Johnson children and I grew up, we became playmates and friends. I would come to their house to play, and sometimes when Mr. and Mrs. Johnson had to be somewhere, my mother would bring the children over to my house. It was quite natural, and color never made a bit of difference.

Actually, now that I think about it, color would sometimes intrude into our play.

When Dick, Hollis, and Mary Anne would come play at my house, the social rules were a little different than when I went over to their house. But those changes were so subtle that the Johnson kids were adults before they even noticed or remembered that things had been different when they played with my black friends at my house.

When these white kids from the upper crust came into my poor neighborhood to play, they always were treated with more respect than any of the regular neighborhood kids, black or white. If the game were tag, the Johnsons never started off being "it." If the game were hide-and-seek, the Johnsons always hid first, and one of the poor kids would be the first one to go seeking.

If any of the games involved someone starting off with an advantage, that advantage always went to the Johnson kids. We poor black kids and poor white kids always deferred to the wealthier white kids. It was the way it was done in those days. We poor kids didn't think twice about it, and the rich Johnson kids never even realized it.

While it might sound like a cliché, my childhood with the Johnsons and their white friends was something like the classic *Little Rascals* comedies where the little white children from all social and economic classes include their little black friend in all their games and mischief. I didn't think anything about my being the only black child playing with them, and neither did they. I can't remember a single instance in my childhood when my skin color came up in the conversation among my white friends. I cannot remember a single time when any of my white friends became angry with me and called me a racial name.

Though we were friends as children, the Johnsons and I never let that friendship affect our character. I was reminded of that by an incident Dick Johnson remembered from a sandlot baseball game that took place more than 70 years ago.

Dick and his white friends had chosen up sides into two teams. Since I was the only black child, it seemed only natural—at least in the minds of the other kids—that I should be umpire. Looking back on it, I guess I should have been doubly proud. Not only were they ignoring my race, but all of them knew that I was Dick's friend. They still trusted me to call the game fairly.

The game was in the bottom of the ninth inning, and the other team playing against Dick's team was up by one run. Two outs were already counted against Dick's team when he came to bat. He was his team's last chance.

I think Dick struck at the first two pitches and missed both of them. His team was one pitch away from either losing the game or having a chance to tie and send the game into extra innings.

The next pitch came, and it was right down the middle of the strike zone. For some reason even he does not recall, Dick never swung the bat.

I had no choice. I called my friend out on a called strike three. The game was over. Dick and his friends had lost not on the field but because Dick's black friend had called him out on a judgment call.

Not one white boy on that losing team—all of Dick's friends—questioned my call. They had selected me as umpire, and they had agreed in advance with the other team that what I said as an umpire would be official. Dick did not question me at all. He knew the ball had been across the plate, and he knew that he had watched it rather than swing at it. No one argued with me. No one called me any names. We just all packed up our gear and walked back to the Johnson kitchen for some soft drinks, me included.

As we children grew older and approached adulthood, the social pressures became more pronounced on both whites and blacks. While white legal officials could turn a blind eye to children playing with one another, it was something else when those children grew into teenagers.

The social standards of the Old South were pretty rigid. Black adults who knew white people could greet them on the street and exchange pleasantries, but black people had to defer to whites. If the sidewalk was crowded, black people had to move into the street. No white acquaintance, no matter how well he knew the black, would ever dare to invite his black friend to eat at a lunch counter. Neither would the black friend ever dare to think about accepting such an invitation.

The same rules, written and unwritten, applied to us. My white buddies could speak and nod at me in recognition when we passed each other on Paducah's sidewalks, but the days of sharing sodas in a home kitchen could not be duplicated in public. While Dick's mother could hand me an ice-cream cone in the privacy of her own home, she did not dare take me downtown, take me inside a drugstore, and offer me the same flavor. Her children—my playmates—could not try the same thing, using the excuse that they were children. Such mixing of the races in an open public setting was literally against the law—which was, of course, much more important than just being against the social norms.

The Johnsons could stand the whispers they got from the white establishment by allowing their black maid to drive their car to the grocery store. That was not against the law. But it would have been foolish for them to buck both social norms and the law by trying to take me or my parents into a white restaurant.

No one, particularly blacks who lived through it, would ever say that segregation made any sense.

Looking back on it today, most people, whites and blacks, think the rules of segregation exposed a silliness and cruelty that even the white people of the day would have a hard time explaining.

Though my father, Lester, cooked for the cream of white society, if he were to walk out the back door, then walk in the front door and into the dining room of the same hotel that employed him, he would not have been served. He likely would have been arrested.

My father could cook for white people, but he could not eat with them. He could be in the kitchen pouring water into glasses for the white patrons of the restaurant, but he could not drink from a whites-only water fountain in the lobby of that hotel. He could point to the bathroom in the hotel lobby when a white person needed it, but he could not use those same facilities himself.

What in the world was the difference between the two acts of serving white people and then associating with them in the social setting of a restaurant? We black folks never figured it out, and I doubt the thinking white folks ever did either.

Safety was certainly not part of the equation. If a black cook had any racial animosity in his heart, he could do much more damage to white folks back in the kitchen than he could eating beside them. The only explanation is that white people wanted to eat only with their peers, and that did not include the black people preparing the meals.

As the Johnson kids and I grew up, our interests shifted to other activities, such as organized school sports. We saw less of each other because we went to separate white and black high schools. Our new circles of friends and girlfriends did not intersect as much as they did when we were more interested in who was "it" during hide-and-seek.

As I grew older and started my teenage years, my mother, Olivia, became more determined that I would "be somebody," as she put it. She wasn't sure what that meant and where it would take me, but she

Look at the difference between me at ages 13 (see photo on page 24) and 15! I grew rapidly in height and bulk in my middle teenage years.

(CLARENCE E. GAINES COLLECTION AT WINSTON-SALEM STATE UNIVERSITY)

knew she wanted me to have every advantage that she and my father never had. My mother was a high-school graduate, and she insisted that I would go farther than she. She knew that education likely meant I would leave Paducah and never return to live, but she also knew that was what it would take for me to become a successful black man in a white man's world.

My mother arranged with a neighbor to teach me piano. Later, she bought a trumpet on time so I could become a member of the Lincoln High School band. At halftime during basketball games, I would not go into the shower room for a rest. I would climb up into the stands and grab my trumpet and join the band.

My parents made sure I understood social responsibility. I became one of the school crossing guards in junior high. I recall they had a hard time finding a helmet and one of those over-the-shoulder belts that would fit me.

When my mother found out that the black high school did not offer typing classes as the white high school did, she bought a second-hand typewriter from a neighbor for a dollar down and a dollar a week. She then found a tutor to teach me typing. She wasn't sure if my future career would ever involve typing, but she knew if learning typing was important for white kids, it would be doubly important that black kids learn the skill as well.

My mother also encouraged me to join the Boy Scouts of America, an association which I maintain today 70 years after becoming a Scout. Experiencing Scouting as a black child during the 1930s took some ingenuity. We were not allowed to camp with the white Scouts at the regular Boy Scout camp, so my mother and my Scout leader, Tommy Withrow, borrowed some sleeping bags and camping gear. They took us down to a makeshift camp on the Ohio River. I am not sure they had permission from the landowner to camp there, but it was only for a weekend, and they wanted us to feel like real Scouts.

I credit Tommy Withrow with being my first role model outside of my family. We called him "Coach," and he taught us sports and how to be responsible young men. As we grew older, we took care of him. Tommy would sometimes drink to excess, so those of us with driver's licenses formed a network to make sure he got where he needed to go without getting behind the wheel. He had kept us safe as kids, so we kept him safe when we became teenagers.

Puberty for me came hard and fast. I had been born a normal-sized baby and had not been much bigger than any other kid in my age group until junior high. Then some genes from both sides of my family must have joined together in a chain reaction. I started to grow. Both my parents were normal sized, so it came as a big surprise to them when I continued to grow into what in those days was somewhat of a giant.

By the time I entered high school, I was almost at my top height and weight of six-foot-five and 265 pounds. Some of my friends called me "Sully," after a large comic-strip boxer named Sullivan.

Though I was bigger than any of my friends and just about everyone in Paducah, I never used my size to any advantage. I was never a bully, never tried to be intimidating with anyone other than on the football field, when being intimidating was supposed to be part of the game.

The only time I can remember ever using my size in high school was when I stopped off at the Johnson house to pick up my mother. My white friend Dick, who had not seen me in several years, since we had both become teenagers, came into the living room. He started playfully slapping at me, trying to goad me into one of our old wrestling matches.

I was sitting down, and my newly found size was not apparent to Dick. And just as puberty had been kind to me in giving me a large, muscular frame, it had been unkind to Dick. He was small—not much larger than he had been when we were both children of the same size.

Dick, oblivious to the fact that the old friend with whom he was now messing had grown into a giant, kept slapping at me, trying to make me stand. Finally, I had enough.

I leaped from the couch, snatched him up, and held him over my head like a weightlifter would clean-and-jerk a 100-pound barbell, which was about what Dick weighed. I extended my arms and held my friend over my head so Dick's back was touching the nine-foot ceiling in his home.

"Are you going to leave me alone, Dick, or am I going to walk away and let you fall nine feet to the floor?" I asked him.

Dick now knew how much I had grown since we last saw each other. I let him down without snapping his back like a twig. There were no hard feelings, just a sense from Dick that he would never underestimate his opponent again. I like to think he was able to use that teenage experience later in his career as a lawyer in Johnson City, Tennessee. Though our lives went in two different directions after we both left Paducah, I still count him as part of my family.

Participating in high-school sports, or at least trying out for the teams in a small town, was expected of most kids whether they were athletically inclined or not. When the coaches saw me walk up for try-outs, their eyes grew wide with anticipation. I have to say that I did not let them down.

I was probably the biggest tackle Lincoln High School's football team had ever had in their history. In fact, I was one of the biggest tackles my conference had ever seen. It was not hard to play good ball in those days, when I would outweigh most other tackles by 50 to 100 pounds. I don't remember my high school's won-loss record. We won three conference championships, and I developed a reputation in the state as a good tackle.

Basketball was a different story. Some folks might find it unusual that I consider my basketball skills adequate but not outstanding. I was just so big that opponents had to find ways to get around me, but I was never a big scorer. To demonstrate how big I was, the school did not have any basketball shorts that would fit me. My mother had to pay a woman to make me a pair of shorts to wear on the court. I probably had the only pair of tailor-made basketball shorts in the history of Lincoln High School. That may still be true. I don't remember any of my high-school scoring records in basketball, which tells me that they were nothing to remember.

During my last three years in high school, my mother and father encouraged me to spend the summers with my mother's brother Lawrence Bolen, who lived in Newark, New Jersey.

Uncle Lawrence was a baseball freak. He loved to watch it at all levels, from the Negro League teams like the Newark Eagles right up to the Brooklyn Dodgers, where we had to sit in segregated bleachers.

But Uncle Lawrence also liked basketball. He was a big fan of the New York Renaissance, named after the second-floor Harlem dance hall where they played most of their home games.

The "Rens," as they were called, barnstormed the country in the '20s and '30s, playing pickup games with local black high-school and college players. Sometimes in the North, they would play white teams. While many people are familiar with the comic performances put on by the Harlem Globetrotters today, the Rens were a real professional

In this photograph, I'm a high school sophomore.

basketball team who played serious basketball. They had a phenomenal won-loss record of 2,588-539. At one time, they won 88 games in a row in one 86-day stretch. Their star players were men like Charles "Tarzan" Cooper, James "Pappy" Ricks, and "Wee" Willie Smith. They were men who could probably go toe-to-toe with the best in the NBA today. The most amazing thing was that there were only seven men, whereas a full squad of college players today is 14 men.

As a wide-eyed teenager in the late 1930s watching these men work magic on the court, I never imagined playing college basketball, or coaching it. I certainly never imagined that one day there would be a national network of professional basketball players duplicating the skills I saw displayed while watching the Rens.

CHAPTER 3

Morgan State College Builds a Boy into a Big House

When I graduated from Paducah's Lincoln High School in the summer of 1941, third in a class of 35 students, I realized that I was about to start on the road to fulfilling my mother's dream that I should "be somebody." My grades in high school had been good, and my football skills were more than good. They were great. Some newspaper reporters called me the top tackle in the state, white or black.

The network of my parents' friends went into high gear trying to find a college that would give me a scholarship, since my parents did not have the money. I did not apply to any white colleges. Most of the white colleges I knew about did not accept blacks.

Before I graduated, my high-school coach, Buddy Ferrell, started writing letters to college coaches describing my skills. He really did not care where I went, as long as I went somewhere. One of the schools he targeted was Morgan State College in Baltimore, because

41

This photograph shows the difference in size between me and Louis Ballard, one of our fastest—and smallest— running backs at Morgan State.

(Photo courtesy of Afro-American Newspapers Archives and Research Center)

it had a reputation among black colleges for its powerful football team.

While my coach could describe my playing skills, he was not the only one helping me make contacts with the colleges. Mrs. Mundy, a lady in my church, Burk's Chapel A.M.E., acted as the unofficial college-placement officer for all of the black kids in our town who had the grades to get into college. She contacted Howard University in Washington, D.C., because she knew that the head of the college's religion department at the time was a Paducah native. Our family doctor, Philip Fernandez, had run on the track team with the coach at Morgan State College, so he called there on my behalf, plus he had gone to medical school at Howard University, so he gave me a contact associated with Howard. My high-school principal, who was a graduate of Lincoln University in Pennsylvania, naturally wanted me to go to his alma mater, so he made contacts with those coaches.

People accustomed to hearing stories today about how high-school sports stars are courted by universities from the time they are in elementary school and junior high have a hard time understanding college recruiting in the 1940s.

Black colleges, even the largest of them, had no recruiting budgets and no talent scouts paid to watch for news coverage or to visit the high-school games to evaluate promising athletes. There were no letters of intent signed in a high-school senior's living room with the press all around to record the moment. There were no make-work jobs at local boosters' companies to ensure the kids had walking-around money. There were no "understandings" made with a recruit's parents to make sure he signed with the highest-paying university.

Black colleges relied on people in communities to send them good prospects. Once the young men arrived on campus, they tried out for the team. If the coaches liked what they saw, they said, "You are on the team. Go get a uniform and then go see about signing up for a scholarship."

Most important of all, those black college teams were composed of true student-athletes. We were students who were in college to learn a profession. There was no dream of playing for a professional football team. Those teams were all white. There were no "football classes" on the theory of sportsmanship, designed to ease the jocks through four years of college. We took the same classes as regular students.

There was not much glamour being a football player in those days. We were poor black kids trying to go to poor black colleges where even the best of the facilities would be rated inadequate by most white college standards. We were going to college to learn how to do something with our minds. Playing sports was one way to get into college so we could get that education.

By the end of the summer after my high-school graduation, I had been accepted academically and tentatively awarded athletic scholarships by all three schools at which I had applied—Lincoln, Howard, and Morgan State. I had not left home to visit any of these three schools. I had never even been in any of the three cities in which they were located. None of the football and basketball coaches at these three schools had ever seen me in any game films. There were no game films. None of the coaches had ever come to my house to meet me or my parents.

My acceptance at the colleges had all been on the strength of my network of contacts in Paducah calling their network of contacts at those three schools and assuring them that I could not only make it academically but also perform on the football field. This method of using trusted contacts around the nation to recruit promising athletes would be something I would call my own once I started my career as a coach.

Some Kentuckians might ask why I did not at least look at any nearby black schools, such as Kentucky State College at Frankfort. I didn't for two reasons: my hometown network had no contacts at that school, and I wanted to spread my wings a little. Like any young man, I was ready to leave home, and Lincoln, Howard, and Morgan State were far away from my parents. I was ready for a little adventure, and it was just as well that my mother was not going to be nearby to monitor those adventures.

My plan for deciding in which school I would finally enroll was quite simple. Since they had all accepted me, I would visit each one and accept the scholarship of the one I decided suited me and my assumed career plans. My major would be chemistry. My mother had already decided for me that the goal to "be somebody" in her eyes would be fulfilled if I became a dentist.

She—I guess I had some say in the matter, but I really don't remember—had decided that getting into dental school after four years of undergraduate work would be easier than getting into medical school.

She—and I—also figured that dentists would always be in demand, like doctors and morticians. Each small town in the South always had a black doctor, a black dentist, and a black undertaker. Those men almost always had prominent civic standing in their communities, and they were generally well compensated because segregation laws virtually guaranteed them a locked-in market.

Most white dentists would not open the mouths of black people, so the financial incentive for me to become a dentist was obvious. While the white medical professionals were splitting the larger white market among themselves, the smaller black market for health services was more concentrated because there were so few black professionals.

That fall, as school and football tryouts approached, I climbed into a car in Paducah with Buster Lee, a lawyer who happened to be home visiting his parents. He worked for the *Pittsburgh Courier* newspaper, but he also had family in Washington, D.C., so he would take me around to the colleges I was scouting.

Once again, the network of black friends would pay off. My parents could not afford to take time off from their jobs to drive me all the way to these colleges in the Northeast, more than 800 miles from Paducah.

As we drove northward, I read through the meager materials I had on the three schools.

Howard, in Washington, D.C., was, and still is, one of the best and most famous of the black colleges. It offered chemistry, and it had a dental school. Lincoln, about an hour south of Philadelphia, was a men-only school, but it had a reputation for turning out lawyers and doctors—the kind of "somebodies" that my mother hoped I would become. Morgan State in Baltimore had only recently become a state college. I was already leaning in its direction because it had a reputation of having a strong football team.

Howard was the first school I visited. Immediately, a glitch occurred in my plans to evaluate the schools. Between the time my friends had contacted him and the fall semester, Howard's football coach had been fired. Though I had no loyalty to the coach, since I had never met him, his firing made me nervous. When I talked to the coach in person, he told me in a roundabout way—without really telling me—that he believed Howard's administration was in the process of de-emphasizing athletics, and that his firing was part of that process. He broadly hinted to me that I could find myself on a football team that might be disbanded during my college career. If the team disbanded, so would my scholarship.

After I crossed off Howard, Buster and I drove the 30 miles to Baltimore and pulled up in front of the athletic department at Morgan State. I unfolded myself out of the cramped little two-door Ford coupe and proceeded to stretch my six-foot-five frame to work out the kinks from riding in the car for several days. By that time, I had probably put on a few pounds over the summer with my mother's cooking. I might have been over 265 pounds, probably the heaviest I had ever been in my whole life.

As I stretched beside the car, the business manager of Morgan State's athletics department, James "Stump" Carter, walked past. He was a little guy, so my height and weight were even more impressive to him. He stopped in midstride, looked me up and down, whistled, and said, loud enough for several people to hear, "Man! The only thing I've ever seen bigger than you is a house!"

Stump and Buster took me in to see Eddie Hurt, who coached both football and track at Morgan State.

I'm not sure what I expected of the coach of the Morgan State College Bears, one of the most powerful and famous black college sports programs in the nation, but it wasn't what I saw in front of me.

Coach Eddie Hurt was a tiny, well-dressed, skinny man who might have weighed 140 pounds if he carried rocks in his pockets. I literally outweighed him by a person—at least 120 pounds.

Coach Hurt was not much to look at, but his looks belied what he had been able to do in recruiting and then coaching his student-athletes. When I came to Morgan State in the fall of 1941, Coach Hurt had

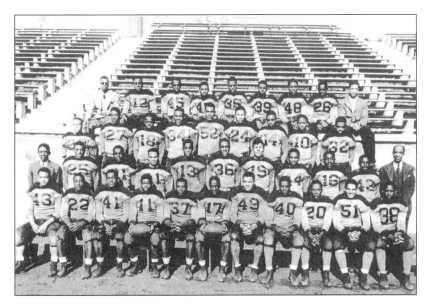

Here is the 1941 Morgan State College football team. I am in the middle of the front row (#49). My friend Alvin "Boo" Brown, who came to Winston-Salem Teachers College as my first assistant coach, is right behind me (#19). The coach on the left is Eddie Hurt. The coach on the right is Talmadge Hill, one of the founders of the CIAA basketball tournament.

been at the school for 12 years. He had already won several Colored Intercollegiate Athletic Association (the original name for what is now the Central Intercollegiate Athletic Association, or CIAA) football championships and several track-and-field championships. Before he left Morgan State, Eddie Hurt, as either coach or athletic director, would win 13 CIAA championships in football, four CIAA championships in basketball, and 15 CIAA championships in track, and his track stars would win 16 individual national championships. In Coach Hurt's career, 11 of his football teams would go undefeated. In 1943, one of the years I played, his team would not allow another team to even score during the entire season.

When Stump mentioned the bigger-than-a-house comment to Coach Hurt, the coach gave a little smile. Most of his football players had some sort of nickname. I had just been given mine, though I had not even put on a uniform.

I didn't mind my new nickname. It was better than "Sully," my high-school nickname. "Big House" had a nice style to it. It fit. I *was* bigger than a house, and anyone who heard the name would know what it meant.

And while I am talking about my nickname, I want to correct a mistake newspaper and magazine reporters have been making for decades. My nickname is "Big House," two words, *not* "Bighouse," one word, but the way it generally has appeared in print. How "Big House" came to be "Bighouse" in the minds of sports reporters is something I have never understood. I never bothered to correct the misperception. It was too much trouble, and newspaper reporters are notoriously hard-headed about correcting their mistakes once they get into print.

I had no trouble making Coach Hurt's team and no trouble capturing the attention of the black sports press. Sam Lacy, the sportswriter for the *Baltimore AFRO-American*—the same man who would cover Jackie Robinson breaking into baseball in 1946—noted my arrival on campus in one of his 1941 columns.

A college football player who tipped the scales at 265 pounds was big news in those days. People wanted to get a look at this huge Kentuckian, so I garnered some fame before any games were even played. One photo from 1941 shows me with my arm extended. Standing under my arm is Louis Ballard, another freshman, who turned out to be a good, if tiny, running back. Another picture from 1941 shows me dressed up in the thick pads that we wore during tackling practice so we would not injure ourselves. I look like a giant version of the Pillsbury Doughboy.

I might have been more of a doughboy than I wanted to admit. Carrying a little extra fat had never mattered much in high school. The boys on the opposing teams had never been as big and as strong as I was, so I was never challenged. But college football was going to be different, and Coach Hurt knew I would be playing against the best from many high schools. He decided to play a little psychology on me.

During one of our early workouts in my freshman year, he began

These pads pictured in this photo were designed to help protect the players. When we didn't have tackling dummies, we tackled each other.

(PHOTO COURTESY OF AFRO-AMERICAN NEWSPAPERS ARCHIVES AND RESEARCH CENTER)

to question my weight, asking me how much of my bulk was fat, how much was muscle, and how much that fat slowed me down.

Even though both he and I knew that I was a fast runner for a big man, Coach Hurt challenged me to a footrace. He wanted to prove, in his mind and in my own mind, that I was slower than I could be because I weighed more than he wanted me to weigh.

I looked at this scrawny little man who must have been at least twice my age. I readily agreed to race him to prove I was not as out of shape as he was claiming. I had forgotten that the man was also the coach of the best college track team—black or white—in the nation. He easily beat me in our one lap around the track. When he finished the race, he was lounging around the finish line, smiling, while I was huffing and puffing my way back to where we had started.

When I returned to campus for my sophomore year, I had gone from a slightly flabby 265 pounds to a solidly muscled, strong-as-a-bull 238 pounds. When Coach Hurt saw what I had become by lifting weights and running, he challenged me to another footrace. In this race in my second year, I beat him, though I recall the margin was somewhat close.

It wasn't until years later, when I was coaching young men to have confidence in themselves, that I began to wonder if Coach Hurt had let me win that second footrace. I never asked him if he threw our race for my benefit, and he never volunteered that he did. Still, from that experience, I learned that a coach can inspire young men by rewarding them for their efforts. It did not always matter if the young man won or lost. In either case, he learned something about himself.

I entered the fall of 1941 as one of Morgan State's 200 freshmen, the largest class in the school's history, with students from 14 states and the District of Columbia. In looking at a picture of about 100 members of our freshman class, I count only 30 men. The rest were pretty girls. That is all I will say about that subject because I have been married for more than 54 years to the woman God intended me to marry, Clara Lucille Berry. I did not meet her until moving to Winston-Salem to take my job as assistant coach at Winston-Salem Teachers College.

Academically, I did okay at Morgan State. There were a few classes that gave me fits. I barely passed calculus. Even today, I cannot quite tell you what calculus is and why it was important for me to learn it.

I did well in my chosen major, chemistry, which I assumed would give me a good background for applying to dental school. But I do remember one incident from my college days when my knowledge of chemistry failed me.

I think it was a homecoming party when a few of us adventurous boys figured it would be fun to spike the punch with some locally obtained gin. We slipped the bottles into the dance hall and poured them into the punch bowl. I'm hazy on the details now, but I know no one felt any effects from the punch. No harm was done, but we also got caught in the act of spiking by one of the college administrators. He sent me to my chemistry professor, who was also my academic adviser.

"Mr. Gaines, do you admit to spiking the punch with gin?" the white professor asked in a slow, deliberate voice as he stared at me over the top of his eyeglasses.

I readily admitted it. I had to. We had been caught with the bottles in our hands. I began to wonder from his tone if I was about to be expelled from school or thrown off my sports teams.

"How much gin did you put in the punch bowl?" the professor asked.

I told him two pints.

"Do you know how big the punch bowl was?" he asked.

I guessed and gave an answer, but I had no idea how many quarts the punch bowl held. All I knew was I had put two pints of gin into it.

"I am disappointed in you, Mr. Gaines. As a chemistry major, you should have known that it would take much more than two pints of gin in that size punch bowl to get anyone drunk. You should have paid more attention in class to our lessons on volume," the professor said as he shooed me out the door.

No punishment was meted out to me on any official level. I don't guess any mention was made of the incident to Coach Hurt, because he never brought it up and did not punish me. As far as I know, nothing was placed in my permanent record.

I was the only starting freshman on the 1941 football team. I don't remember our record, but I do know it was a typical dominating year for Morgan State.

Reporter Sam Lacy of the *AFRO-American* took a shine to me early in my career. After my freshman year, when I had proved to be a good tackle and a fair basketball player, he wrote one entire column questioning why my parents gave me my name of Clarence.

"Kids who were unfortunate enough to have names like Clarence, Ethelbert or Percival tacked onto them were always looked upon as sissies of one variety or another. It was well nigh impossible or so we thought for a guy to overcome the handicap of such a parental misdeed," Lacy wrote.

Even though Lacy wrote in the same piece that I was "a hell-firing football player, a basketball specialist and not at all bad with my dukes," I don't think I ever sent my mother that particular clipping. The article ended with Lacy once again questioning why "Mr. and Mrs. Lester Gaines of Paducah, Kentucky," would ever pick a name like Clarence for their only child.

I don't want to brag, but I dominated my position at tackle. I made All-CIAA all four years and was an All-American for two years. In those days, there was no such thing as offensive and defensive squads and specialists for certain types of offenses. Every player knew how to play both offense and defense. If we were the best players, we were fully expected to play almost the entire game. We might get pulled out once in a while to rest, but it was not uncommon for a player to play both ways all four quarters.

One of the reasons Morgan State dominated our opponents, rarely letting them even score, was because we were so big. One reporter added up the weight of our offensive line and found us to be a total of 1,421 pounds, with an average per man of 205 pounds. I was the heaviest at 265 pounds that freshman year. Our homecoming opponent that season was Virginia Union University. The total weight of their line, which we faced on both offense and defense, was 1,287 pounds, for an average of 184 pounds per man. They weighed an average of 184 pounds to our 205! No wonder we could shove them around the field.

I was a bit of a hero in that particular game when I recovered a

The caption on this photo calls me "a highly regarded tackle." I was just honored that Coach Hurt used me so much my freshman year.

(PHOTO COURTESY OF AFRO-AMERICAN NEWSPAPERS ARCHIVES AND RESEARCH CENTER)

fumble on Virginia Union's two-yard line. The next play, we scored. We won that game 25-0.

It was rough playing football. The pads were thin, nothing like the armor players have today protecting them. The helmets were leather with no face guards. The only protection from getting your nose broken was making sure your opponent's forearm never got close to your face.

One of the toughest players I remember from those days was Ralph Oves, a center and guard at Lincoln. The newspapers listed him at 205 pounds. By all rights, I should have had no problem blocking him or getting past him, as I outweighed him by 60 pounds. But I did have trouble with Ralph. Maybe that was because he was the only white player on an all-black team in an all-black conference. He probably got harassed some by all of the black players he faced, just as the first black players were harassed when they started playing on white teams. Maybe the catcalls Ralph heard made him more determined. I know he was no pushover for me.

It was at Morgan State that I developed some friendships—and rivalries—that continue today. One of those friends was Cal Irvin, who came along one year behind me. For some reason, Cal had never played high-school ball. When Coach Hurt discovered that Cal could run, he had him try out as a running back. He made the team.

As a tackle, it was my job to pull out of the line and clear the way for Cal whenever he would sweep around either end. Cal always trusted me to do that.

"Clarence, if you start running down the middle of the field, I will be right behind you. If you run down the sidelines, I will be behind you. If you run up into the stands, I will be behind you," Cal always told me.

Cal had dreams about following his brother, Monte, into professional baseball, but he never had quite the same skills as Monte, who moved from the Negro Leagues into the Major Leagues not long after Jackie Robinson. Monte eventually became a great ballplayer for the New York Giants, another one of the black pioneers who crossed over into what had been the closed club of white sports.

Cal followed me into coaching. He coached at Johnson C. Smith in Charlotte, North Carolina, before moving on to the school he is most closely associated with, North Carolina A&T in Greensboro. While coaching there, he was a thorn in my side for years, but more about that later.

Another friend I made was Alvin "Boo" Brown, who was a forward

This photo shows the CIAA championship Morgan State College basketball team in 1944-45. Boo Brown is third from left and I am fifth from left. Sixth from left is my skinny buddy, Cal Irvin, who would win fame coaching basketball at Johnson C. Smith University and North Carolina A&T University.

on Morgan State's basketball team when I was the center. We played on two undefeated basketball teams together. I asked him to come down to Winston-Salem to help me as an assistant coach when I was made a 23-year-old head coach. There will be more about Boo later, too.

Though I played on Morgan State's basketball team and we did win CIAA championships while I was there, I always refer to my position on those basketball teams as "right back" rather than center. By "right back," I mean that whenever a forward or guard would pass me the ball, I would pass it right back to them at the first opportunity. My major purpose on the court was to get in the way of the other team's players. Just as I did in high school, I tried to become a big obstacle that they had to overcome to make their baskets.

Sam Lacy wrote elegantly in the *AFRO-American* about my determination to get rid of the ball whenever I got it: "Gaines blossomed into a pivot man that is a pleasure to watch. From it [the pivot] he pours passes to those who move a little faster and shoot a lot better."

Lacy was kind to make me sound so skilled on the basketball court. I don't remember my scoring average, but it had to be on the low side. When sports historians look at my contributions at Morgan State, they rightly concentrate on my four All-CIAA seasons as a football tackle. Though I became a very fair basketball coach, I never excelled at playing the game.

Still, I have to admit that I looked good in the tank top and shorts that were the type of basketball uniform worn in those days. A 1942 photograph of me, after Coach Hurt had convinced me to trim my body fat, shows a handsome young man, if I do say so myself. Imagine a muscular Will Smith or maybe Laurence Fishburne, both Hollywood actors, and you'll get a sense of what I looked like when I was 20 years old.

Once basketball season was over, it was spring and time for track. I was not suited for most of those events. Maybe I could beat skinny little Coach Hurt over the course of a lap, but I suspect he let me win. I was too slow for sprints and too big for long-distance running. I was way too big to jump over hurdles or a high-jump bar or, God forbid, to even think about the pole vault. There wasn't much left to try in track and field. Coach Hurt figured any big man could learn to throw the discus. Coach Hurt was wrong. I never did learn how to throw that heavy pie plate very far.

Of course, World War II always concerned the players. Each year starting in 1941, we lost players who were called into the armed forces. Finally, in 1944, I got a notice to report to the Selective Service office in Baltimore for my draft physical.

I went down to the draft center with a scrawny kid about my age who weighed about 135 pounds. He was even slimmer than Coach Hurt.

I noticed the eyes popping among the doctors conducting the physicals when they saw me walk into the room. I was not only the largest man those bitty young white doctors had ever seen, but more importantly, I was the largest black man they had ever seen.

I passed all of the physical standards, of course, and they sent me into a room with a very nervous, young, white psychiatrist. For some reason, he asked if I liked boys, and I told him, "No, I like girls." He then asked me if I was a joiner. I told him, "No. I am pretty much a loner." I wasn't about to volunteer to him that I was a tackle on the best, most cohesive football team in the nation and that I had plenty of close friends.

The doctor kept asking me questions designed, I guess, to find out if I was suited for army life. Finally, he asked, "Would you like to serve in the army?"

I leaned close to him so he could better sense how much bigger I was than him.

I replied, "No. I don't really care to go into the army. Your army is segregated, and there are not that many jobs you white people will let us black people do. I know if I joined the army at my size, I would probably end up digging ditches. If I am lucky, I might end up driving a truck. If I joined the navy, I would end up as a cook or a steward, as those are the only jobs you white folks let black men do in that branch of the service. I know I am too big to fit into most airplanes, and I doubt you would let me fly anyway, so I don't want to join the Army Air Corps either. If my choices are digging ditches, driving a truck, cooking, or staying in college and finishing my degree, I think I would like to stay in school."

My little speech had the effect I hoped it would have. The white psychiatrist gulped a little as I leaned back in my chair. He made a few notes in my folder before he thanked me for coming down for the physical.

I am sure he must have scribbled that this particular angry, huge black man was not suitable for the armed services. I never got a draft notice, and I never joined. I figured my mother's ambition that I "be somebody" did not include a stint in the army as a ditchdigger.

The little fellow who went down to Selective Service with me was not so lucky. At 135 pounds, he could not look as intimidating as I could. He was drafted. They passed on the 238-pounder and took the runty 135-pounder. They must have figured that skinny black kid would be a whole lot easier to order around than the big black kid.

I ran into that fellow at a bridge tournament some 50 years after that fateful day. We recognized each other and remembered the day both of us went in for a physical. He had no hard feelings toward me or the army because they had taken him but not me. I had no guilt that I had intimidated a handful of white army doctors into letting me finish my college education.

As my final year of college rolled around, I took stock of myself. My grades were good enough to get me into dental school, but the money to go was not there. My living expenses had been taken care of by the sports scholarship, but my pay working part-time at the United States Post Office sorting mail had not yielded enough riches to allow me to pay for dental school.

Looking back on it, I realize now how foolish I was.

I had the grades to get into dental school, but no money to pay for it. For some reason, I and my college counselors never thought about looking for and applying for a scholarship of some kind that would have paid my way. I know now that the demand for black dentists in the 1940s was so great that had I been accepted and started dental school, the school itself would have helped me figure out a way to stay enrolled. Once I was in, I don't think they would have kicked me out because I could not afford to attend.

As I was pondering what to do about dental school, an opportunity came up. At the time, I considered it a short-term fix for my financial problems, something to do until I figured out what I wanted to do.

CHAPTER 4

I Come to Winston-Salem

There I was in the summer of 1945 about to graduate from Morgan State College, and I had no real idea what I was going to do. I wanted to go to dental school, but I had no money. I had not thought about trying to find a scholarship for postgraduate work.

Coach Hurt called me into his office and said that Coach Howard "Brutus" Wilson of Winston-Salem Teachers College in Winston-Salem, North Carolina, wanted to talk to me.

I had met Coach Wilson on a few occasions. He had played quarterback and run track at Morgan State from 1930 through 1934. He would come back to visit Coach Hurt on occasion. I knew he had been the coach at Winston-Salem for four years. He was a short, stocky man who was prematurely balding. I was not at all familiar with the school, though I knew it was a teachers' college populated mostly by girls. I had been in Winston-Salem one time on a weekend trip with a buddy from there. He had not taken me over to see the campus.

Almost as soon as I walked in the door, Coach Wilson said, "I need some help with my program. Coach Hurt says you would make a good assistant coach."

HEAD COACH "BRUTUS" WILSON
(LEFT) AND ASSISTANT COACH
"BIG HOUSE" GAINES

Winston-Salem Teachers College head coach Harold "Brutus"
Wilson may have been short but he was strong as an ox. Notice
how his biceps are larger than mine! This photo was made into a
postcard that cost one cent to mail in 1945.

(Winston-Salem State University Archives)

I was surprised. Not once in the eight years I had been playing high-school and college sports had I even considered coaching, and here was Coach Hurt suggesting to another coach that I should become one.

I knew why he did it. I was a natural learner on the football field. Whenever Coach Hurt would explain some move or strategy to a quarterback, running back, defensive back, linebacker, guard—anyone on the team—I would watch, listen, and learn. I absorbed the role of every position on the team. Coach Hurt noticed that and would sometimes use me to demonstrate what he wanted done. For instance, if he wanted the quarterback to hand the ball off a certain way to the running back, he would ask me to demonstrate it, even though he had no intention of my ever filling those roles.

"What do you say, boy? Want to come back to Winston-Salem to help me?" Coach Wilson asked.

That was pretty much the entire interview. Based on Coach Hurt's recommendation, Coach Wilson, who had never spoken to me directly before that day in the office, offered me a job in the course of a few minutes. In addition to being assistant coach, I would also teach math. Over time, I would also teach courses in family health, physical education, and how to coach sports. I would create the course on teaching driver education.

I don't remember what I said, but I know what I was thinking: I'd help out Coach Wilson for a year, save some money or find a scholarship, and then go on to dental school at Howard University.

Within a few days, I packed up my meager belongings at Morgan State and was on the train to Winston-Salem. The train stopped there, I got off, and I have never left.

Winston-Salem was a bustling place in the mid-1940s. It was a manufacturing town dominated by R. J. Reynolds Tobacco Company, which had invented the commercially packed cigarette with a patent on a cigarette-rolling machine. If manufacturing employees in Winston-Salem didn't make cigarettes, they made textiles or furniture.

This abundance of manufacturing jobs in Winston-Salem had acted as a magnet for black workers starting in the 1870s, when Reynolds first opened its factories. By the time the adjoining towns of Winston and Salem merged into one city in 1913, the black population had grown to 40 percent of the entire city, one of the highest percentages in the state.

As the black worker population in the city grew, so did its professional population. Black doctors, lawyers, and teachers came to the city and established themselves. Black-owned businesses, including bus lines and banks, were plentiful and prospering. Winston-Salem was the place to be for up-and-coming black people in the 1940s.

Still, as good as it was for many black people, Winston-Salem was as segregated as any other place in the South. A north-south highway,

U.S. 52, divided the city into two parts. The black people had begun moving into white-owned homes in East Winston in 1941. By the time I came to the city in 1945, East Winston was almost all black. The racial divide in the city remains U.S. 52.

Winston-Salem Teachers College was located on a hill just southeast of downtown. It had been founded in 1892 as Slater Industrial and State Normal School in a wealthy black neighborhood. The term *normal* was common in those days to describe schools that educated public-school teachers by setting up model classrooms so the teachers could practice their profession under simulated classroom conditions.

The school's founder was a black teacher and former slave named Simon Green Atkins, who named the school after the man who donated the land. Atkins founded Slater with the motto, "Let him be a man, and everything else will take care of itself."

The school had always been coeducational. At first, it taught basic courses, with most of the men learning practical things such as carpentry and brick masonry and the women learning how to be teachers. In 1905, the school started issuing teaching certificates. By 1925, it was a four-year college carrying the name Winston-Salem Teachers College and developing a reputation as the source of some of the best black teachers in North Carolina. By 1945, those teaching graduates were spreading out into other states.

I began to have second thoughts about taking the job when I moved into the men's dorm. That was part of the deal Brutus had offered. I would get a free room and discounted food at the cafeteria. It would be like a continuation of my college days.

Getting the free room and board was not a bad idea. But on reflection, I was not happy with the pay of an assistant coach, which was $1,800 a year. Back at Morgan State, I had worked in the post office sorting mail between the football and basketball seasons. In the winter, I worked from four to midnight in the basement of the dorm keeping an oil-fired boiler working. That turned out to be a great job. When I was alone in the warm basement, I was able to study without any distractions.

Between my pay as a boiler man and a postal clerk, I made more than $1,800 a year as a college student. Now, here I was, a college graduate, making less money than I had when I was a combination student and boiler stoker!

Now, I wasn't happy about the deal Coach Wilson had offered me just a few days earlier, but I had agreed to it. I had told Coach Wilson I would come, and my parents had always taught me to keep my word when I agreed to a deal. I figured keeping the assistant's job for a year would fulfill my word to Coach Wilson. Once my promise was fulfilled, I could look for a better-paying job or a scholarship that would help me achieve my mother's goal for me to get into dental school.

Almost immediately, I discovered a problem with my job. The boys we were supposed to coach were terrible athletes.

I don't mean to denigrate these men, who are now in their late 70s and early 80s. In 1945, they had the desire. They had the enthusiasm. They just didn't have the athletic abilities of my old teammates back at Morgan State.

First of all, the ranks of men—both whites and blacks—on college campuses were greatly diminished. First came the wave of young men who voluntarily joined the armed services. Then most of the rest of the men had been taken by the draft.

The young men who were still at Winston-Salem Teachers College in 1945 were in school because their families either had some sort of political pull with their county's draft board or because the draft board had not found them or did not want them for some reason.

The reason those men were not wanted by the armed forces must have been that they were too short, too skinny, or too fat, or that they had some physical infirmity that would make them less-than-ideal soldiers. As I recall, none of them could have avoided the draft by being classified as a big, angry black man, as I was. None of them was big enough to have intimidated the scrawniest of white draft-board doctors.

A second reason there was a lack of men at WSTC was that this was a teachers' college, and teaching has traditionally been a woman's occupation. In those days, if a black man had the money and the intelligence to go to college, he looked for some better-paying career than education. He got that background in a liberal-arts college, not one that awarded only teaching certificates.

This is the Winston-Salem Teachers College basketball team in 1944-45, the year before I arrived as assistant coach to Brutus Wilson. Left to right: Charles Eaton, Charles Branford, Maxter Allen, William Davis, Romie Avery, Theodore Vines, Charles Wellman, Clarence Cooper, Carl Hargrove, and Coach Brutus Wilson.

Third, WSTC was a small teachers' college of just 550 students, counting the girls, who would not be trying out for men's football and basketball. Coach Wilson and I had fewer than 100 male students from which to pick football, basketball, and track teams. We needed one-third of the entire male population of the school to make a football team.

"House Boy," Coach Wilson used to call me. I don't remember if he ever called me by my given name or even "Big House." It was usually "House Boy."

"House Boy, what are we going to do? How can we field a football team with what we have in terms of talent?" Coach Wilson asked.

How in the world did I know? I was a 22-year-old football player who was wondering how I had gotten myself into such a fix.

We didn't have many outstanding athletes already in the college, and we didn't have much of a chance of attracting any athletic high-school seniors looking for a college. Those boys would want to go to proven teams, not to a girls' school.

The college had created an official sports program only in 1942, so facilities at WSTC were rudimentary compared to what was found on most campuses. Actually, that worked somewhat to our advantage. Our football practice field was filled with rocks. The runners literally had to practice broken-field running because they had to adopt moves to keep from stepping on a rock and breaking an ankle.

The name of our sports teams came in a roundabout way. The first unofficial name of our team was the Red Devils because the red chosen for the uniforms was so bright. The more religious members of the school's administration decided that was not an appropriate name, so they called on the student body to come up with something different. That committee settled on the Rams sometime during World War II, but it was sometime in the 1970s before the news media finally started calling us the Rams and stopped calling us the Teachers.

All in all, I kind of liked the Teachers. It was descriptive of who we were, but it was also a mild-sounding nickname that sometimes lulled the other team into underestimating us. In those days, we needed all the help we could muster in being underestimated.

My first year as assistant coach, our football team went 0-8-1. There was little Coach Wilson or I could do about winning with the limitations we had. I don't even remember what our basketball record was in 1945, which tells me it must not have been all that good either.

After the basketball season was over and my year as assistant coach was drawing to a close, I discovered that there likely wouldn't be any reason for me to even worry about a second season at WSTC. The administration was planning to fire both Coach Wilson and me.

Nearly 60 years later, I am still not clear on the details of what the real situation was—which is not uncommon for coaches who come under fire from their chancellors.

I walked into the administration office one morning around Christmas 1945, and immediately someone asked me, "What is the strike about? Who are the leaders? How do we stop it?"

*I'm pictured here in 1945 at age 22, when I was the assistant coach
of all sports at Winston-Salem Teachers College.*

(PHOTO BY ED SIMONS, COURTESY OF WINSTON-SALEM STATE UNIVERSITY ARCHIVES)

I had no idea what they were talking about. Coach Wilson came in,
and he, too, was puzzled.

That day, a group of students had decided to hold a strike against
the school in protest of the quality of the meals being served in the cafeteria. Since some of the strikers were men, and since both Coach Wilson

This is a photo of the 1945-46 Winston-Salem Teachers College Rams—the first year we were in CIAA competition. Front row, from the bottom: *Clarence Cooper, Wesley Hairston, Jacob Davis, James Ford, Henry Jones, and Theodore Vines.* Back row, from bottom: *Romie Avery, William Davis, Harold Diggs, Charles Wellman and an unidentified player.*

(WINSTON-SALEM STATE UNIVERSITY ARCHIVES)

and I lived in the dorm with the men, the administration believed he and I must have heard about the strike as it was being organized.

The truth was that neither of us knew anything about the strike. I personally had no problem with the meals being served in the cafeteria. The food was as good as I ever got at Morgan State. It was not as good as Momma made back home, but what cafeteria ever serves food that is?

The upshot was that the administration did not believe Coach Wilson or myself. While they did not exactly fire us, they told us our jobs were over and we could reapply for them.

I am not sure if he was trying to call the school's bluff or not, but Coach Wilson took the opportunity to leave and take a job as head coach for Shaw University in Raleigh. That actually worked out well for him because his wife was still home in Smithfield, only about 40 miles from Raleigh, instead of the 160 miles it was from Winston-Salem.

Our 0-8-1 football season did not sit well with the college's boosters. At about the same time as the food strike was happening, a group of men I call "the Peanut Gallery" began to spread stories around Hairston's Drug Store, Winston-Salem's only black-owned pharmacy. The rumor was that I was planning on moving to Bluefield College in Bluefield, West Virginia.

These fellows were the same men who can be found offering their unsought opinions around any college or university campus. They are the Monday-morning quarterbacks, the fair-weather fans, and the rumormongers who always know better than the coaches how to run the sports program. Since sports talk radio came along, they are the men who call in to explain how they could have won last weekend's big game if only they had been coaching the team. Every college, black or white, has such a group of people hanging around waiting for the coach to make a move that displeases them.

I had never had a conversation with or even met a single one of these men. And I had never had any conversations with the administration of Bluefield College about taking a coaching position. On the face of it, this rumor made no sense. I was a first-year assistant coach. More importantly than that, my team had not won a single game that season. Why would Bluefield be talking to me?

The entire story was made up, apparently designed either to get me fired for talking to another college or to convince me that no one in Winston-Salem wanted me to stay around for another season. Since the administration had asked for our resignations anyway because of the supposed food strike, the actions of the Peanut Gallery did not really matter.

I was home in Paducah pondering what to do when I got a call from the college's administration office to come back to school.

Since Coach Wilson was not coming back, would I be interested in taking over as head coach and athletic director?

CHAPTER 5

The Big House Era Begins Slowly

Maybe the WSTC administration was surprised when Coach Wilson found another head-coaching job and didn't reapply for his old job. Maybe they tried to find another head coach, and no one wanted to take over a men's sports program at what every available coach knew was a girls' school. I never found out the true story.

All I know was that Winston-Salem Teachers College offered the head-coaching job to a 23-year-old assistant coach who was still thinking he should just do what his mother intended and apply to dental school.

I thought about it and reached a simple conclusion. If I didn't like the job, I could always quit. If the school decided they really did not like me, they would fire me like they had done just a few weeks earlier. Either way, I would be able to move on to do something else with my life.

Though I still had a little bit of doubt about myself, I did know what a coach should be. On my application for the position of head

I don't recall why the photographer decided to have the new athletic director and men's sports coach pose while sitting on the grass in 1946. It certainly doesn't make me look athletic!

coach, I wrote, "Not only do I consider it important for a coach to follow his chosen career, but he should also be a teacher and a leader in other fields. He should exemplify those traits which deal with character building."

Starting in those early days of my professional career, when getting hired or fired seemed to occur so easily, I decided to adopt a bumper-car theory of living my life. When you ride in the bumper cars at the state fair, you get knocked in new directions all the time. When that happens, you just head off in that new direction and see where you end up.

I decided I would accept the head-coaching job and see how far it would take me.

One of the first problems I had to overcome was that my sole coaching experience was just the one year as assistant under Coach Wilson. In those days, an assistant's duties were hauling out, cleaning, and putting away the equipment, taping injured ankles, even taking tickets at the games. There was not much sitting down with the head coach and figuring out a strategy to win games. Coaching was done by the head coach, who took on all the sports. The assistant did whatever he was told. Over time, the assistant would watch and listen to what the head coach said to the players, and that was how he learned to be a head coach. Coach Wilson had left after just one year with me as his assistant—way too short a time for me to learn much from him about how to inspire young men to push themselves to win at their sports.

Another problem was that I started out as a coach with knowledge of one sport. I knew football very well, but basketball for me was always something to do once the football team stopped playing before Christmas. Once basketball season was over, it was time for track, and my only experience at that sport was my very bad attempts to throw the discus. Every other sport I had played as a college athlete was just a way of staying in shape for football season in the fall.

So there I was in the spring of 1946 as head football coach, head basketball coach, head track coach, head tennis coach, and head boxing coach, making $2,400 a year.

My first real test was in football. We came back from our losing

71

season in 1945 with a record of 3-3-3. Within two years, our record improved to 8-1-0. That was not bad for a team made up of boys going to a girls' college.

Because of my four years of playing football at Morgan State, coaching the WSTC football team came naturally. I could still explain the roles of every player on the football team, just as I had done helping Coach Hurt on the field.

But my role on Morgan State's basketball team had been to be so big that the other players had a hard time getting around me. I had been a center, but not an outstanding one. My game plan was to pass off to the forwards and guards as quickly as I got the ball. As a coach, I had no real idea what happened to the ball once it left the center's hands. I knew the fundamentals of basketball, but not much more.

Once the 1946 football season was over and the 1946-47 basketball season rolled around, I did the only thing I could do. I asked people how to play basketball. And the first people I asked were the members of the 1945-46 team.

I felt no shame in asking those who were playing the game how I could do a better job as coach. For one thing, I was hardly older than my players. For another thing, I had never been trained as a basketball coach. And third, we were at a predominantly girls' school. In those days just after World War II, the play was more intramural level than college level.

I knew, however, that with the war winding down, there would be thousands of young men streaming back into college. Those men would provide the athletic base for my future teams over the coming couple of years. If I could improve my coaching abilities now, before those athletes came back to school, I could get a jump on the competition by learning how to motivate and train the returning service veterans to win ball games in addition to wars.

I also asked my players for help because time was not on my side to build a winning program. I knew from my experience the previous year that the Peanut Gallery would be gunning for me very quickly if we did not start to build a winning program in all sports.

Luckily for me, and just as I predicted, the veterans started coming

This is the 1946-47 basketball team. Front row, left to right: *Will Kelly, Ernest Canady, Herbert Strong, Darnell Newton, Miles Ritchie, and Charles Wellman.* Back row, left to right: *Harold Diggs, Sam Spencer, Wesley Hairston, William Davis, Oris Hill, James Trice, Albert Johnson, Clarence Cooper, and John Martin. Oris Hill became my first player to become a professional basketball player. He played for the Harlem Globetrotters for several years.*

(WINSTON-SALEM STATE UNIVERSITY ARCHIVES)

home from World War II and entering college. What was a trickle in 1945 became a small stream in 1946 and 1947, though the number of men coming to WSTC was still small compared to the number of women in the school.

I knew from early tryouts that real athletes had returned to college. These fellows had fought the Germans and the Japanese as well as racial discrimination in our own armed forces, so they had some pent-up aggression they were willing to let out on the football field and basketball court.

On the downside, I had a few problems with some of these fellows.

73

They were generally my age or older, and they were war veterans who did not always like listening to someone their own age who had not served in the armed forces. I could huff and puff and yell to impress teenage freshmen, but that didn't work well with men who had been dodging bullets. They didn't always go to bed at a decent hour, didn't always abide by the no-alcohol-in-the-dorms rule, and didn't always show up for practice on time.

Still, they were what I needed on the team: seasoned men who had a competitive spirit. You can have players who know all the rules of the game, and you can even have big, strong men who can overpower the other team. But unless you have players who want to win, you are not going to have competitive teams.

Even though I was getting some of these returning GI's on the team, I decided that I was not going to just pick my team from the students who walked on. That was the way it had been during the lean years under Coach Wilson. I was going to recruit, even if it took my own money to do it.

After finishing my first full year of football with my 3-3-3 record and my first full year of basketball in 1947 with a respectable 15-7 season, I packed up my car and headed to the only place where I had existing contacts with coaches who knew about sports talent. That was my hometown of Paducah, Kentucky.

I drove to Paducah, spending one or two nights on an air mattress in my car to save money and the trouble of finding a motel that would rent to a black man. Driving that distance alone gave me time to think. It struck me that I wasn't—and shouldn't be—just trying to find football and basketball players. I had two other duties besides those to my sports teams.

One duty was to Winston-Salem Teachers College. As a coach—and teacher—I should be looking for good students who would graduate to become teachers.

My second duty was to deserving kids of any ability. I had used my athletic ability to go to a good four-year college, and now I had the chance to help others use whatever talents they had to get into college. Once they graduated, they could help others get into college. I realized that the effect of one poor black kid helping others coming along behind him or her could grow exponentially.

When I got to Paducah, I found I had become a minor celebrity because of my years as an All-American and as an All-CIAA tackle at Morgan State. Now that I was a young head coach at another college, I had proven to the home folks and their sons and daughters that education could take a poor kid and make him a success.

My plan of mining my hometown and the surrounding region for good athletes worked just as I imagined. My high-school coaches, Boy Scout leaders, and old neighbors were eager to tell me about talented, deserving kids. Every time I walked down Paducah's sidewalks, I ran into someone who knew at least one kid who wanted to go to college and who had some talent he or she could use once they arrived. I found that many kids had either graduated from high school that year or the previous year and were not in college because their families had no money to send them. Some of the kids were not in school because they did not know how to apply for scholarships.

That first recruiting year, I took 10 students from Paducah and Carbondale, Illinois, 36 miles away and across the Ohio River. They included nine boys and one girl. Most of the kids I needed for my football and basketball teams, but some of them were accomplished musicians I recruited for WSTC's band. The bandmaster had not asked me to find him students, but I knew he could use them.

It is interesting how the word spread that I was in town recruiting. One of my first recruits was James Trice, who had been in junior high when I was a high-school star. He was six-foot-six but only 167 pounds. He looked like a praying mantis, but I hoped I could train him to be a good basketball player.

James already had a scholarship to Wilberforce College in Ohio, but he turned down that coach when he heard that I was looking for players. James knew me, and he had no ties at all to Wilberforce. He had followed my career since he was a kid. He trusted me to help him get a college degree.

James, who happened to be working in Chicago that summer, then told me that his roommate would be a good player. I was a little skeptical, but I agreed to trust this high-school kid's sense of talent. James then convinced his roommate, Will Kelly, an army veteran, to use his GI Bill money to come to Winston-Salem. I never met Will until he showed up for practice in Winston-Salem after taking three buses from Chicago with James.

That first group of basketball players included Oris Hill, a six-foot-seven player who would turn out to be the first of my players to turn professional, if you count playing for the Harlem Globetrotters.

None of the players I recruited from that first Midwestern trip ever did an official tryout for me. I just trusted their coaches' word that they could play.

This use of a personal network to recruit players—rather than any formal, expensive scouting program, as is done today by the major universities—would serve me for 47 years. I found scores of quality players by trusting my contacts' word that the players they sent me could make it in a college environment and could also play football or basketball or both.

Coincidentally, in 1946, the same year that I became head coach at Winston-Salem Teachers College, the Colored (now Central) Intercollegiate Athletic Association began playing its basketball tournament. It was within the CIAA that I and Winston-Salem Teachers College found our greatest successes.

Founded in 1912, the CIAA has become the nation's best-recognized conference for historically black colleges. The makeup of the conference in terms of what colleges are members has changed some through the years, but it consists today of 12 colleges and universities in Maryland, Virginia, and North Carolina. The North Carolina members include Fayetteville State University, Johnson C. Smith University in Charlotte, Livingstone College in Salisbury, North Carolina Central University in Durham, Saint Augustine's College in Raleigh, Elizabeth City State University, Shaw University in Raleigh, and Winston-Salem State University. There's also Bowie State University in Maryland and three Virginia schools: Saint Paul's College in Lawrenceville, Virginia State University in Richmond, and Virginia Union University in Petersburg.

When my Winston-Salem Teachers College team first started playing in the CIAA in 1946 after officially joining in 1945, our opponents also included my own alma mater of Morgan State College; Maryland State (now the University of Maryland Eastern Shore); Hampton Institute and Norfolk State University in Virginia; West Virginia State College at Institute; Bluefield State University in West Virginia; Howard University in Washington, D.C.; Lincoln University in Pennsylvania; North Carolina A&T in Greensboro; and Delaware State University. All of those schools have since joined other conferences, with most of them joining the Mid-Eastern Athletic Conference, or MEAC.

In its first year of 1946, the CIAA basketball tournament was played in the 3,000-seat Turner's Arena in Washington, D.C., near Howard. Played the last weekend of February and sometimes into March of each year, "the CIAA" now attracts 80,000 fans to the tournament venue, putting it just behind the Atlantic Coast Conference in terms of fan attendance.

In many of the years it has been held, the CIAA tournament champion has been decided in the last minutes, sometimes the last seconds, of the game. At times, the lowest-ranked teams—those which have won the fewest games in the regular season—have played exceptionally well in the tournament and have beaten the best teams in the conference in that particular year. I have experienced that myself, both being on the least-favored and the most-favored side of the equation in different years. The most exciting—and frustrating—games of my career have been fought on courts sanctioned by the CIAA. Whatever reputation I might have now was built on those courts during those games. Most of the friends—and opponents—I have had through the years have come from those CIAA courts. Though I retired in 1993, I know that each year for that last week of February, I will be at the CIAA tournament.

So, just as the CIAA basketball tournament was getting started, so was my recruiting. But even as I was proving my coaching abilities on the field and the court to my players and alumni, I also had to prove myself to the college administration. Early in my new career as head coach, I don't think I had the full confidence of the administration. In the same year the school gave me my position of head coach, they also

This photo of me with assistant coaches, Archie Morrow (left) and William Bryant (right), was also made into a postcard. Both of my assistants had graduate degrees, which made me nervous enough to hire my college buddy Boo Brown to watch my back.

(WINSTON-SALEM STATE UNIVERSITY ARCHIVES)

hired two physical-education teachers to "help" me. I was not consulted in their hiring.

One of my helpers was Archie Morrow, who had a master's degree from Columbia University in New York City. The other was William Bryant, who had a master's degree from Iowa University. Both were 10 years older than me, were better educated than me, and had graduated from large, prestigious universities that were predominately white. I don't know if the Peanut Gallery was behind the administration's efforts in their hiring, but I think Morrow and Bryant were brought in to step in if—or once—I stumbled at my head-coaching efforts.

I might have been only 23, but I knew that I needed someone I could trust and who had my best interest at heart, or I could easily find myself out of my second coaching job in two years. The administration might have asked me back once, but they wouldn't do it again.

In the same year Morrow and Bryant were hired, I called up an old Morgan State teammate, Alvin "Boo" Brown, and asked him if he would like to come down to WSTC to be my number-one assistant coach. Boo had been a forward on the basketball team when I played center. We had done pretty well for ourselves. Morgan State was undefeated in basketball my last two years.

To be truthful, Boo should have been the basketball coach at Winston-Salem instead of me. I really knew football, and he really knew basketball.

Still, we made a good coaching team. We thought we were well on our way to building a great basketball team that might even capture the CIAA championship in 1949. Then, one night, we walked into a gym in Durham to play John McLendon's North Carolina College for Negroes (now North Carolina Central University).

Coach McLendon had seen us coming long before we walked through the door of his gym. In a game we felt sure we would win, we lost 119-65. I remember the score, but the rest of the details are too painful to recount. Let's just say that the best team coached by the best coach won that night.

That game was a turning point in my and Boo's careers. We realized—too late to help us in that particular game—that if we were going to play good basketball against really good opponents, we had to find really, really good players.

"Let's go recruit us some good players," I said to Boo as we sat on the bench trying to figure out what freight train had just hit us.

Yes, I had done some minor-league recruiting of students for the past several years, but now I was about to get serious about finding top-notch athletes.

After that basketball game, I also realized two other things. Number one, I realized that I could no longer handle the time demands placed on my being the head coach of both football and basketball. I also realized that recruiting a 10-man basketball team had to be infinitely easier than recruiting a 30- to 40-man football team.

Rather than fight the Peanut Gallery any longer, I voluntarily gave up being the head football coach and chose to become basketball coach, while also retaining the title of athletic director. I left on a winning note, as I was named CIAA Football Coach of the Year in 1949. After amassing a football record of 20-12-4, I helped recruit Thomas "Tank" Conrad, who took over the football-coaching duties in the fall of 1950. I assisted him for several years as his line coach.

While the sting of the loss of that basketball game to Coach McLendon was still fresh, I sent Boo to New York City to recruit from among his contacts, and I returned to Kentucky and southern Illinois. We needed more players and better players, and I was determined to get them.

Boo helped me that one summer, but that fall he got an offer to become assistant coach at Arkansas A&M College. He stayed at that school for a couple of years, then went back to Morgan State as an assistant football coach. Finally, Boo listened to his father, who was a physician, and enrolled in medical school. My first assistant coach became a very accomplished physician who still treasures his playing and coaching days. He still tells me today that the fellowship among athletes is matched only by the feeling shared by musicians. No other set of friends or professionals can create the same camaraderie found among athletes who have played on the same team.

I agree. Teams I had more than 50 years ago still keep track of each other, still help each other. When one dies, his teammates still come back together from all around the nation to bury him.

Once Boo and I decided we needed to find better players, I also realized that I had to learn how to be a better coach.

When I was home in Paducah on a recruiting trip, I heard about a basketball coaches' clinic being held at Murray State College, a white college in Murray, Kentucky, about 50 miles away. The featured speaker at that clinic was going to be Clair Bee, the famed basketball coach at Long Island University, one of the few colleges that was mixing blacks and whites on the same team.

I called the college to ask about registering for the clinic. There was some hesitation on that end of the phone line when I told the Murray State coach that I was a Lincoln High School graduate. Anyone in Murray would have known Lincoln was black. The coach grew even more nervous when I confirmed to him that I was a black coach who coached at a black teachers' college in North Carolina. The coach told me he would call me back once he checked with his president, an excuse I expected.

He did call me back, which I did not expect. This was the late 1940s, when segregation rules were very strict about blacks and whites mixing in public. The president of the college had agreed to invite me. I wonder how many college presidents were ever bothered by coaches asking if they could invite a certain type of coach to their clinic.

On the day of the clinic, I climbed up into the stands of the gym and sat in the middle of the other coaches. There must have been about 50 white men there, mostly from high schools and a few small colleges. They kept glancing at me curiously, but no one shied away from me. Finally, after the lunch break, some of the men came up to me and asked if I was a college janitor interested in basketball.

"No, I'm not a janitor," I said politely. "I graduated from Lincoln High School in Paducah, went to Morgan State in Baltimore, and now I am head coach at Winston-Salem Teachers College down in North Carolina. I need some help teaching my players to be more competitive. When I heard about this coaching clinic, I thought it would accomplish that purpose. So far, it has."

With that explanation, everything was fine. Once the mystery of my presence was solved, the other coaches treated me with the same respect they gave each other. Mind you, they didn't invite me to dinner or to drink from their water fountains, but they accepted me as another coach.

I had just learned another little thing about white people. If you act like you belong with them, they are more likely to accept you.

I had done all the right things in planning to attend the clinic. I hadn't crashed their event. I had called ahead and registered. I even told the organizers that I was black, so there would be no misunderstandings or confrontations at the check-in table.

Once I got to the gym, I simply climbed into the stands and blended into the group, right into the middle of them, just as if I belonged there all the time. I was as much of a coach as they were, with the same responsibilities of winning basketball games and molding young students into men.

Just as Jackie Robinson showed white people that he belonged on the baseball diamond, I was determined to show white people that I belonged in any formerly white coaches' clinic. It wasn't arrogance. It was simply doing what was right.

CHAPTER 6

Coach John McLendon Changes the Way Basketball Is Played

The inventor of basketball, Dr. James Naismith, might not recognize his game of slow walking and precise passing as it is played today.

The improver of basketball, Coach John McLendon, would recognize the fast-breaking, running, and shooting game that is typical of today's college and professional teams. He would smile and say, "That's my game!"

Naismith, born a Canadian, was teaching future physical-education instructors at the School for Christian Workers—which later became the Young Men's Christian Association—in Springfield, Massachusetts, in 1891 when the headmaster came to him with a problem. It was a problem all high-school, college, and professional coaches know well.

Some of the P.E. majors were proving to be unruly. They had too much nervous energy from being cooped up inside the gym because

When we played a big rival such as Greensboro's
North Carolina A&T University, we would hold the game in
Winston-Salem's Memorial Coliseum.

(Winston-Salem State University Archives)

of the cold weather outside. It was Naismith's assignment over the course of a week to dream up a new sport that would keep these students occupied. He settled on a game where putting a ball in a goal would be the object.

Naismith thought the game would be something like hockey, but he decided against using sticks to pass the ball because he thought the boys might use them as weapons against each other. They were already keyed up enough, and he didn't want them even more aggressive with sticks in their hands. He decided against any tackling like that used in football because the gym's floor was hardwood. He decided that intentionally trying to hurt someone by pushing or tripping him to the floor would be a foul that would result in that person being ineligible to play until the next foul was committed by the other team.

Because Naismith could not find the boxes in the equipment room that he had intended to be the game's goals, he had the school's custodian nail peach baskets to the bottom of a running track that was 10 feet off the floor.

That is the short history of why we have basketball and not boxball and why the rim is 10 feet from the floor.

The game has changed in the 100-plus years since Naismith invented it with the posting of 13 rules on the wall of that gym. He did not mention anything about dribbling, only that a player could not run with the ball. He never mentioned anything about shooting foul shots, nor did he assign two points for a basket and three points for a long-distance shot. There is no mention of "paint" or "lane" in the original rules. There is no mention of lines on the floor at all. All those parts of the game came later.

Naismith envisioned a game where teams of nine men—three forwards, three centers, and three backs (now guards)—on a side would play on a court 50 feet by 25 feet (now 94 feet by 50 feet) for two halves of 15 minutes each (now 20 minutes each in the college game). The object of the game was for one team to pass the ball from one man to another until someone got close enough to toss the ball into the peach basket. Play would stop long enough for the "goal tender" to retrieve the ball and toss it to the single referee. That referee would then walk to center court to toss the ball up for the jump ball. Basketball was designed to be a slow, deliberate game where passing and shooting accuracy determined the winner.

Then along came Coach John McLendon.

Actually, there were a few changes in the rules before McLendon came along to exploit those changes. By 1910, the rules had been changed to allow a basketball player to hold onto the ball by dribbling, which was against the original rules of 1891. In 1910, that ball handler still could not shoot for the basket. He had to pass off to someone else, who would shoot. Within another few years, the rules were changed again so the dribbling player could shoot. More changes allowed a fouled player to shoot a foul shot and then a second shot as a bonus if he made the first one. By the 1920s, the game had changed further. The old style of play of passing from one well-positioned, static player to another had changed so that running, passing, and shooting on the run were now important.

If I can credit one man with giving me most of my basketball knowledge, it would be John McLendon, who coached at North Carolina Central University, Hampton Institute, and Tennessee A&I State Teachers College (now Tennessee State University).

(CLARENCE E. GAINES PERSONAL COLLECTION)

And that is where my friend John McLendon came into the sport and changed it forever.

John was born in tiny Hiawatha, Kansas, in 1915, to sharecroppers who wanted him to go on to better things. He integrated the University of Kansas and became an early civil-rights activist while attending the university by integrating the college's pool when he jumped into it. The day after he jumped in the pool, he saw school janitors draining it. As soon as it was filled up, he jumped in again. The janitors, under orders from the college administration, drained it again. It took a petition signed by about 1,000 white students confirming that they didn't mind swimming with a black student before the administration stopped draining and filling that swimming pool every time John jumped into it.

While in college, John was not allowed to play varsity basketball because of segregation rules barring on-court competition between blacks and whites. Instead of playing, he sat down with famous Kansas coach Forrest "Phog" Allen to learn about the game. When John wasn't quizzing Coach Allen, he was talking to the man himself, Dr. Naismith, who had been hired by Kansas as a professor of physical education. Neither man offered to put John on the varsity team, since it was illegal. But both coaches saw nothing wrong with talking with this bright young man who seemed so interested in becoming a coach.

John's first job after college came in 1935 when Dr. Naismith helped him get a job as coach of the black team in a mixed-race high school. Two years later, John found a job as assistant coach at the North Carolina College for Negroes (now named North Carolina Central University) in Durham. In 1940, he was named head basketball coach.

It was in Durham where I first got to know John in the fall of 1945. I had known about him when I was a student at Morgan State, but I had done little more than nod at him before and after games.

Physically, John McLendon was an unimposing man, only five-foot-eight and 135 pounds. No basketball coach in his right mind would have picked him for even a junior-varsity high-school team. Shoot, he wouldn't have been picked for a schoolyard pickup game. John was too short, too skinny, and too mild looking.

But John had quick eyes. He saw everything that was going on around him, which is necessary in a basketball player.

The best thing John had going for him was his mind. He had one of the best-organized basketball minds I have ever seen. He was able to motivate his players to do just about anything possible with a basketball. His championships prove that.

He also had the ability to convince college administrators to do just about anything he wanted. The tournament he helped create proves that.

In 1946, John McLendon, Talmadge Hill of Morgan State College, Harry Jefferson of Virginia State College, and John Burr of Howard University finally created something that had been talked about since the founding of the Colored Intercollegiate Athletic Association in 1912—a postseason basketball tournament that would crown a CIAA champion. At first, the idea of creating a tournament had been defeated by the presidents of the other schools, but these four coaches would not give up. They went on a lobbying campaign and got a revote. Creating the tournament passed the second time around. The organizers pooled their own money at $100 a pop to finance the first tourney. Today, that tourney generates millions in income and economic impact.

John had a great mind for behind-the-scenes political maneuvering that would go far beyond just organizing the CIAA tournament. In a few years, he would use his skills of organizing and pressuring to suggest changes to the white basketball sanctioning bodies that would result in them finally accepting black basketball teams into their tournaments.

It was after John's team whipped my team's butt 119-65 in 1949 that I made him my friend rather than my opponent. I decided then and there that I might not be able to beat him on the basketball court, but I could learn a lot from him about how to beat other people.

What I learned—what everyone in basketball learned—was how to play the high-speed style of basketball. Until John McLendon came along, when a team sank a basket at one end of the court, they leisurely trotted back to defend their goal. While the defending team was easing into position, the attacking team was walking back up the court with the guards eyeing the defense and making a selection about which moves their team would employ to get close to the basket. It might be 30 seconds before the attacking team even walked close enough to the goal to begin attacking the basket.

John read over the rules and saw a way he could put his stamp on the game. He saw nothing in the rules that prevented him from drastically speeding up the game. As soon as the ball came out of the net after his opponent had scored, one of his players would retrieve it and then toss it up the court to a teammate, who would pass it on to a shooter running full tilt toward the basket. He called it a "fast break."

All his opposing coaches, including me, read the rules, and we couldn't find anything to stop what John was doing. So instead of fighting him, we had to join him and teach our players an entirely different game. No longer did your team saunter back to protect their little part of the court. Now, your team had to run to catch up to your opponents, who were running as fast as they could up the court to attack the basket!

John McLendon turned a somewhat mild passing game into a running game. The effect was dramatic. Coaches had to change their practices to include a lot more running and conditioning just so their teams would not become exhausted before the game was over. We had to teach how to defend on the run, how a defensive player could take away the ball from a fast-moving, advancing player without fouling him.

John could play the opposite kind of game, too. Dean Smith, retired coach of the University of North Carolina, is credited with the invention of the game-slowing four-corners offense, in which, before the 35-second clock was instituted, the team that was ahead simply passed the ball to each other, rather than taking a shot at the basket. Dean and John were not coaching contemporaries, but John McLendon's North Carolina Central Eagles were using that four-corners offense a good 15 years before Dean Smith's Tar Heels. John was using both the fast-break and the four-corners offenses against every team he played in the '40s and '50s, before Dean Smith was even elevated to head coach at UNC in the '60s.

I feel confident in saying that what is accepted as standard basketball today at both the college and professional levels was introduced into the game by John McLendon.

The best decision I ever made in my career was teaming up with John for recruiting trips.

No one can imagine the coaches of North Carolina and Duke, or Kentucky and Louisville, climbing into the same car for a two-week road trip looking for recruits. No coaches today would trust the others not to steal their prized prospects. But that was the way John and I started to do it in the late 1940s and early 1950s.

John thought we were riding together to save gas money, but the truth is that I wanted to get him alone to talk about basketball plays, strategy on the court, and how to motivate players to do exactly what I wanted them to do when I wanted them to do it. John seemed to have no trouble with all those coaching skills, while his opponents were standing around scratching our heads as his teams ran up the score on us.

When we headed to my territory of western Kentucky and southern Illinois to talk to high-school coaches, prospects, and their parents, John would sit beside me and not say a word as I pitched Winston-Salem Teachers College as the best college those young men could attend. When we got back in the car and drove on to Chicago and Kansas City, where he had coaching and recruiting contacts, the roles were reversed. I would not say a word as he pitched North Carolina Central as the best college those young men could attend.

Maybe those prospects assumed that the other man sitting with their coach was an assistant coach, but neither John nor I ever directly lied to the coaches, prospects, or parents. We just never corrected any misimpressions they may have had about who that other man was.

As amazing as it might seem to people wondering about competition for hot players, neither John nor myself ever sandbagged the other. We never tried to recruit the other's prospects. Even if that prospect showed no interest in the primary school, we never tried to go back and recruit him for the other's school.

How good was John McLendon as a basketball coach? His teams won 264 and lost only 60 while he was at North Carolina Central. He won eight CIAA tournaments between 1941 and 1952. He moved on

(From left) H. Douglas Covington, the chancellor of Winston-Salem State University from 1977-84, myself, Eugene McCullers from Coca-Cola, Coach John McLendon, and another old rival, Coach Bobby Vaughn of Elizabeth City State University, help me celebrate my induction into the Basketball Hall of Fame in 1984. Coach McLendon was the first black basketball coach ever named to the Hall of Fame.

(CLARENCE E. GAINES PERSONAL COLLECTION)

to Hampton Institute and won 32 and lost only 14. Then he moved on to Tennessee A&I State University in Nashville, where he won 149 games and lost only 20. While at Tennessee State, he won three straight National Association of Intercollegiate Athletics (NAIA) championships.

His basketball coaching was amazing, but so were his negotiating skills.

The road to integrating the NAIA championship was rocky, and the deft political maneuvering the black coaches used to accomplish it is interesting. And right in the middle of all of that was my friend John McLendon.

The first crack in officially sanctioned segregation in college basketball appeared in 1946, just after thousands of young black men began to reenter society after fighting in World War II. In one of the first postwar college tournaments, a forward playing for a majority-white school from Iowa was not allowed to participate in a National Association of Intercollegiate Basketball (NAIB) tournament because he was black.

This callous treatment of the black player, who was a war veteran, outraged some NAIB members, including Al Duer, the white athletic director of George Pepperdine College. Almost immediately after the tournament was over, Duer wrote to the NAIB executive secretary that he was "ashamed" the player had been excluded from play.

By 1947, the pressure increased when the United States Olympic Committee told the NAIB that its members would not be allowed to participate in the upcoming Olympic trials because of their stance against black players.

That was the straw that broke the camel's back—in a good way. In a vote taken just two days before that year's tournament was to begin, the NAIB board voted to allow black players on the court. In that tournament, a reserve guard playing for Indiana State University became the first black player to play in an NAIB postseason tournament. The coach of that team in 1947 was John Wooden, who would go on to win 10 NCAA championships, including seven in a row starting in 1966.

But discrimination did not end just because the NAIB decided to allow a black player on the court with white players. Allowing one or two black players on a white team was much different than allowing entire teams of black players from small black colleges into the tournaments. That was still banned by both the NCAA and the NAIB.

In 1950, three coaches from the CIAA—Eddie Jackson of Howard University, Harry Jefferson of Virginia State College, and John McLendon of North Carolina College at Durham—started lobbying both the NCAA and the NAIB to allow black colleges to play in their national tournaments. These three coaches started with a very large endorsement. They secured the unanimous support of the National Association of Basketball Coaches to allow black colleges to compete in postseason tournaments with the white college teams.

There was resistance from both associations. The NCAA's board of directors flatly turned down the idea when they were approached by the three black colleges. The excuse the NCAA gave was that the organization had no mechanism to include small schools. The real reason might have been even more basic and something that Jackie Robinson would have understood. One NCAA official told Coach McLendon that "the fans might not accept or appreciate the kind of game you play, and your coaches might not be competent enough."

Talking about "the kind of game you play" must have meant that the white coaches were afraid of the fast-breaking, hard-running kind of basketball that McLendon had made common among most black colleges. "Your coaches might not be competent enough" needs no explanation. The NCAA in the 1950s did not think much of black men as coaches.

The black college coaches were not going to simply walk away. Instead, they approached the NAIB, which was then headed by Duer as executive secretary. To move matters along, Mack Greene, the athletic director at Central State College in Wilberforce, Ohio, applied for membership in the NAIB. It was the first black college to apply for membership in what had always been a white association.

Duer and Greene met several times in 1951, with Duer warning that basketball fans in the NAIB's hometown of Kansas City might not be ready to see a team of black players on the floor in a national tournament. Greene replied, "Some few fans may be lacking in the training for tolerance and decency, but we believe they have a conscience, and we know their conscience is on our side."

I don't know if Greene was consciously following the strategy Branch Rickey and Jackie Robinson had used to integrate professional baseball in 1946, just four years earlier. Greene told Duer that the black players were willing to endure any catcalls because he believed that the majority of white basketball players and fans wanted to see the best brand of the game they could see. That included seeing black teams playing white teams.

On March 12, 1952, the NAIB's board of directors approved membership for all black colleges that met the same standards as white colleges. They also approved recognition of a tournament then sponsored by the black colleges and agreed that the winner of that tournament would be eligible to compete in the NAIB national tournament in Kansas City.

Greene wrote to the coaches at small black colleges a letter in which he said, "The door is now open to all colleges for Negroes to world competition in basketball. Let's prepare ourselves for all that it means!"

While it is true that the NAIB opened the door to the small black colleges, they also installed a screen door through which all the black colleges had to pass but that the white colleges could bypass.

To handle the application of the black colleges to the NAIB, their executive committee created an at-large district—District 29—into which all of the black college teams were placed. I don't think that most of us black coaches thought much about it at the time, but what the NAIB really did was create a more palatable type of segregation. All of the black colleges, no matter where they were located geographically, were put into District 29. In effect, rather than allowing the black colleges to compete against the white colleges on a regional basis, the black colleges decided their own national-champion team, then sent that team to the Kansas City championship play-off. The black colleges eliminated each other to get one national-champion school, while all of the other members of the NAIA (which changed its name from the NAIB in the middle of this) sent regional champions.

The winner of that first District 29 championship in 1953 was Tennessee A&I State University, coached by Clarence Cash. When the team—described in a magazine as having "extra protective cutaneous pigmentation"—took the court, they were met not with boos but rousing cheers of welcome, as loud or louder than the 31 white teams at the tournament received. Just as Jackie Robinson had proven seven years earlier, the fears that the fans would not accept black players were unfounded.

The Tennessee State team won its first and second rounds but was defeated in the quarterfinals.

This single appearance ended the major attempts by NAIA schools in trying to hold onto segregation with regard to tournaments. Even a white team from Mississippi Southern voted among themselves to play the black team from Tennessee State if they met in tournament play. That did not happen, as both teams were eliminated in the quarterfinals.

When called on the question by the black coaches, the NAIA board reconsidered the idea of segregating the black schools into one district. In a short time, putting black schools into the all-inclusive District 29 was eliminated, and more reasonable regional districts were adopted.

With the prohibitions against interracial play falling, white coaches slowly began calling black coaches to schedule games. At least this was true in the North. Not many changes occurred in the segregated South right away. Some invitations that had never been issued in the past were now given to black colleges to play in Christmas tournaments. In 1954, the downtown Kansas City hotels agreed that they would house the black teams coming into town for the NAIA Tip-Off Tournament, which was won by McLendon and Tennessee State. Previously, the black teams had been put up in black hotels in other parts of the city.

Once allowed to compete on a national level, the small black colleges proved their worth. Tennessee State, still coached by John McLendon, won the NAIA national title in 1957, 1958, and 1959, the first time in college-basketball history that any team—white or black—had won a national championship three consecutive times. It was only four years earlier that the first black team had even been permitted on the Kansas City floor.

The success of the NAIA tournament in Kansas City did not go unnoticed by the NCAA. In 1957, the board that had once told black coaches that fans would not appreciate their kind of play formed their own small-college tournament with no racial restrictions. That tournament would eventually become the Division II, or small-college, championship.

The NCAA would not have changed their stubborn stand on even creating a tournament for small colleges if not for that handful of black coaches and an even smaller handful of white college and sports administrators who realized the time had come to let black athletes play against white athletes.

If not for coaches like John McLendon, Eddie Jackson, Harry Jefferson, and Mack Greene—men who were never given the chance to play or coach at the highest levels of college or professional basketball themselves—there might never have been national college tournaments for black players to showcase their talents for the professional scouts.

What those black coaches did was begun because they wanted fairness between the races. What they could not have known at the time was that what was best for individual black players would eventually prove to be bad for their own small black colleges.

My friend John McLendon later added another first to his resumé by becoming the first black professional coach, joining the American Basketball Association's Denver Rockets in 1969. His contributions to basketball were recognized in time, and he was named to the Basketball Hall of Fame in 1979. He died in October 1999. I am proud to have known him and to have called him my friend. Whenever the CIAA tournament rolls around in February, I still look for him, though I know he is not there. All of us in black college basketball greatly miss the man who changed the game forever.

CHAPTER 7

Recruiting Northeastern Players Begins in Earnest

Not long after I established myself at WSTC, a friend of mine suggested that we go meet the new girls in town. He had heard that a couple of new female instructors had arrived to teach in Winston-Salem's school system, and he wanted to check them out. As teachers ourselves, we couldn't date our own students, so I was ready to meet an interesting young woman who had nothing to do with the college.

The person I met was Clara Berry, a West Virginia native and the daughter of a United Methodist minister and a homemaker. Clara, a graduate of the University of Pittsburgh, had been hired to teach Latin to the black students in Forsyth County's public-school system. That tells you a lot about her intelligence and the level of education that was in our public schools at that time.

Clara says the first thing she remembers about me was that I filled the doorway of the house where she was staying. I was taken with her.

*This photo shows Clara and me on our wedding day in
Annapolis, Maryland. I may still have that same suit. I know I
still have my same wife.*

(CLARENCE E. GAINES PERSONAL COLLECTION)

I don't know anything about love at first sight, but we were married in 1950. We have two children—Lisa and Clarence Jr.—and four grandchildren—Loran and Ryan (Lisa's children with husband Raymond Eugene McDonald) and Olivia and Garrett (Clarence Jr.'s children with wife Cheryl Newman Gaines). We also have two godchildren, who we like to think of as being as close as any of our own children. One is Caroline Lattimore, who holds a doctorate. The other is Kevin G. Wallace of San Francisco, the son of one of my former coaches, Cleo Wallace.

Being a coach's wife is not something most women would enjoy. When the team is winning, the coach is loved. When the team is losing, the coach is not nearly so popular. I was loved most of my career in Winston-Salem, but it was my wife who heard the catcalls on those days when Big House couldn't do anything right. I rarely heard the shouts and remarks because I was concentrating on the team. Clara heard them. She could do nothing but listen to them. She would never respond to them. She says hearing the things people were saying about her husband made her a stronger woman by ignoring them.

Clara has watched me drive off to away games when I might come clomping back into the house early the next morning. She has been awakened in the middle of the night by telephone calls telling me something about one of my wayward players. I never intentionally brought my coaching problems home to her, because home was home, and coaching troubles were supposed to be left at the office. She never complained.

I would bring home coaches to play poker and players to eat pizza. I never asked her to mother my teams, and she never volunteered. Most of those young men had mothers, but some of them didn't have fathers. Clara didn't mind my playing their surrogate father, even if it meant taking some time away from my own family.

Through it all, Clara has been there. Maybe it is because she treats me just as she did her Latin students. She never put up with any nonsense from her students, and she has never allowed me to get away with any either. After more than 54 years of marriage, she still calls me "Gaines," the same last-name address she used with her students. It is

*This is a portrait of my family in 1977—(from left) Clara,
Clarence Jr., me, and Lisa.*

(NOTTINGHAM STUDIO PHOTO IN THE CLARENCE E. GAINES PERSONAL COLLECTION)

not "Mr. Gaines" but "Gaines." I answer to that name when she calls. I always have.

I also want to take a few lines to talk about my daughter, Lisa, and son, Clarence, who grew up surrounded by basketball and football players and university employees. I treated my children much as I treated my players. Clara and I taught them to be independent thinkers with few hard-and-fast rules. We instilled in them what was right and what was wrong and allowed them to sort out for themselves the gray areas between those two realities. Clara and I figured that was part of allowing them to grow up. They both seemed to instinctively know what was expected of them. I can't remember ever being disappointed in them.

I guess it says something about how independent my kids were that Lisa grew up more interested in reading books than she was in watching basketball games. Clarence did get interested in sports, but not enough to follow his daddy into coaching.

My kids have fond memories of life with Big House. Both of them would come onto campus after school to help out around someone's office or to watch me conduct practices. I might have been gone at night on occasion during the basketball season, but I was always able to keep an eye on them when they got home from school. I guess I was lucky in the sense that my kids could come and watch their daddy at work, while he made sure they got a start on their homework.

In a school of barely 500 students where the males numbered just under 200, most of the young men on my early teams had no illusions that they were anything more than students who played at being athletes. Most of them simply wanted to play a sport like basketball for fun, as a diversion from their studies to become teachers. In the days before black kids were invited to play professional basketball, there was nowhere else they could take their ball-handling skills after high school but to college, where they hoped to learn a career in class, not a career on the court.

Sure, playing basketball was fun for the future teachers I had on my teams from 1946 to 1949, but I reasoned there was nothing preventing my working to attract real student-athletes, convincing excellent high-school basketball players that they wanted to be teachers.

I had done some minor recruiting in 1946, but my standards were lower in those early days. I was looking for players—any players—to fill out my team. I went to where I knew coaches and family members, to western Kentucky and southern Illinois. I bumped it up a notch in 1949, when I sent Boo Brown to New York and I went back to the Midwest. Now, as the 1950s began and I finally knew what I was doing as a coach, I wanted to find really good players. I needed to boost my recruiting another notch.

I convinced the president of the school, Dr. F. L. Atkins, to give me a little money to use to find student-athletes who might be persuaded to come to our little teachers' college in North Carolina. By "a little money," I mean a very little money, just enough to pay my gasoline and food expenses on recruiting trips. The college did not have any wealthy boosters, no rich graduates who could funnel secret payments to players to convince them to come to our college. All we had was my powers of persuasion.

I had already rejected the idea of recruiting only from North Carolina or even the South because segregation had kept the sport of basketball from growing in the black community. Most towns in the South did not spend money on municipal recreation programs for minorities, so there were no indoor recreation centers or even many paved outdoor courts. The only time black kids would play basketball was in their school gyms during the fall and winter basketball seasons. The rest of the time, those gyms would be used for other forms of recreation, and were maybe even closed in the summer, when there was no school. Basketball in the South was a seasonal sport.

I needed to recruit athletes in a place where basketball was a way of life among black teenagers.

I could do that in southern Illinois. For some reason, they played more basketball on the north side of the Ohio River than the kids did on the south side. But I had been selling the college in that area since 1946. With the 1950s approaching, I was like a salesman who has pitched just about everyone in his territory. I needed to open some new territory.

There was another place where I knew kids played basketball year-round—the Northeast. I decided to center on New York City and Newark, stretching up north into Connecticut, west out to Trenton, New Jersey, and then down into nearby Philadelphia, Pennsylvania. It was an area with a 100-mile radius.

This was not unfamiliar territory for me. For three summers in my teenage years in the late 1930s, I had lived and worked with my uncle Lawrence Bolen as he delivered food to restaurants for the Uco Food Company from his home base in Newark. As the union foreman, he had his choice of routes. He would vary those routes so he could see more of the Northeast every day, rather than just driving up and down the same city streets. I would help him load and unload the groceries and take in the urban scenery. Working in and around New York City was quite an experience for a boy who had just 35 classmates in his high-school class and who lived in a city with fewer than 30,000 people.

I didn't know it at the time, but those summers were some of the most important days of my life. While riding around in the truck with Uncle Lawrence, I learned how to navigate the biggest cities in the United States. We might be driving in Newark one day, in Harlem the next day, in Manhattan the next day, and in Brooklyn the next day. At the end of the week, we might be in Trenton. I saw where all of the high-school gyms were. More importantly, I learned where all of the neighborhood recreation centers were, which is where the kids played basketball when they weren't in school. Once in a while, those playgrounds were near a restaurant. While my uncle was talking to the store managers, I might shoot a few baskets with the locals. I came to know those inner-city neighborhoods just as I knew the dirt streets back home in Paducah.

Now, more than a decade later, here I was riding those same streets again, looking for those same basketball playgrounds. I had to find some players who could help me.

I needed help in order to face teams like John McLendon's North Carolina College at Durham and another powerhouse in the CIAA, West Virginia State College at Institute. The Yellow Jackets, coached by Mark Cardwell, had gone undefeated in the 1947-48 season and had won the CIAA tournament two years running, in 1948 and 1949.

Their best player in those years was Earl "Big Cat" Lloyd, who had come out of an Alexandria, Virginia, high school. I don't know why he didn't go to an in-state school like Virginia State, Virginia Union, or Hampton. It would not have mattered. My team would have had to face him anyway, as those schools were all in the CIAA.

Lloyd was a six-foot-six, 220-pound forward who averaged 14 points and eight rebounds a game during most of his college career. I don't remember if we ever beat West Virginia State on their home court, but I do know one thing. I never told my team that Lloyd had been named All-Conference in high school. Later, as he matured and became even better, I never told my teams that he made All-CIAA and All-American in college. I tried to keep my kids as ignorant about West Virginia State and Earl Lloyd as I could.

Warning those boys about Lloyd would have only made them even more frightened of him. Nearly 60 years after my 1947 team played West Virginia State, one of them, James Trice, still remembers the final score. West Virginia State beat us 66-25, and they could have beaten us worse if they had really tried. That was the year that West Virginia State was the only undefeated college basketball team in the nation.

Lloyd was so good as a college player that the professional teams could not ignore him. Just as the time had come in 1947 for Jackie Robinson to integrate professional baseball, the time had come in 1950 to integrate the National Basketball Association. Lloyd, Harold Hunter of North Carolina College at Durham, Chuck Cooper of Duquesne University, and Nate "Sweetwater" Clifton of the Harlem Globetrotters were all offered professional contracts with the NBA in the summer of 1950. Earl Lloyd was actually the first black player to play in an NBA game, beating out the others by a day or so. Of the four, Lloyd had the best and longest NBA career, at 10 years. Cooper stayed for seven years. Lloyd went on to coach the Detroit Pistons in 1970. I should note that two of the first four black players came out of the CIAA, and that one of them was trained by John McLendon.

All in all, things could have been worse for me in the mid-1940s. Before Chuck Cooper played for Duquesne, he had served a hitch in the navy. But before he was drafted, he had been accepted at West Virginia State. If Cooper had not been drafted by the navy and had taken that scholarship offer from West Virginia State, my team would have faced both Lloyd *and* Cooper for four years.

There was one other aspect I did not like about playing West Virginia State and Bluefield State College, also in West Virginia. Those colleges had tough teams to beat, but more to the point, those places were damn hard to get to in the 1940s, before there were any interstate highways. I used to put the most talkative player on the team beside me on the front seat of the station wagon I drove when we went to faraway games at West Virginia State, about 220 mountainous miles from Winston-Salem. That player's job was not to talk over basketball strategy on the way to the game or to figure out why we won or lost after the game. That player's job was to say anything that would keep me awake driving those twisting, steep mountain roads. My players did a good job, as I never wrecked coming back from any of those games.

There I was in 1950, wondering how I would find players who were as good as Earl Lloyd. My solution was to search out those New York City and New Jersey playgrounds I remembered from the 1930s. On those playgrounds, I could see kids playing any hour of the day, any day of the week, any week of the year. I rarely talked to the inner-city high-school coaches or asked to see the kids' high-school won-loss records. I could watch them on the playgrounds and see if they had the skills that I needed for my college teams.

This was essentially a continuation of the strategy I had developed the previous year, when I sent my assistant coach, Alvin "Boo" Brown, to New York City, his old stomping ground, to start looking for talent. Boo had hit on talent almost immediately, finding me a tall man for center, six-foot-seven Willis Johnson, who would play for WSTC from 1949 to 1953. He would be captain of the team in his senior year, 1953, which was the year we won our first CIAA championship.

The story of how Boo came up with Willis is typical of how we found many of our players. Boo had been looking for a friend of Willis's who was supposed to be a good player, when Willis showed up on the playground. Sizing up his height, Boo suggested Willis try out, too. Willis, from the Bronx, had already planned to go to City College of New York, but when Boo and I invited him over to a high-school gym in New Jersey for a formal tryout, he came just to see what we were about. We liked what we saw. To our surprise, Willis also liked what we had to say. Instead of taking the slot at CCNY, Willis came down to Winston-Salem. He decided he liked the city so much he stayed there after graduation. Willis was a pioneering recruit for me, one of the college's first recruiting successes out of New York City.

Boo got a job offer from another college about that time, so I lost

*Here is the 1952-53 CIAA championship team, my first. Sitting,
left to right: Arthur Crockett, Leon Whitley, James Jones, Willis
Johnson, Donald Asctwood, Marshall Emery, and Robert
Claybrook. Standing, left to right: Clarence Jones, Nathaniel
Potts, Fred Parker, James Price, Millard Harris, William Vance,
Fred Blyther, and Nathaniel Robinson*

(Winston-Salem State University Archives)

my main contact in New York City. But I kept up with the recruiting
myself after entering Columbia University in New York City in the
summer of 1950 to pursue my master's degree in physical education.
Making the rounds of the Harlem playgrounds was easy, as that is
where Columbia is based. On weekends, I would head over to the
Bronx or to Newark, tracking down those recreation centers I remembered from my days delivering food with Uncle Lawrence.

The best place to find players in 1950 was a Harlem playground at
128th Street and Seventh Avenue managed by a New York City parks
supervisor named Holcombe Rucker.

Rucker, who was only a couple of years older than I, was better than a junior-high or high-school coach when it came to evaluating talent. He took an interest in every kid who came through the chain-link fence surrounding his playground. Even if a kid couldn't play at the same level as the best players on the court, Rucker still learned his name and his home life, determined how smart he was in school, and demanded that he treat every person he encountered on the playground with respect.

In exchange, Rucker gave his time to coach these young boys and teenagers on how to play proper basketball. What he actually did was allow them to mix their self-taught street-ball skills with the discipline he knew was required of ballplayers who would play in college for no-nonsense coaches in front of omnipotent referees.

In 1947, Rucker had so many kids from other neighborhoods coming to his recreation center that he organized a regular tournament, inviting the kids to form their own teams and then to play against each other. Over the course of a few months, all types of clubs, from YMCA and church teams to neighborhood pickup teams, began to show up at his playground. Teams of players from all of the other New York City boroughs came to Harlem just to play on Rucker's courts. Sometimes, teams from across the Hudson River in New Jersey showed up.

In time, the league of amateur teams was divided into a high-school and a college division. The college division really was based on age, as it attracted both college players who were home on vacation and kids old enough to have gone to college but who may have flunked out or who had been left behind because they did not have the academic credentials to get in and stay in school. In time, Rucker was even forced to add a professional league because he had so many NBA players showing up who wanted to relive their days on the playgrounds.

The scene during weekend games at this recreation center was amazing. Thick crowds of people surrounded the park, jockeying for any open spot in which to stand and watch the sports action. This was no school gym with bleachers. The recreation center's courts were simply outdoor basketball courts surrounded by a chain-link fence.

Rucker's requests to the city's recreation department to add bleachers were repeatedly turned down. This was during the days when any request from uptown, black Harlem went to the bottom of the stack, compared to any request from downtown, white Fifth Avenue. No matter how popular Rucker's little Harlem park was with the public and how much it was used by the kids, it always appeared shabby compared to the garden spots you could find in downtown Manhattan.

Racism existed as strongly in New York City as I ever experienced it in the South. The difference was that in the South, we blacks knew the rules because the signs were out in the open where we could read them, like "Colored Waiting Room" and "Whites Only" drinking fountains. The people in the North never wrote anything down as they did in the South. As a black man in the North, you never could know for sure when you were crossing a racial line until you crossed it.

That was one thing I noticed about Rucker's tournaments. There never seemed to be any discrimination. I saw teams of white kids and Jewish kids playing teams of black kids. There might have been some taunting and teasing, but I never saw any racial incidents on those courts.

Since the weekend tournaments were mob scenes where you could not always see because of the crowds, I would come around to watch the kids play on their own after school. I was not the only black coach who was looking for raw talent. The players would sometimes notice a few men standing around watching their practices, so they would show off their fanciest moves to try to impress us college coaches. I would pick out the players I wanted to see again and then would arrange for my own private scrimmage to see how they did against each other.

Basketball fans familiar with NCAA rules may wonder if that sort of scouting was within today's rules. At that time, the NCAA had not admitted black schools into membership, so I was not bound by any of their rules.

I don't know what the rules were for white colleges, but for black colleges there was no recruiting season, no signing deadline, no rules about how many visits a prospect could make to a school, no rules about how much contact a head coach could have with a recruit—none of that stuff. I certainly didn't have any money to offer them above the table, much less under the table, so financial ethics never were a consideration under the circumstances in which I was operating.

I don't think I saw a single New York kid play a single high-school game. For one thing, the high-school season pretty much tracked with the college season, so I was busy with my own playing schedule when they were playing high-school ball. For another, it was a long drive or train ride to New York from Winston-Salem, and my tiny recruiting budget simply did not allow for that kind of special trip. And finally, I really didn't need to see how they played against another team in order to judge their talent. I was never overly impressed with awards like All-City. I could judge if a kid had mastered the fundamentals of playing basketball within a few minutes of watching him play anybody. I didn't need to see him in a regulation high-school game. I knew he was going to play just as hard on the playground as he would on the high-school court—maybe harder, because he knew when he was playing in front of me that he was trying out for a college scholarship.

It took awhile for my reputation to build on those playgrounds, but by the mid-1950s, the black kids in the boroughs of New York knew that the man who fit the description of Big House was a college coach looking for players with basketball skills who had the brains to make it in college. It helped that kids like Willis Johnson, a veteran of the Rucker tournaments, were succeeding in college and that word of Willis's success was filtering back to the younger players in his neighborhood. It wasn't long before the best of the kids were making sure they were at the top of their game when they found out which playgrounds I was scouting.

Though I was starting to shift my attention to the Northeast, I didn't neglect the Midwest. I still would recruit in my home region, as much to drop by and see my parents as anything. Still, there was talent to be found.

One player I found who never quite worked out to his full potential was Tommy Reynolds from Carbondale, Illinois. Tommy never seemed to grasp the discipline that was necessary for a basketball team to be successful. Twice he went home on his own, and twice I sent my mother over to Carbondale to put him back on the bus to Winston-Salem.

My mother got tired of that.

"Clarence, this is the last time I am going to get Tommy. The next time, you can drive out here yourself and get him," she told me in a telephone call.

My parents were enjoying my chosen career in college athletics, even though I had not become the dentist my mother hoped I would be. Both of them followed my career as best they could from the scattered newspaper accounts they could find. Even though I was a hometown hero, it still did not make much sense for Paducah's newspaper to carry news about a small North Carolina college basketball team.

My mother liked to dig me about my varying successes at basketball.

"Clarence, what does it feel like to lose?" she would ask me.

"Why do you ask, Momma?" I would say, knowing the answer I would get.

"Because I never lost a single game when I was playing high-school basketball. I don't know what it feels like to lose," she would always answer with a little smirk on her face.

I never could figure out a good comeback. My mother really was a great basketball player in high school, and her team was undefeated in her entire career. She really did not know what it was like to lose. I would learn quite a bit about losing in my career on my way to winning my 828 games.

My parents' lives got better once I graduated from college, thanks to their entrepreneurial skills. They bought the Metropolitan Hotel at 724 Jackson Street in Paducah in 1951 and renovated it back to the way it had been in its glory days when it was built in 1909. At the time they bought the hotel, there was a lot of construction occurring on the Ohio River, and they realized that the black workers who would be finding jobs would need a place to stay.

In addition to the long-term guests, the Metropolitan was also one of the few black hotels in western Kentucky. In its heyday in the '50s and '60s, it was often filled with celebrities. My parents hosted entertainers such as Louis Armstrong, Fats Domino, B. B. King, and Ike and Tina Turner. One of my mother's vivid memories was

My parents bought The Metropolitan Hotel in Paducah, Kentucky, after I left home. They played host to all kinds of famous black entertainers in the 1950s and 1960s, since The Metropolitan was one of the few black hotels in that part of the county. Everyone from Louis Armstrong to Ike & Tina Turner enjoyed my parents' hospitality.

(CLARENCE E. GAINES PERSONAL COLLECTION)

of Louis Armstrong using her bureau to lay out an array of white silk handkerchiefs that he used to hold his trumpet. Luckily, I was in Winston-Salem, or my not-shy mother might have suggested that Louis ask me to play a duet with him, since I had learned to play the trumpet in high school.

Though I was in Winston-Salem when most of those celebrities passed through the hotel, they still had an influence on my family. I remember dropping my daughter off with my parents at the Metropolitan while Clara and I went on our own vacation. I left behind our four-year-old daughter, Lisa. When I returned, I picked up our four-year-old Tina Turner.

My father passed away in 1975 and my mother in 1983. My mother, the undefeated basketball player, passed away while my team was playing in Virginia. I think we won that night, so she must have been watching over me.

When I look back on my raising today, I know there is nothing more that I could have asked of my family than what I received.

CHAPTER 8

A Northern Scandal Sends Black Recruits South

During the midwinter of 1950-51, a scandal erupted that destroyed the lives of a handful of college basketball players but which proved to be a golden opportunity for me and several other coaches in the CIAA.

The stage was set in the spring of 1950, when the team from the City College of New York won both the National Invitational Tournament and the NCAA championship. Today, the NIT is run like a consolation prize to the "March Madness" conducted by the NCAA, but in 1950 both tournaments were about equal in standing. For one team to win both tournaments was outstanding. It demonstrated the strength of the CCNY team.

CCNY was at the top of its game. It started the tournaments with a 17-5 regular-season record by beating both the defending NIT champion, San Francisco, by 19 points and the defending NCAA champion, Kentucky, by 39 points, the worst defeat of a Kentucky team coached by Adolph Rupp. This was in the days before television carried many professional sports, at a time when people had intense loyalty to their home-state or hometown college teams. I have read that CCNY was actually more popular than the New York Knicks. Knicks tickets were easily obtained, but the dearest tickets to purchase in those days were for those CCNY home games.

I went to some of those games and read about all of them. Like any other basketball fan, I thought I was seeing some great basketball. Still, as a basketball coach whose business was to watch players sink baskets in practice and during games, some things did not always seem right. CCNY would win some games by small margins that should have been blowouts. At the time, I did not think much about what was really happening.

What was happening was that the success of CCNY and other basketball schools such as Manhattan College, Long Island University, and even Kentucky had caught the attention of New York's extensive network of gamblers. These men were intensely interested in the point spread.

The concept of beating or coming in under the point spread was simple. Bookies would take bets on not only if the dominant college would beat a weaker team, but by how many points the stronger team would win. If a gambler bet that CCNY would win a game and the school lost, the bookies would keep the gambler's money. But CCNY rarely lost, so the bookies did not make much money under those circumstances. If the gambler bet that CCNY would win by 10 points and the point spread was 10 but the team won by only nine points, the bookies would keep the gambler's bet. That was where the bookies could make big money, when CCNY did not cover the point spread. Since CCNY was such a dominating team in 1950, the only way to make sure the players did not cover the point spread was to convince them to "shave points," or lose by less than the point spread.

According to the newspaper accounts that came after the scandal broke, during the summer before the basketball season started, the bookies had started contacting the basketball players they thought they could influence. Most of the players worked as waiters in hotels in the Catskill Mountains, where they would put on exhibition games for the hotel guests. The gamblers made a circuit around the hotels, feeling out which players they thought would listen to their pitches of making a few hundred or thousand dollars per game to still win, but win by less than the point spread. The players were too competitive to lose games intentionally. They wanted to win and wanted to be champions. But they figured if they could still win the game while shaving points and making a little spending money on the side, no one would be the wiser.

I remember being as surprised as anyone else when I opened the newspapers and read the headlines in January 1951. I was so removed from the idea of gambling that I had to have the Lincoln College coach explain the concepts of point spread and point shaving to me.

The case had been broken by one honest black player. A white bookie who had been a Manhattan College center approached a current player, Julius Kellogg, the first black center the college had ever had, with a bribe to shave points. Kellogg reported the offer to his coach, who informed Manhattan College's president, who told the police. The police started their investigation and arrested the bookmaker. The bookmaker then started talking, and the house of cards that was college basketball in New York City began to fall apart.

Several players from CCNY were arrested and charged with fixing a game that had taken place more than a year earlier. Two days later, black players from Long Island University, one of the first white universities to court blacks openly, were arrested. At the time, LIU was 20-4 and expected to be competing with CCNY to win one or both of the NIT and NCAA tournaments.

For a while, it seemed that every day brought news of another college player from a New York City-area college being arrested for accepting a bribe. As a fan and coach, I was appalled at what I was reading. College basketball was supposed to be about student-athletes doing their best while attending college and learning a career. College was not supposed to be a vehicle for gambling.

Then Adolph Rupp brought race into the story.

Coach Rupp of the University of Kentucky said it was only "niggers and Jews" who would be caught in a point-shaving scandal. He went on to say that the gamblers "couldn't touch my program with a 10-foot pole." He put his foot in his mouth very deeply because several months later, in the fall of 1951, three of Kentucky's best players, all white boys, were arrested for fixing a game that had taken place in Madison Square Garden in 1949. I heard from coaching buddies that Rupp was so angry with the arrested players that he did not speak to them for the rest of his life.

The arrests ended, but the effects lasted long afterward. Thirty-two players from seven colleges were found guilty of having fixed 85 games in 22 cities over a period of two years. Some of the players went to prison for a short time in a judicial effort to show how serious a crime they had committed. Some of the best college players of their day were banned from returning to their college teams and were also banned by the National Basketball Association from applying to turn professional. They were left in complete limbo.

That part was sad because I knew every single one of the black players. I had seen them on the playgrounds. Great players like Sherman White of Long Island University and Ed Warner of City College of New York lost whatever chance they had at taking their talents beyond their brief college careers.

Of course, this judicial show of putting a few kids in jail had little effect on the men who started the scandals. The bookies did not go away, nor did betting on college basketball games. It just returned underground, with the bookies a little wiser about who they would try to recruit into their scams.

We black college coaches who had been recruiting on the New York City playgrounds were surprised by what happened next, after the college students went to prison.

Although it was a black college player, Julius Kellogg, who went to the police and blew the scandal open, it was the black high-school athletes who followed him who suffered for his act of bravery in doing what was right for the game.

Instead of focusing only on the white and black college players who had been caught in the scandal, the white college coaches and presidents believed that the problem must have started with the sassy attitude of the fast-breaking street-ball players. In a twisted logic that we black coaches found racist, the white schools decided that since these black playground teenagers had little respect for the old way of playing basketball by standing in one place, passing the ball to teammates, and then taking carefully aimed shots at the basket, they must be more likely to get involved in gambling. Once the newspapers turned to other stories, the recruiting of black high-schoolers in New York City by white colleges essentially stopped.

It was the gamblers who recruited the college players, but the college administrations blamed the high-school players, who had nothing to do with either the gamblers or the college players!

The change in attitude by these white colleges was dramatic. In 1950, I used to see white men I didn't recognize hanging around the playgrounds of Harlem, the Bronx, and Newark all the time. I am sure they were Northern college coaches or scouts for those teams who were doing the same thing I was—looking for undiscovered talent. I never talked to them, since they were not my friends and since, most important of all, they were after the same players I needed for my team.

In the spring of 1951, after the point-shaving scandal had been covered by the newspapers, those white men disappeared. The only coaches I saw recruiting were the ones I knew and sometimes played against. Some of the CIAA coaches were recruiting, as were coaches such as Leonidas Epps from Clark College in Atlanta and John Brown from Benedict College in Columbia, South Carolina.

When we black coaches talked about the disaster that had befallen college basketball, it dawned on us that the scandal had a good side. Now that the white Northern colleges were ignoring them, these high-school players had nowhere else to go but to our small, black Southern colleges. The point-shaving scandal was forcing the athletes to consider schools they had never heard of, in cities they had never visited, and in a region of the country that frightened them.

We were approaching the situation from an entirely different viewpoint than the white college presidents and their coaches. The white colleges were worried about angering their alumni, who were worried about the admission of dishonest black students. My fellow black college coaches and I didn't care about the reputations of those white colleges. Our concern was educating black high-school students—and

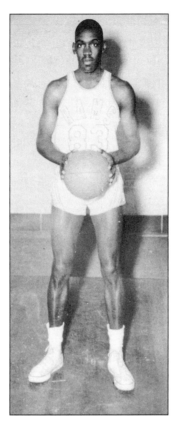

One of my early stars from New York City was Jack DeFares.

maybe winning a few basketball games. We recognized what the white Northern college coaches did not. The hundreds of athletes coming out of New York City high schools were entirely innocent of any scandal, and they deserved a chance.

Judging from my own experience of recruiting in New York City from the late 1940s through the mid-1970s, I would say the point-shaving scandal delayed the integration of black athletes into the mainstream of college education by at least a decade. Looking back on it 50 years later, I know it sounds odd to say that the scandal was good for me and my fellow black coaches, but there is no doubt that it helped build our programs. We might have competed with each other for student-athletes, but for at least 10 years we didn't have to worry about the major Northeastern schools recruiting "our" athletes.

I don't feel sorry at all for the white colleges who ignored those black students. Those college presidents, athletic directors, and basketball coaches chose the racist route of blaming those high-schoolers for what happened on their college campus. They ignored the talent those kids had both on the court and in the classroom and abandoned them without thinking twice about who would educate them and how they would work their way out of the inner city.

At the same time, I don't think being barred from those white universities hurt those inner-city students at all. The coaches of the small black colleges had only one thing to offer those players —a college education. That was what we promised them, and that was what we delivered.

In the years immediately following the betting scandal of 1951, I would say half of my players came from either New York City or parts of New Jersey and Connecticut that were close to New York City. I brought to Winston-Salem Teachers College players like Jack DeFares, who had been on several of New York's All-City teams. Coming with Jack was his best friend, Carl Green, who was our leading scorer in his freshman year and also made All-CIAA. Coming, too, was center Willis Johnson, who captained my first CIAA championship team in 1953, and Wilfred John, who had a field-goal percentage of .596 and who once hit 17 fouls shots in a game in CIAA competition. Other New Yorkers included Bobby Brown, Charles Riley, Ernest Brown, Sidney Lawson, and dozens of others too numerous to list. Coming from close by the city were Tommy Monteiro of Jamaica, New York, who once scored 17 straight foul shots to help us win one game, and Marshall Emery, who came from New Haven, Connecticut. Marshall played for us from 1950 to 1954 and was recruited by track coach Archie Morrow to play both basketball and run track.

I never met most of these players' high-school coaches, never saw them in a high-school game, never even met most of their parents. In those days, particularly among the small black colleges, there was no dancing around by the coaches trying to impress the recruit's families, as you see today with top prospects. Many of those young men

Another early star was Wilfred John.

did not have a stable home life. Most came from one-parent households where paying for college would have been impossible. For someone like a college coach to come along with the promise of a college education and a degree that would lead to a professional job was a dream come true.

I knew what kind of players I needed, and I could tell how they would perform just by looking at them when I saw them on the playground.

Good basketball players have big hands—big enough that they can grip a basketball with their long fingers. If a player can't hold a basketball out in front of him by gripping it with his fingers, he will never be a good ball handler.

Great ballplayers have to be equally comfortable shooting, dribbling, and passing with either hand. They don't have to be truly ambidextrous, but if both their right and left hands are equally strong, that helps.

They have to have strong, thick ankles and big feet to stand the shock of jumping and landing at sometimes odd angles. Good knees are important, but maybe not as important as people may think. Earl Monroe was knock-kneed, and his legs did not look like the legs of a ballplayer, but he turned out to be great.

Ballplayers have to have stamina. A ballplayer who got tired after running up and down the court a few times was not the player I wanted. When I put a team of five men on the court, I expected them to stay there the entire game. As long as the game was going well, I rarely substituted unless someone got in foul trouble or got hurt.

Past the physical characteristics, players should be concerned with teamwork but also possess some selfishness mixed in with a strong sense of confidence.

A shooter has to be somewhat selfish. That is the whole point of the position. He is the one who is supposed to make the most points. The only way he can do that is if the guards get him the ball. A guard has to be unselfish, willing to play a supporting role by constantly feeding the ball to someone else who he knows the fans consider the star player.

Finding the right psychological mix created a challenge in sorting out all of these characteristics in New York street-ball players. These kids had not been brought up on the fundamentals of being able to shoot different styles of shots from different parts of the court. They were fast-break players accustomed to shooting on the run and even carrying the ball all the way down the court if they could get a step on the defense. All of them thought they were stars. Most of them were selfish. Even when they played as a team, they would have preferred to perform as individuals. I had nothing against fast-break ball. I had learned that lesson from John McLendon's North Carolina College at Durham team. But I had to have a team who knew that the fast break never could overshadow the fundamentals of the game.

Finally, I looked for players who naturally would be leaders on the court and for other athletes who would be willing to follow their leaders. Coaching basketball from the sidelines during a game is highly overrated by the media. I always believed my job was to condition the players in preseason and during practices, remind them of the fundamentals of the game, and then permit them to play the game as it developed. I couldn't get on the floor and shoot the ball for them. I could shout in a play now and then or tell them when the other team's defense had changed, but I still wasn't the one going up against the defenders. I needed leaders on the floor who could read the flow of the game and make adjustments. I needed athletes who knew instinctively what to do when the game was going their way and when it wasn't. You can't coach leadership into an athlete once he is a member of the team. You have to find that sense of leadership in the athlete and then develop that characteristic.

At the same time, I had to develop the sense in the other players that they had to trust that leader on the court. Maybe they had been leaders themselves on their own teams, but once I decided who would be my leader on the team that year, I needed the rest to follow him.

In answer to the obvious question of why I did not talk to the high-school coaches to find out each player's characteristics, I will say that was because there was little time for formal contact. Besides, I already knew from my own observations and research that some of the players were outstanding.

For instance, DeFares and Green, who had been friends since they were 11, were the only black kids on New York's All-City basketball team in 1953. They were from different parts of the city and had been cross-town rivals at different high schools. Everything I could find out about them made me think that they would make great teammates. They knew each other's strengths and weaknesses and the way the other would move on the court in different situations.

I first met both of them after watching an intense Rucker tournament game. I grabbed one player by the shoulder and asked him if he could tell me how to find Jack DeFares and Carl Green. The boy looked me up and down and asked back, "Who wants to know?" He thought I was a huge black cop who suspected that the players were on their way to a dice game—which they were.

The person I had grabbed admitted that he was Carl. Once I told him I was a college coach scouting talent, he called over Jack. We talked for a while, and I got them to agree to go over to Newark to a YMCA gym where I was setting up tryouts. Neither one of them had ever crossed the Hudson River to Newark. I doubt either of them had ever been out of their own uptown or downtown neighborhoods except to visit each other. As Carl explained it, and as I was learning myself from living in New York City, neighborhoods were sacred things. Kids just did not cross neighborhood lines unless they had someone from that neighborhood along to introduce them.

From that one private game I staged at the gym in Newark, I found four players from Newark and five from New York City who I thought would make good players for Winston-Salem Teachers College.

Why didn't I talk to my prospective players' parents? Again, there were the issues of time and budget. I was in New York to study for my master's degree, not to be on a recruiting junket. More importantly, many of these young men did not want me to know about their home life. Most of them did not have fathers, and some did not have mothers. Some were living with extended family, such as their aunts. They were embarrassed by their poverty and did not want me seeing their dangerous neighborhoods.

Their escape from that environment was the playgrounds. They excelled on the basketball court, and just like anyone from the upper crust trying to impress a Harvard recruiter, they wanted to put their best foot forward when they heard I was a college coach interested in seeing them play and maybe offering a scholarship. In many cases, I was the only one talking to them. They knew they had to do all they could to impress me.

How did I know that these prospects could do college-level

coursework? I didn't. I sometimes asked them to bring me their report cards or records from school. I would find that some of them had low Scholastic Aptitude Test scores and low grade-point averages. If their low school production was matched by a low opinion of themselves, I knew they had no chance to make it in college. But if the boys had a positive spirit about themselves, a sense that they conveyed to me that they could do college-level work, I kept after them. Low high-school grades or not, if I thought they had the drive to make it in college—and if they could help my basketball team—I was apt to give them the chance. If I hadn't brought them to college, they would not have gone. They would have had to look for a job that required no more than a high-school degree.

I was never dishonest with any of these early prospects, but I will confess that I did not tell them the whole story either. Winston-Salem Teachers College in the 1950s was exactly what it sounded like. The only degree you got from the college in those days was one that qualified you to teach in the elementary and secondary schools.

When I talked to prospects, I emphasized that they would leave the college with a four-year degree that would take them anywhere they wanted to go. Granted, that was usually into an elementary or high-school classroom, but it was still a college degree.

My competing coaches at North Carolina College at Durham and North Carolina A&T in Greensboro worked for liberal-arts colleges with many more degree programs that educated students in business and the sciences. If a student asked me specifically about business or the sciences, then I would suggest he contact those colleges. But if he were satisfied with the scholarship leading to a degree from Winston-Salem Teachers College, I never pressed him.

Another thing that I never made a point of warning these New York recruits about was what life was like in the segregated South. If I had, they may have skipped college entirely.

CHAPTER 9

The Team
Starts to Jell

The first inkling my New York recruits had that life was going to change for them for the next four years of their lives was when they changed trains in Washington, D.C. In the station, a conductor gathered all of the black people from all the cars and took them to the colored cars.

These New Yorkers had no idea why they were being moved to other cars until the conductors told them that it was the law in most Southern states that black people could not ride in the same train cars with whites. In Winston-Salem and throughout the South, they would learn that there were two standards in most public facilities—one for whites and one for blacks.

That was a culture shock. Most of these kids had gone to all-black schools because they lived in black neighborhoods, but they had played white high schools throughout their high-school days. Some of them had played on integrated YMCA teams or were accustomed to playing with white kids on the playgrounds. Few of them had ever been out of the city of New York, but they were used to riding buses and subways side by side with white people, with neither race thinking much of it.

One of my players got a rude shock about the culture into which he had moved when he first arrived in Winston-Salem and decided to take a walk downtown to see what the city was like. He was walking with two students from South Carolina when a white cop drove up, rolled down his window, and ordered them off of the sidewalk. The two Southern-born guys immediately complied, but my New Yorker did not. He was not being disrespectful to the officer, but he had no idea why the cop had yelled at them. He thought he had somehow misunderstood what the cop had said, so he was waiting for some sort of clarification. He understood when the policeman pulled out his pistol, pointed it at him, and told him again to get off of the sidewalk.

Some of the players were surprised to learn that the school had fewer than 800 students, but they felt better once I told them that about 600 of those students were girls. The players liked the looks of the new Whitaker Gymnasium, though it sat just 2,000 people, about what an average game at a Harlem tournament would draw in standing-room-only crowds.

Seeing the campus and the city did dash the dreams of some fellows. Carl Green and Jack DeFares came down in 1953 hauling trunks full of tailor-made suits that they intended to wear nightclubbing. I had to break the news to them that their dreams of finding a place like Harlem's Cotton Club would not be fulfilled in this Southern town.

The athletes I recruited from Kentucky, southern Illinois, and southern Indiana had less of a culture shock when they climbed down from the bus. The Kentuckians most easily adapted. Separation of the races and inequality of services based on one's race were encountered daily in their towns. Just like me, they had grown up with segregation. And just like me, they realized that while it might be unfair to them, there was not much they could do about it on their own. They adapted, hoping that one day the climate would change.

Though life was easier on the north side of the Ohio River, those Midwestern kids still saw their share of racism. There were places where blacks were supposedly welcome, but where in reality they were not.

For instance, black athletes going to college in southern Illinois could go to classes on campus, but they could not live in the dorms.

I found it curious that there were cultural differences between the Midwesterners and the New Yorkers based on how they played sports. All of these athletes were black, all of them were poor, all of them were good basketball players, and all of them wanted something better in life. That was no problem. The problem arose because the two sections of the country had entirely different ways of playing basketball.

The athletes I had recruited from around my home region played the traditional style of basketball, with the emphasis on waiting until everyone was in position, then passing to the open shooter, who would take aim at the basket with one of his selection of shots. This was the type of game that Dr. Naismith had taught at Kansas and which every high-school team—black or white—was accustomed to playing in the Midwest.

The New Yorkers paid little attention to that type of deliberate basketball. They wanted to grab the ball just after it dropped through the net, then run toward the other end of the gym before the opposition's defense had time to get set. As high-schoolers, they had played the fast-break type of game that John McLendon had been adapting for his college teams.

When I mixed these two kinds of kids on the gym floor during practice, they did not exactly mesh. The street kids from New York City laughed at how precise the Midwesterners were in posting to their corners, then aiming their set shots. The Midwesterners wondered if the game the New Yorkers were playing could even be called basketball, since the city kids' playground game looked nothing like the rules said it should. While the analogy may not be quite right, I'll always remember that these athletes from two different regions of the country with two different views on playing the same game sometimes re-fought the Civil War.

I brought both sides together when they discovered they did have something in common—they were afraid of me. I was not some old high-school coach who had been hanging around the gym for decades. I was barely out of my 20s, so I was not even 10 years older than some of them. At six-foot-five and anywhere from 250 to 265 pounds, depending on how much I was eating and how often Clara was demanding that I stop eating, I was as big as or bigger than all of them. While they may have called me "Coach" to my face, I knew that among themselves, some of them had changed my nickname from "Big House" to "Big Nasty."

That was okay by me. Players are supposed to fear their coach at times, love him at times, and hate him at times. It is up to the coach to demonstrate to the team that they should respect him and what he is trying to do to bring about cohesion and win games.

A coach may not have winning seasons every year because his teams' talent may not be good enough to produce those wins. But if a coach can't create a team spirit, he needs to find something else to do. I may have had some losing seasons toward the end of my career, but I never lost sight of the need to make my bunch of athletes into a true team. I think that is the reason my teams dating back to the first one in 1946 still think of themselves as small fraternities of men with shared experiences.

One of the coaches who helped me fulfill my role as athletic director at Winston-Salem Teachers College was Wilbur Ross, who served as track coach from 1953 through 1959. I originally hired Wilbur as an assistant basketball coach, but when Archie Morrow took another job, I asked Wilbur to step into the role as track coach. He agreed without thinking too much about one little problem. WSTC did not have a 400-meter track. It had few starting blocks, hurdles, or even uniforms. Most of the school's training was done on a hard-packed grass field, while most of our competitors had real running tracks, a luxury that we could not yet afford.

Wilbur started building the team's reputation immediately. In the first meet the school ran, WSTC garnered only one point. Each year, the school improved, until in 1959 WSTC won the NAIA national track championship by one point over a much larger team. The amazing thing was that it was done with only three athletes: Elias Gilbert, Godfrey Moore, and Russell Rogers. Gilbert won all three hurdles events. We won the national championship though we still did not have a proper track.

When I am asked to name a coach who did more with less, I always point to Wilbur Ross.

Though most of my basketball recruiting was out of state, I did meet one tall 14-year-old in 1952 in High Point, North Carolina. I tried to convince him to keep Winston-Salem Teachers College in the back of his mind when it came time to go to college.

High Point was hosting the national YMCA basketball tournament, and I saw an extremely tall kid who also played good ball. I did have some knowledge of him because he had a cousin attending WSTC. Somehow, I convinced him to ride with me over to Winston-Salem to see our campus. He would not be entering college for another three years, but it was not too soon to start pitching.

The young man was not impressed by our little campus. In 1955, he entered the University of Kansas. In just two varsity seasons, he averaged 30 points and 18 rebounds a game, with a high of 52 points scored against one team and 36 rebounds in another game. In his first year playing NBA basketball, Wilt Chamberlain would be named the Rookie of the Year.

I think that even at 14 years of age, Wilt was smart enough to know that the bigger colleges, even the white ones, would come courting him, so he never even considered playing for my little school. Still, I had tried. You never know what is going to happen until you try.

Over 47 years of coaching basketball, I emphasized three things that I believe led to my teams' success on the court.

I believed in conditioning the players. I made them run over to the football stadium every morning in the dark. I made them run wind sprints in the gym during practice. They may have hated practicing, but they thanked me for it after playing the games. Our game was about running and shooting, so they had to be ready to do both.

I believed in playing my best guys. My friend Cal Irvin at North Carolina A&T believed in having a "platoon" team, where he had a bench full of substitutes who could jump into the game at any time and be expected to perform as well as anyone coming off of the court. I believed my best players earned their slots in practice, but I expected them to prove it by playing the entire game unless they got hurt or ran into foul trouble. If they got tired, then they were not conditioned enough.

And finally, I believed in practicing the fundamentals of the game, whether or not the fundamentals were used on game night. If my boys could not sink a basket from any part of the forecourt, if they could not outrebound the other team, or if their passes were intercepted by the defenders, then we had not practiced those fundamentals enough.

I had good recruiting years in the early 1950s as I began my quest to become more competitive in the CIAA. At that time, the CIAA was dominated by four schools. One of them was John McLendon's North Carolina College at Durham, which had just dropped "for Negroes" and changed its name in 1947. John's team had won the first CIAA tournament in 1946 and had won again in 1950. Also strong was Mark Cardwell's West Virginia State, which had won the tournament in 1948 and 1949, with Earl Lloyd leading the way. Earl's value had since been recognized by the NBA. In 1947, Virginia State, under Coach Harry "Big Jeff" Jefferson, had won the tournament. The most dominating team of all was Virginia Union of Richmond, coached by Tricky Tom Harris, who had won the tournament in 1951 and 1952.

Winston-Salem Teachers College had not done well in the CIAA tournament up until that point. We had lost 42-33 in the 1946 tourney; we didn't play in the second; we had been slaughtered 81-41 in the third by Virginia Union; we didn't play in the fourth or fifth; we had lost to Lincoln 74-60 in the sixth; and we didn't play in the seventh, in 1952.

Though we had not won a trophy, I was proud of what my teams had done. Even in my first year of coaching, 1946, when I had to convince almost 6 percent of the entire male enrollment—10 out of 188—to come out for the team, we had what I considered a surprising 15-7 record. That team was a mixture of players I had brought back with me from a trip home to Paducah. They had formed an interesting mixture—walk-ons who had been too sickly or meek to be taken by the armed forces, along with some hard-drinking, hell-raising veterans ready to blow off some pent-up steam.

This is the 1953-54 team. Kneeling, left to right: *Carl Green, Jack DeFares, Marshall Emery, Clarence Jones, James Sessoms, Fred Parker, and Ed Sherrill.* Standing, left to right: *Jodie Wilson, Sidney Lawson, Harry Rogers, Don Bradley, Millard Harris, Calvin Price, Charles Riley, and Otis Hunter.*

(WINSTON-SALEM STATE UNIVERSITY ARCHIVES).

After six years, my record was 80-55. That wasn't a great record, but considering that the women outnumbered the men at my college by a ratio of three to one, and considering that we still had fewer than 1,000 students in the entire school, I thought it was pretty good.

Things all came together in the 1952-53 season. We won the regular-season CIAA championship in the last game of the year by beating Shaw 72-69. That gave us an 11-1 conference record and a 20-4 overall record.

That record sounds like it should have been good enough for a conference title, but in those days we used the Dickinson system of determining the championship. Dickinson was a college professor who devised a mathematical system that valued wins based on your opponents' records. It was complicated to keep up with, but it determined which teams had the hardest schedules, and thereby which teams deserved the championship. For instance, under Dickinson, a win over an opposing team with a winning season was worth more points than a win over an opponent with a losing season.

WSTC was tied in points with North Carolina College going into the final game, but they lost the same night we won. That plus the fact that we had beaten them twice during the regular season secured the championship for us.

The Shaw game was very exciting, with both teams taking turns tying the score in the closing seconds. Willis Johnson, my New York City center, tied it up for the final time with 12 seconds to play to send the game into overtime.

In overtime, Shaw and my players traded baskets, but then Marshall Emery, my Connecticut Yankee recruited by my track coach, Archie Morrow, scored a basket and a free throw to make the score 70-67. At that point, I had Johnson and a forward named Jim Jones freeze the ball by passing it back and forth for a minute and a half. Of course, that was in the days before the shot clock forced offensive players to try for the basket. As the game clock wound down, Johnson sank one more field goal. He led the team with 28 points.

The leading scorer for Shaw was a freshman named Sam Jones, who scored 17 points. But he was not *the* Sam Jones of North Carolina Central, whose name basketball historians probably recognize.

The story of *that* Sam Jones is another one where my old buddy John McLendon snookered me. While I was in New York City looking at street-ballers, Sam Jones was attending Laurinburg Institute, a private boarding school in North Carolina for promising black kids. When Sam graduated in 1951, he enrolled at North Carolina College. He would score 1,770 points in his four-year career and would win CIAA All-Conference recognition three times. Sam would be drafted in the first round by the Boston Celtics. In his 12-year career with them, he would help win 10 NBA championships. Of the black athletes turning professional in the mid-1950s, Sam was probably the most successful. But I didn't know about him until John McLendon sprung him on me.

Actually, we did pretty well against North Carolina College in Sam's freshman year. We beat them both times we faced them.

A few days after beating Shaw in the regular season, we started the CIAA tournament in Durham at North Carolina College's gym. When the tourney started, I had a sinking feeling, as we drew West Virginia State, who we had not beaten in regular-season or tournament play for three straight years. In our two regular-season games, we had lost to them 73-58 and 69-57. The games had not even been close.

But our players were up for this tournament game. The Yellow Jackets stayed ahead most of the game, but my team scrapped back, with Leon Whitley hitting his only field goal of the night to tie it at 53. The lead changed hands several times until my team finally sank three baskets in a row. We won 68-61.

One of the reasons we won, of course, was that Earl Lloyd had graduated one year earlier.

Our next tournament opponent was Morgan State College, my alma mater. Again, we trailed most of the game, but once again Whitley, a sophomore guard, sank his only basket of the night to tie the score. Marshall Emery sank two more baskets, and Whitley got a foul shot to put us ahead by five points. Once again, I told my team to freeze the game, and they passed the ball around. Against my orders, Willis Johnson went in for a layup with a minute left and scored a basket that sent the score to 49-42, but Morgan State had plenty of time to make something happen.

Morgan State got two quick baskets to come within three points. I told the team to freeze it again, and Morgan fouled Marshall Emery. He sank a foul shot to make it 50-46. Morgan State sank another basket, and we tried freezing again. Once again, Emery was fouled, and he sank a shot to make it 51-48. Just 20 seconds were left, but that was more than enough time for Morgan State to do something. I knew. I used to play for them.

They did it. Morgan State sank a very long basket to bring the score to 51-50 with just 10 seconds left. They stole the ball and tried another very long shot, but our James Jones, who scored only five points in the entire game, knocked it out of bounds as the game ended. We won the semifinal 51-50.

What a defensive game that turned out to be! Our high scorer was guard Willis Johnson with a whopping 12 points. Morgan State's high scorer was a guard with 10 points. I used a lot more players than normal. Nine different players scored points.

The tournament final was even more exciting. We played Saint Augustine's of Raleigh, normally a team that the stronger CIAA opponents considered a pushover. We had beaten them three times in the regular season. They were no pushover in this tournament. Neither team was ever more than five points ahead of the other. With just 25 seconds left in the game, Saint Augustine's went ahead 67-66. The always-reliable Willis Johnson tied the game at the buzzer with a free throw.

Twenty-four points were scored in the overtime. The game was tied with three seconds left when a jump ball went our way. James Jones got the tip and threw in a basket as the buzzer sounded. Saint Augustine's tried to say that the buzzer had sounded before James took his shot, but the referee ruled that the ball was in the air when the buzzer sounded. We won 77-75 to take our first CIAA crown.

What a season Winston-Salem Teachers College had! We won both the regular-season championship and the tournament. That was the first time that had happened since the CIAA tournament was founded in 1946. We won the most games in the school's history, won the conference championship for the first time in our history, and won the tourney for the first time in our history. It wasn't easy doing all three. We won the tourney by the skin of our teeth. In three games, the winning margin was just nine points total.

All that recruiting Boo Brown and I started had paid off. I was proud, and the school was proud. The whole city could have—should have—been celebrating, but the white people of Winston-Salem barely noticed. Though we had brought a multistate college conference championship to the city, notice of our win in the *Winston-Salem Journal* was placed below news of high-school sports wins. There were

Willis Johnson, one of my first recruits from New York City, and I share our first CIAA trophy.

(WINSTON-SALEM STATE UNIVERSITY ARCHIVES)

no photographs of the winning team or individual players. There were no photographs from any of the games.

You could tell how much status the college had with the local news desk by looking at our placement on the page. On the day we won the regular-season CIAA championship, the news was placed below several pictures of white small-college students who would be competing in a state tournament in the city that weekend. Our news had already taken place, while their news was still to come. Our win was news, while the white colleges had not made any news at all, but there we were below them! Winston-Salem Teachers College had beaten more than a dozen black colleges along the East Coast, and we still were not as important as the white athletes who had not played a single tournament game.

I was used to this kind of treatment by the newspaper, but it still irritated me. When I first came to the city in 1945, the only news black people got was in "Activities of Colored People," a column that covered everything from church socials to engagements. Winston-Salem Teachers College was in town, but the newspaper editors did not believe that anyone really cared much that we were there. Now, seven years after I had come to the city, "Activities of Colored People" was still the major source of news about black folks.

Still, the newspaper did occasionally put in photos of black people. On the same day that the *Journal* covered our first CIAA championship, it printed a photo and a small story about one of our track sprinters, Eugene Walcott. Eugene had won a local talent contest playing the violin. He was so good that he had been invited to play on a national television show. Eugene would later start using his given first name, Louis, and he would change his last name to Farrakhan. He is now the leader of the Nation of Islam.

For the next several years, WSTC joined the ranks of the elite CIAA teams. In 1954, we finished 25-8 but lost to Virginia Union in the championship game by a heartbreaking score of 56-55. In 1955, we went 21-6, finishing second to Virginia Union again in the tournament, by a score of 85-80. In 1956, we went 23-7 and finished in second place in the tournament to Maryland State, getting blown out by an embarrassing 106-76. I think that might have been the first time that any

Here I am with one of Winston-Salem Teachers College's sprinters in the 1950s, Eugene Walcott. Eugene went on to dedicate himself to his religion. He is now known as the Honorable Minister Louis Farrakhan, leader of the Nation of Islam.

(CLARENCE E. GAINES PERSONAL COLLECTION.)

CIAA championship game went over 100 points. I hated that my team was on the losing end.

We had finished as runners-up in the tournament three times in a row. I think that was some sort of record for losing, but I consoled myself and my team by pointing out that no one else had as good a record as we had over the last four years.

Nineteen fifty-seven was a better year. We finished the regular season 21-6, but we went into the tournament as underdogs to North Carolina College, since they had lost only three CIAA games. Our offense was ranked first, though we were fourth in defense and field-goal shooting.

We upset North Carolina College by a score of 63-54. That school no longer had my old nemesis and friend John McLendon, who had moved on to Tennessee A&I. My New Yorkers—Wilfred John, Charles

137

Riley, and Laurence Harrison—controlled the boards. John led the scoring with 20 points. We controlled the entire game, and I had the team slow it down as much as they could once we got ahead.

In the semifinal game, we stomped North Carolina A&T 81-61. That felt good because they had beaten us twice during the regular season. Wilfred John again led us with 26 points and 21 rebounds. He hit 10 of 14 field goals and seven of eight free throws. Harrison and Riley backed him up with good performances.

The final against Virginia State was a slow game, but we won it 48-42. This time, Charlie Riley was the high scorer, with 16 points, followed by Jack DeFares with 15. Wilfred John managed only 11. It was a very slow, defensive game. We were ahead 30-24 at the half, and we never gave up the lead, but if anyone had come to see action, they went to sleep. Wilfred John was named Most Valuable Player of the tournament for his 57 points and 54 rebounds.

During the entire tournament, I substituted just one player, and that was in the first game. As I said, I liked to play my best players, and they had better be ready to play as long as they were needed.

That year, the winner of the CIAA tournament was eligible to participate in the District 29 championship of the NAIA. This was the new championship series that John McLendon had worked hard to create, so black colleges could get a chance to play for a national championship. The winner would move on to Kansas City to play in the NAIA national championship.

The tournament brought in two teams we had not seen previously: Tennessee A&I, which was the Midwestern Athletic Conference champion, and Grambling State College, which was the runner-up in that conference.

I knew we were in a little bit of trouble when I read that Grambling's two pivotmen were six-foot-six and six-foot-nine. My tallest rebounder was Wilfred John at six-foot-three. I would have to rely on my New York street-ballers, DeFares and John, to keep the game running fast, as I could not count on our catching many rebounds against those giants up front.

I need not have worried. DeFares and John were hot, each hitting

25 points for the game. In fact, we led the entire game, once going ahead 22-10. The tall players from Grambling were good, but my street-ballers were better. In the end, we beat them 94-74.

That meant we had to face McLendon yet again. The game was like a dream match-up, the old master against the man who had been his willing student.

In fact, it turned out to be more like a nightmare than a dream for me. Tennessee A&I led all the way. We could never get closer than 10 points. In the end, Tennessee A&I won 100-80. Johnny had beaten me once again.

I do have to smile about that butt-kicking. John's team went on from being District 29 champion to being the NAIA champion in 1957, the first time that a black college won the NAIA championship. In winning the NAIA, he put to rest any lingering feelings among white college coaches that black colleges could not compete with them on an equal basis.

John McLendon went on to win the NAIA championship in 1958 and 1959. Of course, I wish I had won those years, but I am glad John did. He was the man who really taught me how to coach basketball, and he deserved those wins.

So there we were in 1957 with our second CIAA tournament championship and a runner-up finish for District 29 of the NAIA. Our playing was going well, and our recruiting was going even better. No longer would I have to go on my own to scout the playgrounds of the Northeast. My recruiting for the next 20 years would rely on a network of former players who knew what kind of talent I needed in Winston-Salem and knew how to find that talent on the playgrounds.

Things were about to get better. I was about to get one of the best college players who ever played the game. I say "get" rather than "recruit" because I never saw the kid play in high school and never saw him play on a playground. I never saw him at all until he arrived at my campus. He was recruited for me by a WSTC alumnus.

CHAPTER 10

I Get My
First Superstar

I am not perfect, and sometimes I am not lucky. Sometimes, those two facts collide, and I make a mistake.

For example, in 1956, Waltin Young, a WSTC graduate, called me to suggest I recruit a hot teenager from Newark. When I heard the athlete was a guard and only six feet tall and 175 pounds, I thanked Waltin but told him I would pass. I had all of the guards I needed. I wanted bigger, heavier men than that slight guard.

Waltin did not easily let his suggestion drop. He had been too small himself to play basketball, but he had volunteered to keep score for us during the games from 1950 to 1954. He had seen a lot of basketball and knew how to evaluate talent. After graduation, Waltin had taken a job with the recreation department in Newark. That put him in the perfect position to watch for good college prospects for me. He had read in the newspapers about this guard's high-school career and then had seen his skills on the playground. Waltin was convinced the guy was the best who had ever tromped on his playground.

While watching and evaluating the athlete's ability, Waltin grew impressed with the young man's kind, gentle ways with the younger kids. This hot teenager would take the time to instruct the small fry how to play the game. Waltin thought that showed that he could be a leader on the floor.

I thought about Waltin's prospect some more. Sure, the kid might be a kind, thoughtful person who could play basketball. He could be a leader on the floor, someone every basketball coach always needed. But he was only six feet tall! Even in the mid-1950s, that was not tall at all. An attacking six-foot-three forward would be able to jump over a six-foot guard to get to the basket.

"No, Waltin," I said. "I'll let this player pass on to someone else. If you see someone else you like who is a little taller, then call me again."

Waltin has never let me forget that fateful phone call. I don't know that the player ever knew Winston-Salem Teachers College was considering him, but when I passed on him, he signed with Cal Irvin over at North Carolina A&T in Greensboro.

The kid was Al Attles, who proved to be an outstanding college player and an even better professional player, taken in the fifth round by Philadelphia in 1960. He played 11 years and scored 6,328 points, which sounds low, but he was always a defensive player. I once heard Al joke that one of his Warrior teammates ruined his perfect night in 1962, when Al hit eight baskets in eight shots. The teammate who ruined Al's moment in the spotlight was Wilt Chamberlain, who hit 100 points that night.

Al stayed with the Warriors after his playing days and became the team's head coach, a position he held from 1970 to 1983. He turned out to be a good coach, which Waltin Young had recognized back in 1956 when observing him instructing younger boys. In 1975, Al Attles became the first black coach to win an NBA championship. He is still with the Warriors (now the Golden State Warriors) as an assistant general manager, giving him an astounding career of 45 years with one pro team. On the rare occasions when I see Al now, I kid him that he could have gone far if only I had recruited him for my team. He kids me back that I had my shot at him and blew it.

When Waltin called me again one year later, in 1957, with another prospect he had found, I was willing to listen to him more intently than I had when he was describing Al.

Waltin said he had been watching a kid on the playground ever since he was a junior-high-school player. Now, he was a senior, and he had not signed with a college at that time. In talking to the player, Waltin had found that he wanted to go to college but that his grades would probably be an issue.

When I asked how tall the player was and how much he weighed, I shook my head as Waltin was talking on the phone. The kid was only six-foot-one and 185 pounds. He was barely bigger than Al Attles, who I had rejected one year earlier for being too short. I realized I had been wrong about Al. I was leaning toward giving Waltin the benefit of the doubt on this second player.

But then Waltin told me there was a catch to landing the kid. He wanted to play on a college team that would accept both him and his best friend. The real catch was that the best friend may have been five-foot-seven if he stood on his toes.

To get a kid who stood only six-foot-one, I was going to have to take a kid who stood five-foot-seven!

"What?" I remember asking Waltin. I may have said a few curse words, too, but my memory is thankfully dim with that kind of recollection.

Waltin told me I had better hurry and make a decision. Wilberforce College in Ohio had already tried to recruit the kid, but since that coach would not take his small friend, they had both returned to Newark. They were now planning to walk on at Shaw University over in Raleigh. And if Shaw didn't take them, Waltin had heard that my old buddy Cal Irvin at A&T would give the kids a shot at making his team.

A few days later, the kid and his little buddy showed up unannounced in my office asking if they could try out for the team. When I saw the athlete moving around my gym, I knew I had to get him in school. Even the short one looked good. He might have been small, but he could play ball good enough that he could make my team.

I am a big believer that some things just fall into your lap. I call it "stumbling into a good deal." And that is the short story of how I

Dr. Kenneth Williams, chancellor of Winston-Salem Teachers College, presents an award to my first real star, Cleo Hill. This photo was taken in the Winston-Salem Memorial Coliseum, probably in 1961. Notice two things in the background; there are a number of white people watching two black colleges play, and nearly every man is wearing a coat and tie to a basketball game!

(Winston-Salem State University Archives).

stumbled onto Cleo Hill, a player who was one of the two best athletes who ever suited up for me in 47 years. Had Cleo been given a fair chance to compete in the NBA when he broke into the pro game in 1961, he may have become the first Michael Jordan—20 years before *the* Michael Jordan came along.

Cleo had been a star at Southside High School in Newark, averaging 29 points a game. He had crossed over the river to play in the Rucker tournaments, so he was building a reputation in the New York area when Waltin told me about him. Cleo was beginning to get some looks from the black colleges, though apparently no white college was pursuing him. When Wilberforce and Shaw passed on taking both him and his little best friend, Arthur "Artie" Johnson, I promised we would take them both.

Getting Cleo enrolled in school posed a bit of a problem. As Waltin had warned me, Cleo did not have the best grades. But after talking to him, I sensed much more to him than what the report card showed. I believed if I could get him enrolled in school and push him through some remedial courses to bring up his reading ability, we could make him a college student.

Actually, getting him down to school was another story. On the day before he and Artie were supposed to be driven down to Winston-Salem by Waltin Young, Cleo hurt his knee in a pickup game, so he stayed home to recuperate while Artie came to WSTC. Artie kept after Cleo until he finally came down, and we got him registered.

The first thing I did for Cleo was to enroll him in remedial English to bring him up to college level. He did very well in the class, and the learning ability I suspected was locked in his head broke free. As a freshman, Cleo needed those remedial classes. By the time he was a senior, he was tutoring English to other athletes in the dorm. What we found out at Winston-Salem Teachers College was that Cleo was much smarter than his high-school teachers and administrators had ever imagined. He had just never been pushed by anyone to use his brain. We pushed him.

If what I saw of Cleo's abilities in the classroom pleased me, what I saw of his abilities on the basketball court amazed me. Soon after he arrived in Winston-Salem, I invited him over to my house for dinner. While Clara was making the meal, I took him to a nearby city park that had a basketball hoop. I watched him make something like 20 straight shots from what would have been half-court on a basketball floor.

I started testing him some more. He could shoot with either hand. He could shoot any type of shot. He was particularly good at the old-fashioned set shot, where a player plants his feet, sees the basket, and lets it fly without any fancy moves. He made those shots almost every time. When he jumped, he made himself the size of a man several inches taller than he really was.

One of the most amazing things I saw was watching him practice in a gym by himself. I am not even sure if he knew I was in the building. He turned out all of the gym lights but one behind him. It was so dim in the gym that I could barely see the basket. He made shot after shot after shot from all kinds of angles.

When I asked why he was practicing in a dark gym, his answer made perfect sense. He was duplicating his playground experience. Once the day was over and the recreation directors had gone home, dedicated street-ball players like Cleo would continue to play on the asphalt courts. As it grew dark, the only lighting would come from the nearest streetlight. Cleo was simply re-creating the way he practiced back home on the Newark playgrounds. The effect of that kind of practice in dim light was that he was both honing his depth perception by shooting at a hoop he could barely see and developing a sense of where that hoop was in relation to where he was on the court. Once he knew where to find the hoop in the dark, he would not even have to see the hoop in a brightly lit gym.

Over the years, I have come to realize that Cleo was one of the most scientific players I ever encountered in my whole career. That includes the 400 or so players I coached and the thousands of competing players I saw on the court over 47 years.

For instance, Cleo would sink a basket using a particular type of shot he had selected. If I asked him to tell me about how he sank that particular shot, he could tell me how many times the ball had rotated on its way to the hoop. If he had wanted to, he could have adjusted the number of times the ball had rotated by controlling how fast or slow it rolled off his fingers as he shot it.

Most kids loosely aim and toss the ball, hoping that it will go in the basket. Cleo was figuring angles, distances, velocities, trajectories—doing all kinds of complicated math and geometry in his head to make sure it went into the basket. This was a boy the high-school teachers said was not a good student!

He not only analyzed his own shots at the basket, he analyzed his opponents. He would notice how often a player cut left or right when faced with a defender on different areas of the floor. He would notice how often they made baskets when shooting from the left or right foot. He would notice which players liked to take chances on jump shots and which players did not. He would see if players gripped the ball by the seams, which gave them more control, or if they just tossed it. If a player took enough care to grip the ball, as Cleo did himself, Cleo would pay more attention to him, as he was the same type of careful player Cleo was.

As a freshman in the 1957-58 season, Cleo did not add a lot to the team, as we finished just 13-12, our worst season since 1952, when we ended 12-11. I used Cleo sparingly, and he scored only 300 points in his freshman year. We did not even win enough games to qualify for the CIAA tournament. Looking back on it, I am still amazed. In 1957, we won the tourney. But in 1958, we couldn't even qualify. It was the first time in five years that we had not finished first or second in the conference.

In 1958-59, we bounced back a little to finish 17-14. Cleo more than doubled his points, to 772. He finished the year as the leading scorer in the CIAA and was fifth in the nation, just behind future Los Angeles Laker Jerry West.

Still, we did not have a good season, just one of those off seasons every coach has. We even lost the opening game of the 1959 CIAA tournament to North Carolina College, 77-72. That was an odd game. Cleo set a single-game tournament record with 43 points, but our only other player in double figures was Tommy Monteiro. North Carolina College had five players in double figures.

Later in February 1959, we missed on a chance to go to the NAIA tournament when we lost 73-70 to the Hampton Pirates. That was another odd game. We were ahead 68-62 with just two minutes left. All we had to do was stall it, but Hampton was able to steal the ball, and they eventually went ahead to beat us.

It was in one of the first home games of the 1959-60 season, when Cleo was a junior, that an event occurred that would start me, Cleo, and the city of Winston-Salem down the path to a peaceful integration of the races.

The game was just about to start when I looked up and saw a white teenager glancing around Whitaker Gym on our campus. It was easy to see him. He was the only white kid in a crowd of 2,000 black folks. Puzzled, I looked at him closer and recognized him from photos that I had seen in the *Winston-Salem Journal*'s sports section.

He was Billy Packer, a guard that Wake Forest College in Winston-Salem had recruited from a Northern high school. His father was the coach at Lehigh University in Pennsylvania.

I walked over to him, introduced myself, and said, "Son, why don't you sit down here with me, so you can ask me any questions you want?" I didn't ask him why he was there. I knew why. He was there to watch good basketball, and I needed no other explanation of what one lone white person was doing on the black side of town.

Billy sat down beside me and then asked me which of my players was Cleo Hill. News of Cleo's skills was beginning to reach a white audience, even if that audience was another college basketball player who lived and breathed the sport.

Just as I pointed to Cleo on the court, the game began. Cleo got the tip and immediately threw the ball up toward the basket—a very un-Cleo-like move. The ball never even came close to the basket. It was as big an air ball as any kid who had never played basketball could make.

Without saying a word, Billy glanced at me with maybe a touch of pity or skepticism in his eyes. I knew what he was thinking. *This is the great Cleo Hill I have been hearing so much about?* was written all over Billy's face.

But Cleo soon removed that look from Billy's face and replaced it with one of awe as he began to regularly sink 15-foot hook shots, two-handed set shots, and every other kind of shot there is in the book. Cleo was great on defense, too, even goaltending and getting away with it.

Billy didn't say much to me, but I knew exactly what he was thinking. He was thinking that the black kids in a tiny girls' college in the tiny CIAA played better basketball than the mighty North Carolina, North Carolina State, Duke, and Wake Forest in the mighty Atlantic Coast Conference.

Billy later told me that he thought the ACC probably had more

Pictured is Whitaker Gym, built in 1953, where early Winston-Salem State games were played.

(WINSTON-SALEM STATE UNIVERSITY ARCHIVES)

overall talent spread over the entire league, and that Len Chappell, Wake's center, was better than our center. On both those counts, I would probably agree. The CIAA's smallest schools struggled to field consistently good teams, and Chappell was an excellent player.

But Billy went on to say that he had never seen anyone like Cleo for leaping ability. Most importantly, he said the overall athleticism and speed of our team was something that he was not accustomed to seeing on white basketball courts. Without quite saying it, Billy was saying that my little Winston-Salem Teachers College team could hold their own with—if not beat—some of the big-time university teams.

The next day, Wake Forest's coach, Horace "Bones" McKinney, casually asked Billy how he had spent the previous evening.

"Watching Winston-Salem Teachers College play basketball," was Billy's reply.

Bones just nodded. He was trained to be a Baptist minister and had secretly worked behind the scenes to smooth the way for Sam Jones of North Carolina College to be drafted by the NBA in 1957. I know Bones didn't harbor any ill will toward blacks and probably didn't have any ill feelings toward anyone. Well, maybe he did have ill feelings toward the University of North Carolina at Chapel Hill, which had beaten Wake for the ACC championship in a 1957 game decided by a controversial call.

A few days later, I stopped at my office in the gym on my way to church on a Sunday morning. I heard basketballs being dribbled and shot. I would never call a practice on a Sunday morning. In fact, I urged my players to take Sunday off and go to church to get right with God.

I opened the door to the court and looked inside. There were my black players taking on the white Demon Deacons from Wake Forest in a pickup scrimmage. There were no coaches and no fans—just a white team playing basketball against a black team. Perhaps most importantly, there were no referees and no students in street clothes acting in that role. The kids were depending on each other to call and admit to fouls.

I watched for a few seconds, then closed the door before anyone noticed me. I went on to church.

What I had witnessed was probably illegal. In most Southern towns, it was literally against the law for black athletes to play white athletes. In 1947, when Jackie Robinson had tried to play professional baseball in some Southern cities, the local governments had closed those facilities rather than allow him to play. Now, here were 20 or so black and white college students in my gym playing basketball.

Billy, without asking Coach McKinney's permission, and Cleo, without asking my permission, had arranged for the two teams to play each other whenever travel and class schedules permitted. Billy would later tell me that he had told his teammates about the phenomenal play he had seen in our game, and how the conversation had drifted around to wondering how the Wake team would perform against our players.

One thing led to another, and soon the entire white Wake team from the ritzy west side of town was regularly driving over to the poor east side of town to scrimmage. Sometimes, my black players would cram themselves into a couple of cars and make the trip over to Wake.

Dozens of these unauthorized scrimmages occurred in the early to the mid-1960s, thanks to Billy Packer, who started them as a player and then continued them when he graduated and returned a few years later as a Wake Forest assistant coach.

What Billy and his teammates and Cleo and his teammates did was unofficially integrate Winston-Salem. According to Billy and Cleo, there was never any conflict between the two races on the basketball court. There were no racial taunts, no macho displays, no fistfights, no violence of any kind. Coach McKinney and I wouldn't know. We were never invited to attend any of those scrimmages. I don't think a single one of them was ever supervised or even witnessed for the full game by a coach on either team. This was the players' idea, and I think both coaches instinctively knew that it should stay their idea.

In one sense, those scrimmages were amazing. In 1959, in a South where racial segregation was the social and legal norm, there were 20 or so black and white young men slamming into each other on a court in an intense basketball game. Despite all this physical contact, there was no violence.

Contrast that with what would happen two years *later* in Greensboro, when several male students from North Carolina A&T staged a famous sit-in at a Woolworth lunch counter. When the black students refused to leave after they were refused service, several angry white men started pulling at them and hitting them. Those students were arrested for trying to eat breakfast.

The calm way Billy Packer and Cleo Hill introduced their teams to each other tracked with what I had seen when Jackie Robinson started playing baseball. When Jackie proved he was a good player, the white fans accepted him because they wanted to see good baseball.

Those white Wake Forest kids not only wanted to see good basketball, they wanted to learn from the black kids who were playing it. Once Billy described for his teammates what he had seen in a normal CIAA-sanctioned game, the Wake Forest team realized they could learn how to be better players by playing against Winston-Salem Teachers College.

With the help of Cleo Hill, Billy Packer staged the first scrimmages between the Winston-Salem Teachers College Rams and the Wake Forest Demon Deacons. When he returned to Wake Forest as an assistant coach, he reinstituted the games. Billy (#34) is shown here playing against ACC opponent, the University of Virginia.

And my black players realized that scrimmaging against the white players, who played a slower, more controlled kind of game closer to the original rules of basketball, could only enrich their experience. True, they were unlikely to encounter the white kind of play on a CIAA court, where fast breaks ruled, but they would at least learn what playing white basketball was like.

I don't think the newspaper editors ever got wind of the scrimmages. If they did, they chose not to send reporters to cover them. I know the police never got wind of the games. If they had, they might have sent a squad over to break them up, and maybe even to arrest me for knowingly allowing the races to mix on the basketball court. The games remained a secret known mostly to the players themselves.

Billy went on to do pretty well for himself. After leaving coaching, he became a college basketball play-by-play announcer for television. I remember watching Billy on his first college broadcast, a game between Maryland and North Carolina in Chapel Hill. Billy was interviewing Maryland coach Lefty Driesell when he made some kind of comment about how "we don't think much of you down here in North Carolina." Lefty just stared at him, not sure what to say.

I knew what to say. Billy tells me that no television executive called him up to critique his first performance, but I did. I told Billy just one thing and then hung up: "Don't ever insult a coach to his face to get a reaction."

Billy's done much better since that rocky night. I think he is one of the best college-sports commentators working on network television today. I call him one of my millionaire friends.

In 1959-60, WSTC came back with a season of 19-5. The season was officially one game short, thanks to a peculiar game that was officially erased off the record books.

On January 16, 1960, we played North Carolina A&T in Winston-Salem's Memorial Coliseum in order to accommodate the large number of fans who wanted to see Cleo play. With 2:28 to play, Cleo put us ahead 66-65. We then stole the ball, and Charley Riley was fouled under our basket. A&T took a time-out.

I don't recall why—I know it was not intentional—but when the time-out was over, Cleo lined up at the foul line instead of Charley. Cleo made a one-and-one and put us ahead 68-65. A&T put the ball inbounds, and we stole it again. Cleo got it and got another basket, making the score 70-65.

At this point, Coach Irvin of A&T told the referee about Cleo shooting for Charley. The referee reset the game back to that point, wiping four points off our lead. A&T got their momentum back and "won" the game 71-68.

I protested to the CIAA, citing the rule book, which said it was the official's fault that the wrong player shot the foul shot, and that no harm should come to the team that made the mistake. After reviewing the rule book, the CIAA agreed, and the game was officially regarded as "no-contest." Both WSTC's and A&T's seasons were one game shorter.

We won our third CIAA tournament in March 1960. As any good coach should, I did not rely solely on my star, Cleo Hill.

In the opening game of the tourney, against Virginia Union, Charley Riley and George Foree joined Cleo in carrying the day. All three of them played the second half with four fouls, so they had to be very careful in rallying us from six points down with just four minutes to go in the game. Between the three of them, we kept stealing the ball and sinking our baskets to win the opening game 79-74.

The next night, the hero of the game against Hampton was Bobby Williams, who was a walk-on from nearby Atkins High School in Winston-Salem. We were ahead by just one point with 1:36 to play when Bobby went on a tear. He scored six straight points—four foul shots and a layup—to put the game away. Cleo scored 30 points in the game, 21 coming in the second half. Tommy Monteiro led in rebounds with 13, plus he scored 20 points.

In our third game, we easily whipped Saint Augustine's 65-44 to win our third CIAA tourney championship. Saint Augustine's had earlier upset top-seeded Johnson C. Smith and Virginia Union to win a place in the finals. They must have been tired, as they seemed to give us no trouble. Had they won, they would have been the first eighth-seeded team in the history of the tourney to win the championship. I rested my top players and substituted players, as I knew we would be representing the CIAA in the District 29 championship the next week.

An injury to George Foree, our main rebounder, doomed our chances for going for our first NAIA national championship. In the third quarter against Tennessee A&I, he pulled a groin muscle. With

This photo shows the 1959-60 CIAA Champions. Kneeling, right to left: *Charles Riley, Bobby Williams, Arthur Johnson, Edward Thompson, and Cleo Hill.* Standing, right to leftt: *Bobby Rowe, Tommy Monteiro, George Foree, Louis Parker, and Emmett Gill*

(WINSTON-SALEM STATE UNIVERSITY ARCHIVES)

him out of the game, Tennessee A&I was able to control the boards. Up until that point, we had been on a comeback from a 41-31 halftime deficit. We had tied the game and then gone ahead 50-46 when George got hurt. We eventually lost that game 81-74.

Cleo had an off night, scoring only 21 points, seven below his average, but I still think our main problem was having to play the game in A&I's hometown of Nashville. I didn't think their team was as strong as it had been in previous years, and we could have matched up to them if we had played that game in a neutral city. During the game, and to reporters afterward, I complained about the "home cooking" of the officiating. My Rams were charged with 22 fouls, while A&I was charged with only 14. The other team got 19 foul shots to our 12, enough to provide the winning margin.

My 1961 team had some interesting characters, as well as some great ballplayers who would come into their own later. One thing I did that was different for me was to start a couple of freshman on a regular basis.

154

Fred Parker, part of my 1957 team, had convinced his younger brother-in-law, Willie Curry, to come to Winston-Salem Teachers College. Fred was from Indiana, a player I found as a result of my days of recruiting in the Midwest, where I had contacts from my playing days in Paducah. Willie was from Fort Wayne, and I thought he would make a good end on the football team until I saw him work out on the basketball court. Somehow, I had missed the fact that he had helped take his high school to the finals of the state basketball championship.

In Willie's first game as a freshman in 1960, he scored 25 points—the same number as my graduating senior and star player, Cleo Hill! I hadn't let Cleo play all that much as a freshman, and here was this kid I had almost ignored matching him point for point!

Another thing that was unusual for Willie was that he was left-handed. His favorite shot was a left-handed jump shot from way back on the court. Since he could do that, I had the team focus on feeding him and Cleo.

The other freshman who would start to shine that year was Richard Glover from Newark, Cleo's hometown. Richard was born with a heart murmur and was banned from playing high-school basketball. The only place he could play was on the playground, where no doctors were checking him. Cleo's friend and former teammate Artie Johnson first spotted Richard and told me about him. I made a trip to the Newark playgrounds and saw that Richard was kind of gangly and skinny. Still, even knowing that he had heart problems in his past, I decided to take a chance on him. He was the first player I ever had on my team who had never played a single day of high-school basketball.

Richard was six-foot-four, and I used him as a rebounder. He was a little short for that position, but he had such great hands and leaping ability that he did well against taller opponents. Most coaches would think I was taking a chance of pitting him against taller players. But when I saw him on that Newark playground, he was playing against much bigger men and some great ones like Sherman White. Sherman had been an All-American at Long Island University until getting caught up in the point-shaving scandal of 1951. He loved the game so much that he still hung out at the playgrounds, training

Teddy Blunt screens Richard Glover's jump shot in 1963.

(Photo courtesy of Winston-Salem State University Archives)

younger players and teaching them how to defend against dominating players like himself.

My 1960-61 team had 20 regular-season wins and only four losses, thanks to the play of Cleo, the two freshmen, and upperclassmen Tommy Monteiro and Charley Riley. We finished second in the regular-season championship, based on that complicated Dickinson system, but we went into the CIAA tourney as a favorite, along with Virginia Union. The games would be played at Winston-Salem's Memorial Coliseum.

Oddly enough, Virginia Union was beaten in their first-round game by last-seeded Virginia State. We beat Delaware State 91-84 in our first-round game. We dominated most of the game, but Delaware State came back a couple of times when we let down our guard.

In the semifinals, we played North Carolina A&T. My boys sank an amazing 32 free throws in the second half to win the game 82-73. This was a sloppy game. Every time I thought the boys were ready to put it away, they would throw the ball away. At one point, A&T sank nine straight points on us. I was irritated at the sloppy play. Much was expected of us. We had been in the finals of the CIAA tourney for seven of the last nine years.

The final game, against Johnson C. Smith on March 4, 1961, was exciting to fans and gray-hair-inducing for coaches. We won 106-105 in overtime when one of my substitutes, Bobby Williams, sank two free throws with eight seconds left. Bobby came in because my two biggest stars, Cleo Hill and Charley Riley, fouled out. Bobby sank only four points in that whole game, but two of them were the winning points. What made the game special for Bobby was that he was one of my few players from a local high school. He played at Atkins right in Winston-Salem. My two freshmen, Curry and Glover, did a great job, but Johnson C. Smith kept coming back to tie us. They must have tied us four or five times in the final minutes.

This was a great tournament for Winston-Salem Teachers College. It was the first time in CIAA history that a host team had won the tournament. I was named coach of the tournament, and Cleo was named player of the tournament. Attendance at the games was listed at 18,000, a record.

At the same time that we were winning the CIAA championship, Wake Forest was winning the Atlantic Coast Conference championship. On the day after we won, there was a cartoon that ran on the *Winston-Salem Journal*'s sports page showing two basketball players shaking hands and doing a victory dance. One player was labeled "Wake Forest" and the other "WSTC Rams." Curiously, both players had the same skin color—white. From the cartoon, you could not tell that the Rams represented a black college. I still don't know what to make of that cartoon. You would think the artist could have at least put a little shading to the player's skin to make him look black. At that time, Wake Forest was still all-white.

Our next game would be for the District 29 championship, which we would have to win to go to the NAIA championship in Kansas City. The team we would have to beat was our old enemy, Tennessee A&I (the name would change to Tennessee State in 1968). Coach Harold Hunter had taken over for Coach John McLendon, and the team was as strong as it had ever been. They were ranked number two in the nation among small colleges, and they were champions of the Mid-West Athletic Conference. They had won three of the last four NAIA titles.

I did have hope. We had beaten Jackson State in the Georgia Invitational Tournament in Atlanta, after Jackson State had beaten Tennessee A&I in the same tournament. Another thing we had going for us was that the game would be played in Winston-Salem.

The game was played in Whitaker Gym, which sat 2,000, rather than at the coliseum, which sat 7,000. I chose to bring the game to the WSTC campus because I wanted our players to feel as much at home as possible. Another reason was that the coliseum was so expensive to rent that I didn't think the school could make as much money as we could in our own facility.

I had to go to man-to-man coverage with A&I, and that was a tough assignment for George Foree, who had to guard a center who was seven-foot-one. That kid was huge. This was in the days when a player of Wilt Chamberlain's height was still considered unusual.

We won in an upset, though the margin was a wide 92-82. It was the first time we had won the District 29 championship. Cleo had a hot night, hitting for 38 points, more than 10 over his season's average. Tennessee A&I used five different players to guard Cleo, and none of them figured out how to do it. They even took one of their top scorers to guard Cleo, but that didn't work either. Tommy Monteiro was another hero. He sank 14 of 15 free throws in the last five minutes of the game.

We went to Kansas City for the first time on March 13, 1961. Our first opponent was Westminster College of Salt Lake City, Utah. Since this was our first time in the tourney, we knew absolutely nothing about them, other than they were tall, judging from the statistics. They were also religious. Their nickname was "the Parsons."

We beat Westminster 95-70, with my freshman Richard Glover leading the way with 24 points. We were very sluggish because the game did not start until 10:30 P.M. Kansas time, or 11:30 Winston-Salem time. That was a time when my team should have been in bed. Still, we had no trouble outshooting them and outrebounding them. I played the entire bench once it was obvious that we would handle them.

Our next opponent was Westminster College again! This time, it was Westminster from New Wilmington, Pennsylvania, the top-ranked team in the tournament and the reigning NAIA champion. We played them on March 16, 1961.

Who says white boys can't play basketball? They handled us exactly the way they wanted. We lost the game 35-33! The score was 15-9 at the half! Two nights previously, we had scored 95 points, but this night all we could manage was 33. Westminster completely shut down our fast break and slowed the game to their pace by repeatedly stealing the ball and keeping it from us.

We fought back and actually went ahead 29-26 at one point. We tried playing their kind of game by freezing the ball while we were ahead, but Westminster continued to show that they could steal the ball on us.

What an odd way to end our season at 26-5! My seniors—Cleo Hill, Charley Riley, Tommy Monteiro, and Emmett Gill—all graduated without getting a national championship. Cleo, the best player in the

CIAA, managed only two goals and four points for the entire night. Charley Riley was high scorer with 12.

With the 1960s dawning, I and my teams were about to enter an interesting decade where we would see a national championship and the dismantling of segregation.

CHAPTER 11

White People Discover Black Basketball

Racial relations began to change—or at least to be examined—in the South and in Winston-Salem in the late 1950s and early 1960s. Black people were far from being treated as equal citizens, but at least the debate about how to treat us was happening.

I guess it may be hard for people of any color under the age of 50 to understand how black people were treated in those days.

In my youthful days, black people simply deferred in all ways to white people. We rode in the back in public transportation. We had separate water fountains and bathrooms. We even got off of the sidewalks when white people walked past. We did not question their authority, and we put up with their irrational laws, such as the one making it illegal for black women to try on hats in white-owned stores in downtown Baltimore or Washington, D.C.

Still, there were ways around segregation. One of the ways I made sure my teams were treated well—better than those of most other black coaches—was my retention of what I called my "white representatives."

I didn't actually have white boys on my team, but I had two blacks who were white enough to fool most white people.

The whitest of my representatives was Cleveland Dobson, who drove our bus when the school finally purchased one, rather than having the team drive to games in two old station wagons. Cleveland could easily "pass," as we called it in the South. I always kidded Cleveland by asking him if he was absolutely positive he was a black man. It was too inconvenient being a black man!

If I ever had to deal unexpectedly with a white person on the road, such as in making an unplanned stop at a gas station or a store, I would send Cleveland in to talk with the proprietors. He never reported to me that he had any problems. Either they were very polite to a black stranger or they thought they were talking to a white man. Then again, we would often park the bus out of sight, so the store owners might not have even known that Cleveland was driving a bus filled with tall black kids.

The other person I had was my trainer for many years, a student named Nathaniel Wiseman. Nathaniel was very light skinned but obviously a Negro. But as with Cleveland, I had noticed that light-skinned black people did not frighten white people nearly as much as darker-skinned blacks did. More importantly from the white people's standpoint, they were less worried by a normal-sized, light-skinned young man than they might have been by a black young man who stood six-foot-six or taller. So if Cleveland wasn't along, I would send Nathaniel in to deal with the white folks for such things as ordering sandwiches and soft drinks for the team. If Cleveland or Nathaniel were on the trip, they could go in the front door of restaurants to get food. If they weren't, I had to go around to the back door to get the same food.

Most of the time, we had no trouble on the road. We knew what gas stations had black bathrooms or had nearby bushes where the players could "hide their waists," as I told them to do. In traveling up the East Coast to Maryland and beyond, we knew the two black hotels in downtown Richmond that would serve sit-down meals to the team.

Moving my team around a segregated South really was not all that bad. In my years of coaching, I really cannot remember encountering any racial incidents that frightened or angered me or my players.

Personally, on the other hand, I have many bad memories. It is not hard at all for older black people to remember specific hurtful, embarrassing incidents.

Sometimes, it could start at home. Once, when our daughter, Lisa, was very small, she was lying in bed with Clara and me. We were just enjoying the quiet with Lisa when our daughter put her arm next to Clara's. Clara is lighter skinned than Lisa. Lisa compared her black arm to Clara's brown arm and casually said, "I like Mommy's skin color better than mine."

Clara and I were shocked. At first, we didn't say anything to each other or to Lisa. We couldn't think of anything to say. We had never said anything at all about skin color in our family. The only thing I can assume is that Lisa had been absorbing news about race and skin color from television coverage about integration battles, or from little friends who had been hearing about it from their parents.

How do you answer a small child who has just announced that there is something about herself that she does not like, and it is something that she can never change?

When we recovered our voices, we told Lisa that God makes children in all kinds of colors, and he scatters them all over the world so there can be a great variety among the people. The important thing for her to know was that God loved her and her color, and we loved her and her color. It was the best we could do on short notice, and she seemed to accept our answer.

Clara and I can't remember Lisa ever bringing up the subject of skin color again.

That does not mean that other people did not bring up skin color. I remember gassing up our car in Asheville, North Carolina, during a family trip to see my parents in Paducah. I gave Lisa some money to walk over to the McDonald's next to the gas station to buy herself some ice cream. In a few minutes, she came back in tears. The employees of McDonald's had refused to draw some ice cream in a cup and hand it to a little black girl.

I knew from my daughter's tears that I had to do something to correct not only the immediate hurt but to make sure that Lisa did not think there was anything wrong with her as a person. It was not long after that incident that we were driving on the Blue Ridge Parkway, a national park that is also a scenic highway in the mountains of North Carolina. We stopped for gas at a convenience store that I knew was licensed by the National Park Service.

I gave Lisa some money and told her to go inside for an ice-cream cone. She refused. She remembered what had happened the last time I told her to get ice cream. I insisted, knowing that any store under the control of the United States government would be serving everyone. She came back with a smile on her face and an ice-cream cone. She had learned that not every white person she encountered was bad and that laws were coming to protect her right to be just like every white person she would meet in the future.

Eventually, companies in the South realized the damage racism was doing to their business, so they started changing their practices. It certainly had an effect on Lisa. She now runs her own market research company near Chicago. She has completed professional projects for McDonald's during her career, but for nearly 20 years after that incident when she was a child, she refused to walk into one of their stores.

I took every opportunity to reinforce the idea to Lisa and her younger brother, Clarence Jr., that equality was for everyone. Whenever we would travel to Maryland to see Clara's parents, the family would always stop at the same restaurant in the same town. It was only a half-hour to the children's grandparents' house, where we knew plenty of food and treats would be waiting, but we always stopped at this same restaurant. It was a family tradition.

Lisa and Clarence Jr. must have thought Clara and I stopped there because the food was good. Actually, the food was mediocre at best. We stopped at that restaurant because when we walked in, we were treated just like every other dinner guest. Every time we stopped, we were immediately seated among all of the other customers. There were no second looks, no scowls, no mumbling from the employees. The white waitresses sat this black family of four next to white families of four and took our order. No other diners complained. No one scooted their chairs away from us. No one paid us any mind.

That was the lesson we wanted the children to realize. They were equal to anyone else in the restaurant. They were so equal that no one even gave them a second look. That sort of experience went a long way to making the children ignore silly and hurtful treatment.

Still, segregationist habits died hard. Tanglewood Park in Forsyth County, the county in which Winston-Salem is located, was once a country estate owned by Will Reynolds, brother of the founder of the R. J. Reynolds Tobacco Company. In 1951, the estate was left to Forsyth County with instructions from "Mr. Will" that it should be used as a county recreational park—but that the park could admit only white people. Old Mr. Will didn't want black people walking around on his property after he was dead! That wish lasted for years, until the national mood changed and county lawyers realized that a dead man's wishes could not conflict with federal discrimination laws.

I don't remember the year Tanglewood's admission requirements changed, but I remember the day of the week. The county set a specific date, a Monday, on which Tanglewood would open its gates so that people of all races could drive out and enjoy the lakes and open spaces. I loaded up the family and drove out to the park on a Sunday, the day before the park would officially be opened to black people. I never dreamed that we wouldn't be allowed into the park one day early.

The gatekeeper wouldn't let my family into the park because we were black.

I didn't challenge the white gatekeeper. I didn't get angry. I didn't get confrontational. I told the kids that we would come back another day when the park would be open to us.

Once again, my children had learned the lesson that they were a little different from white people, and that the difference sometimes meant discrimination. I couldn't protect them from it forever and obviously couldn't predict when they would encounter it.

Change was coming, but it seemed like it was coming slowly, and some in the South were resisting. On the same day in February 1959 that Winston-Salem Teachers College was about to compete in our last game of the 1958-59 season, the newspaper carried a story about how the Southern senators had spoken for 100 hours straight and were about to start a second 100 hours. The issue was a law that would ensure that black people had the right to vote in elections. They wanted to block it by talking.

But every time I read something like that in the newspapers and wondered if black people would ever get equal treatment from whites, I would read something else that would tell me that cracks in the dam holding back integration were appearing.

Just a day or so after reading about the filibuster, on the same day we were preparing for the CIAA tournament, I read another article that showed me that Jackie Robinson's plan of using sports to integrate society could work.

The article said that the student body at Mississippi State University had voted overwhelmingly to support their basketball team if they made it to the Southeastern Conference championship of the NCAA. What drove the student body to hold that vote was that some racist organizations in the state were demanding that the team boycott the tournament. The reason was that if the Mississippi team was good enough to go on to the conference championship, they would inevitably face black players, who were sprinkled among the other top teams competing for the championship. I remember one name mentioned as one of the blacks who Mississippi State would have to meet in that championship race—Oscar Robertson from the University of Cincinnati. "The Big O" had led the nation in scoring that year. In a couple of years, he would become one of the first black superstars in the NBA.

In the end, the turmoil in Mississippi didn't matter. Their team was defeated before they ever faced a team with black players. Still, it was important that the college student body and the college team itself told their college president that they did not mind playing black players. It was the hard-core racists, many of whom might not have even gone to college, who were objecting to playing blacks.

Times were changing. Appropriately, it was the younger people who were leading those changes.

Here in Winston-Salem, black people were getting their photographs in the paper more, though most of the news about black people was still relegated to the same page in the newspaper. It was as if we black folk were a separate club within the larger society. We would have preferred not to be singled out in that way, but at least they were finally printing our news.

On the plus side for me as a coach and for the college, the newspaper had hired a black sportswriter, Luix Overbea. Over the years as we started winning games, coverage of the college had been creeping higher on the page, though we generally were still second-page sports news, compared to first-page coverage for the University of North Carolina, North Carolina State University, Duke, and Wake Forest.

That was now changing because Overbea must have had the respect of his editors. By 1960 and 1961, I could find articles by Overbea on the opening page of the sports section describing games we were about to play. On occasion, you could even find a photograph of one of my players. I was sometimes quoted—usually complaining about the officiating when we lost a game, but quoted all the same. To a coach, every game is important. Every loss brings him closer to getting fired by the college chancellor.

It was Overbea's regular coverage of Cleo Hill that must have caught the attention of Winston-Salem's white people. Sometimes, Overbea would just give straight facts about Cleo, such as mentioning in an article that his 24 points per game was ranked 10th in the NAIA. In other articles, Overbea would mention Cleo's "superior" rebounding. I know on several occasions, the reporter slipped in adjectives such as "amazing" when describing Cleo's play.

I started noticing white people coming to Whitaker Gym—our gym, the gym for a black college on the black side of town! There were not many, so they stood out in a sea of black faces, but the newspaper was bringing white fans out to see black basketball players. They were coming to see my players and specifically Cleo Hill.

For several games in the 1960-61 season, Cleo's senior year, we moved the games to Winston-Salem's coliseum, which sat 7,000 people, more than three times what we could seat in Whitaker Gym on WSTC's campus. The reason we rented the bigger facility was because we were getting so many black fans coming from the bigger CIAA rivals, such as North Carolina A&T, who wanted both to support their team and to see Cleo.

What surprised me when I watched those fans streaming into the coliseum before the games was that even more white folks were intermingled with the black folks. I've talked with white fans who remember those days who estimate that as many as a quarter to a third of the seats would be taken up by white people sitting side by side with black people. The coliseum was general admission, which meant there was no way that official segregation, practiced in many places around town, could be enforced. Nor could separate concession stands be set up. In other words, on those nights, official segregation in Winston-Salem did not exist.

White people were coming to see two black colleges play each other! I looked over at my bench and realized that there was no mystery about this mixing of the races in a public place. Everyone was coming to see the "amazing" Cleo Hill.

In Cleo's senior year, he scored 826 points. Over four seasons, he scored 2,530 points, breaking Sam Jones's CIAA record at North Carolina College. If I had played Cleo more as a freshman, when he scored only 300 points, Lord knows how many more points he would have scored in his career.

More importantly for him, Cleo would have never scored anywhere near the points he did had I let him slip through my fingers and go over to North Carolina A&T as Al Attles had done. Cal Irvin's platoon style of substituting players all the time would have kept Cleo's points so low he might never have been noticed.

I say this about Cleo to get back at Cal, who has never let me forget Al Attles. And I say it so Cleo will always remember the coach who allowed him to play all the time.

Another thing that Cleo did for us beyond scoring was his constant analysis of other players. We were playing Johnson C. Smith College one night, and he saw that one of his old YMCA buddies from Newark was playing. As Cleo watched him, he realized that his buddy still had an old playground habit of shooting off-balance, by setting the wrong foot behind him. Cleo told his teammates that if they could force the player to move left all the time, they would throw off his shooting.

It worked. The player's shooting percentage tanked after Cleo told his teammates how the kid could be messed up on the court. Later, Cleo's buddy laughed at how Cleo had "given up all my secrets."

The only problem I ever had with Cleo was one day when he threatened to leave the school—two days before the 1961 NAIA tournament was to begin.

On Tuesday, March 7, Cleo was in the registrar's office clearing up some questions about his upcoming graduation when someone in the office told him that he was missing some English courses. Until he took them, he could not graduate. That was news to Cleo! He had already arranged for student teaching that spring, and for his graduation. The school was telling him after he had been there for four years that he was not going to graduate in a few months, as he had always assumed.

Cleo went to his dorm room, packed his bags, and told his roommate he was heading home to Newark because Winston-Salem Teachers College was treating him wrong.

Cleo did not come to me at all to straighten things out! The first I knew of the situation was when some frantic people interrupted a class I was teaching to tell me my star player was on his way to the bus station.

I did not panic. In fact, I told everyone I expected Cleo to show up for practice at 6:30 that evening. A college professor, Dr. Joseph Patterson, a calming influence on the campus who I frequently depended on to fix problems, tracked Cleo down and brought him back about 6:00 P.M. Everything was worked out, and Cleo was ready to play. I found out later that Cleo probably would not have left Winston-Salem. He didn't have enough money to buy a bus ticket home. He was bluffing, knowing his threat would get the registrar moving. It did.

The story of what happened to Cleo Hill after leaving Winston-Salem Teachers College would be a sad one had Cleo not gone on to become a schoolteacher and later a good college coach.

Cleo was drafted number one in the 1961 draft, the first time a player from a small black college had ever been drafted that high. He went to the St. Louis Hawks with a one-year, no-cut contract for $7,500. He would help them fill a gap by acting as an outside shooter from the backcourt. That role fit Cleo to a T. He could hit from anywhere on the court, and he was an excellent defensive player.

Immediately, problems occurred with the established team members. Cleo was a black star from a black college team who was accustomed to playing fast-break basketball. The Hawks' front court was composed of three white veterans—Bob Pettit, Clyde Lovellette, and Cliff Hagan—who were accustomed to playing a slower game and doing all of the scoring for the team.

The contracts for those three were structured such that they made more money if they scored more points and kept their scoring averages high. Then Cleo came on board and demonstrated how powerful he could be in the preseason games. He shot and made baskets, which naturally cut down the numbers for the front three. If Cleo's play kept up, they would make less money over the course of the year.

In an exhibition game against the Philadelphia Warriors at Winston-Salem's coliseum that I promoted in the fall of 1961, Cleo scored 21 points in the win against Wilt Chamberlain's team. The Hawks' Pettit scored 30, but the other two front-court men scored only 11 and 10.

I promoted that game by promising both teams a total of $10,000 if they came to Winston-Salem. I did everything to promote that game, including selling most of the tickets myself. To demonstrate how small the NBA was at the time, the *Winston-Salem Journal* did not even mention the game in its sports section until the day of the game. In a small racial victory, I was able to house the visiting professional players in the biggest downtown hotel, the Robert E. Lee.

When the professional season started, it appeared that the front three players for the Hawks were intentionally not passing the ball to Cleo. The coach, Paul Seymour, threatened the other players with fines if they did not pass the ball more to Cleo. The threats did not work. Eventually, the Hawks' owner fired the coach, who was Cleo's biggest booster, and Cleo was relegated to being a substitute. After averaging more than 20 points a game in the preseason, he ended the season averaging just 5.5 points a game.

Then, after practicing all summer and preparing for what he hoped would be a better year, he was cut from the squad before his second season began.

There were rumors that the Hawks quietly sent word around to the other NBA teams not to hire Cleo. I don't know if those rumors were true, but I know no team ever tried to talk to the player who had broken the scoring record set by Sam Jones, who was then playing with the Boston Celtics. I don't know all the reasons why Cleo had problems adjusting to the Hawks, but I suspect jealousy and money were at the root of the problems. Cleo was a heralded star, the number-one pick. When he started, he took away headlines from the established players. When he played well, that meant they would lose money. It is not hard to figure out that their loyalty lay with each other, not with the new member of the team, whether he was white or black.

Nineteen sixty-two was well before sports agents played major roles in personnel selection. It was Cleo's responsibility to find another team which would hire him. Since he was not experienced in how to do that, his NBA career ended after one year. It was the biggest waste of basketball talent I have ever seen. Perhaps the most talented basketball player I ever coached was not given a fair chance to make it in the professional ranks.

I do not weep for Cleo Hill, however. He went on to do what he was trained to do. He became a teacher, and an excellent one. The student who had to take remedial classes when he first arrived at Winston-Salem became the head coach and athletic director at Essex Community College in Newark. He also sired good basketball talent. His son, Cleo Hill, Jr., also became a basketball coach, first at Shaw University, where he took the team to a 2002 CIAA championship, and now at Cheyney University in Pennsylvania. My only problem with Cleo Jr. is that he attended college at my old nemesis, North Carolina College, instead of playing for me at Winston-Salem State University. He helped that school beat me a few times.

What Cleo Hill did for me and Winston-Salem Teachers College put our basketball program on the front page of the sports section in our city. Once white sports fans read about Cleo's exploits, they wanted to see him in person. To see him in person, they had to go either to Whitaker Gym or to the coliseum. To actually watch him in a game, they had to sit next to black people. Once they sat next to black people, the whites in Winston-Salem—at least the ones who went to our games—realized that integration was not as bad as they had been led to believe by their political and business leaders. Black people were not that much different from white people. We black folks were not going to attack them or threaten them. We didn't want their white women. All we wanted to do was watch good basketball with them.

Well, actually, we also wanted to drink out of the same water fountains, use the same restrooms, and sit down to eat in the same restaurants, but we didn't have to bring all of that up right away when we were trying to watch the same basketball game.

By just watching an amazing player like Cleo Hill on the court, white people were beginning to think that those were not unreasonable requests. The Jackie Robinson theory of what white people wanted—to see good sports—first tried in 1947, was still working in 1961.

Chapter 12

How I Trained Winners at Basketball and Life

By the early 1960s, my network of graduates who were my recruiting scouts was firmly in place and regularly sending me tips on players who could help Winston-Salem Teachers College. After recruiting for myself from 1946 through 1955, I could now count on a growing family of former players and supporters who would feed me prospects who would play basketball for me for four years and then would pursue teaching and educational administrative careers. Once those players graduated, they would join my network of basketball scouts who had loyalty to me and the college.

Of great importance to both me and the college was the fact that this network did not cost my slim athletic budget a dime. These scouts would often drive recruits down themselves or buy them train tickets to Winston-Salem. They were never reimbursed by the college. There was no budget for such a thing. These scouts were primarily concerned with educating young men at their alma mater. If it cost them a hundred dollars or more to get those athletes in school, they figured it was their alumni contribution.

The system started working in 1957, when the school captured its second CIAA championship, using a mixture of players I had recruited and who had found me through the network. The championships in 1960 and 1961 came with players almost exclusively found by my network.

My network of scouts was really wide ranging. I even recruited players from the Philippines and Maine. Actually, that was one player, Tim Autry. In 1958, Tim was in the United States Air Force when he was stationed in the Philippines and then discharged in Caribou, Maine. A Winston-Salem Teachers College football graduate, Herman McNeil, had written me about Tim and told me how to reach him through his air-force overseas address. I tracked Tim from the South Pacific to Maine and kept after him, telling him to come down and prove that he was as good as Herman said he was. Tim did come and play for me from 1959 to 1963. He later became a good college coach and athletic director at South Carolina State University in Orangeburg.

By the early 1960s, I had graduates in New York City, Newark, Philadelphia, and at least a dozen other Northeastern cities. While I still did not concentrate on recruiting in North Carolina, since the kids just did not play basketball enough to become as proficient at it as they did in the Northeast, I had contacts in the high schools scattered around this state, who regularly called me with tips.

I listened and sometimes bought. In my first 20 years of coaching, most of my players came from the Northeast, but I also picked up players from North Wilkesboro and Leaksville, two tiny North Carolina towns. One of my more dependable players, Bobby Williams, came from Atkins High School, no more than five miles from our campus. His high school was named after the man who had founded Winston-Salem Teachers College.

With the burden of recruiting shifted from my shoulders, I could concentrate more on training players to become winners on the court and in the classroom. My past players would find me the teenage kids.

I would turn those teenagers into college basketball players and responsible young men. Those young men would eventually go on to become male role models in the elementary schools and high schools around the nation.

During the early days of recruiting players, I concentrated on teaching the fundamentals of the game—how to shoot from any part of the court, how to defend without fouling, how to pass without getting intercepted. My early recruits needed those fundamentals. In the mid-1940s, my service veterans were more accustomed to handling carbines and wrenches than basketballs, while the males who hadn't been in the service were often the second-stringers from their high schools, if they had played basketball at all.

By the mid-1950s, the war was a distant memory for the players. I was getting good basketball players again. The athletes I was getting fell into two categories: those who knew plain old basketball by the rules and those who knew street ball but to whom the rules were a little fuzzy. With these athletes, I had to teach them how to play fast-break ball by the rules that the referees would be enforcing.

By the early 1960s, the prospects I was getting were extremely good players. We had already won two championships in the 1950s and were on our way to winning two straight in 1960 and 1961. What I needed to train these players to do was stay strong on the court and not wear out. I also needed them to remain confident in themselves.

I keep going back to the age-old basketball question: Should you recruit 10 good players and substitute when they get tired, or should you recruit 10 good players but keep the five best players in the whole game? There is no right or wrong answer to this. Cal Irvin won basketball championships at North Carolina A&T by using the platoon system of moving players in and out. I won CIAA championships by keeping my five best players on the court for the entire game and substituting only when one or more of them got in foul trouble or was having an off night.

To keep those five players in the entire game, and to make sure the substitutes were ready if something happened to one of the starters, I had to strengthen them until nothing could tire them. I did that by running them—and running them, and running them. They got up at 5:00 A.M. and ran down a long, steep hill to Bowman Gray Stadium, where our football team played their home games. It was a long, steep climb back up to the gym. I know that hill was steep because the car I drove to follow my team would coast down when heading to the stadium and would chug climbing the hill on the way back.

Yes, I drove a car while I was training my teams. I didn't go in for that "I wouldn't ask you to do something that I can't do myself" routine. I was in my 30s and not about to run up and down a hill every day with a bunch of teenagers. On the days that I could not make sure my players were making that predawn run, I trusted the captain of the team to get his teammates out of their beds. As far as I know, no team ever cheated on their expected runs.

And then there were the rope drills.

I am not sure of the exact year I started the rope drills. I know I wasn't doing them in the 1940s or mid-1950s because the players of those eras don't recall them. They would have had vivid memories had they experienced them. I must have started the drills in the early 1960s because those players and all the players after them still have bad dreams about falling off of ropes.

They didn't, but they well could have.

The rope drills were simple. I got all of the players onto the court and told them that all we were going to do for that practice was shoot two kinds of baskets. They were going to shoot layups or jump shots. It would be their choice. The only catch was that each time that they missed a shot, they would have to climb a rope and touch the ceiling of the gym.

Every year, the freshmen would look at me with puzzlement. They had their choice of shooting either easy layups or more difficult jump shots? I was not ordering them to shoot a particular shot?

"What is the catch?" they would ask me.

"No catch. Shoot the shot you are most comfortable making," I would answer, tossing them the ball. "Once you miss, however, you have to climb the rope and then shoot some more. We will keep shooting and climbing the rope until the team is tired."

I learned so much about my teams and individual boys by that simple drill.

The most confident and most skilled players would start off shooting jump shots. They knew that the jump shot was most valuable to the team because they would not often get the opportunity to take a shot at an undefended goal by using a layup. That type of shot generally came when a fast break got past the defenders. Considering that most colleges in the CIAA played fast-break ball, that would not happen very often. The jump shot went over defenders' heads and was hard to defend. It was the type of shot that would most often occur during a game. It was also the shot that permitted the athletes to show off their skills.

The players who were less skilled and less confident in themselves would shoot the layups. They knew their shot selection was easy, a "gimme" that would virtually assure them that they would not have to pull their bodies up to the ceiling. They were thinking of their own self-preservation, not what would make them better players on the court. They were less willing to take chances. But what I knew was that it is chance-taking that wins close games. I would always prefer a player who was willing to take chances over a player who wanted to remain in his safety zone.

I had some players, such as Earl Monroe and Bill English in the mid-1960s, who played my ploy perfectly. Earl and Bill would start off shooting jump shots but would switch to layups when they got tired and sensed that their aim was becoming shaky. They knew when it was time to move on to the easy layups.

Look at what I learned from that one drill!

I saw the basic skills of my players. With the jump shots, I saw how each kid could read the angles to the basket. With the layups, I saw how they set up the most basic of shots. If one of them consistently missed his jump shot, I knew I had a problem that had to be ironed out immediately. If one of them consistently blew the gimme of the layup, I had an even bigger problem to fix.

I saw how confident my players were in themselves and their playing abilities. If a player never, ever took the chance on a jump shot,

William (Bill) English grabs a rebound as Ronald Plant (#34) blocks out. English set a single game record of 77 points against Fayetteville State in 1968 that still stands.

(WINSTON-SALEM STATE UNIVERSITY ARCHIVES)

then I knew he did not have full confidence in himself and his playing abilities. If my player were frightened of missing a shot and climbing a rope in an empty, quiet gym, how would he react when faced with a six-foot-six, 200-pound man waving his hands in a gym full of cheering or jeering fans?

I saw how well my players could think through a situation. If a kid was not making his jump shot, was he stubborn enough to stick to it until he made it, or was he willing to switch off to the easy shot?

This was something that was harder for me to evaluate. Stubbornness can be a good trait in a player, but at the same time, you want a player who is willing to recognize that something he is doing is not working out right. I didn't want a player who continued to stick to the same shot but who had the ball batted down each time. That did not put points upon the scoreboard. Neither did I want a player who insisted on passing the same way, only to have the ball stolen every time he passed it. That player was going to let the other team pile up points on the board. Players have to adapt to different conditions as they occur on the court.

Finally, the rope drills showed me how flexible players were in their thinking, how willing they were to try something new. Sometimes, jump shooters would run through a few layups just to tune themselves up for another round of jump shots. They knew when it was time to change the shot selection just to keep off the ropes. Earl and Bill fell into this category. They were bold enough to have confidence in their jump-shooting ability, competitive enough to keep shooting jump shots as long as they knew they could make them, and smart enough to know when they were growing too tired to make them, so they would switch to layups.

I loved those rope drills as much as the players despised them. Ask any of my players what they hated about me and my practices, and the rope drills will be the first thing mentioned. I had one player return to school for homecoming not long ago. He made a special trip over to Whitaker Gym just to see if those old ropes are still hanging from the ceiling. They are. He told me he gave a little shudder when he saw them, as they brought back all the bad, painful memories of missing those shots and climbing to that ceiling.

Of course, playing basketball was not the real reason they attended the college. They came to learn to be teachers, or at least to get a college degree, so they could carry that into the work force.

I think one of the best things I did to teach these young men how to be adults was *not* to place rules on them.

That seems like an odd thing for a coach to say. Colleges and college towns are full of temptations. There are drugs. There are bars. There are loose women. I was not going to be around to tell my players when to go to bed and when to get up. But my players knew the morning run was coming. They could have stayed up all night if they wanted, but they also knew that I would expect them to be just as fast in the morning run as they would be after a full night's sleep.

When they arrived on campus and we had our first team meetings, I told those teenagers that there would be few rules that I would personally enforce, but that what I did expect of them was that they conduct themselves as gentlemen and students. That was a big charge that pretty much covered all types of behaviors.

Sometimes, an athlete would really screw up and would find himself in trouble with the police. That didn't happen often, but in 47 years of coaching, I was bound to have a player or two who found himself on the wrong side of the law. Even in the days of segregation, however, the police in Winston-Salem were often willing to give my players a break. The police would sometimes call me up and describe the problem and ask me what I wanted to do. I would often tell the police to keep my player overnight, and I would come down and get him in the morning. There are few things more instructive to a young man about maintaining good behavior when away from home than staying overnight in a jail cell with a few strangers.

One of the ways I discovered the character of my players was to invite them to my home to have a home-cooked meal prepared by Clara. Many of these males were not accustomed to seeing an intact family. I wanted them to see that black folks could live the same way they assumed white folks did—Mom and Dad and the children sitting around a dinner table talking about what they had done that day.

Some of these kids who I learned about over the dining-room table

Teddy Blunt advances the ball against Prairie View College in the
Georgia Invitational Tournament in 1965.

(WINSTON-SALEM STATE UNIVERSITY ARCHIVES)

I later trusted to baby-sit my children. One of these was Teddy Blunt, who became a school administrator and city commissioner in Wilmington, Delaware. He learned to handle my children, knowledge which came in handy when he had to handle millions of dollars in a city budget.

Sometimes, I would invite the team to my house to play a game of penny poker. I would count out 50 pennies for every team member around the table, and then I would find some excuse to leave the table for a few minutes. I would walk upstairs or outside for several minutes, leaving the kids alone with my pennies. When I got back, I would count my pennies. Sometimes, there would be a few missing.

"When I left here, I know I had 50 pennies. Now, I don't. Who took my pennies?" I would ask.

Usually, the thief would confess. He would try to joke his way out of it, but I would have none of that.

What I was testing was basic honesty. If I could not trust a team member in my own home with 50 of my pennies, how could he win the trust of his teammates and, more importantly, the trust of the students he would one day be teaching? I caught a few kids at that game, and I forgave a few, but I was always disappointed when I caught them. It revealed a weakness in them that I would have to watch.

Another test I used involved soft drinks. I had a good relationship with the Coca-Cola distributor in Winston-Salem. Knowing that I often entertained players at my home, he would give me six-packs of Cokes that I kept in my garage. The games I would play with the students were always in my finished basement. When the game was over, they would walk out through the garage—right past those stacks of six-packs.

I always knew how many six-packs of Cokes were in my garage. I would count them before the party began, and I would count how many we would put on ice. On Monday morning, I would count those six-packs again. Sometimes, I would find some missing. One or more of the boys would have picked up a pack on their way out of the garage.

I would hold a team meeting when I got to school, and I would simply confront the players in a soft, quiet way. I never yelled about the missing drinks. They were worth only a couple of dollars, so their theft from my garage was not financially damaging to me. But I made it a point that someone had stolen from their coach's home. Usually, the offender would come forward, sometimes at the meeting but more often in the privacy of my office.

I was not laying a trap for these students but was trying to emphasize to them that honesty with me was my only policy. Some of them may have come from a bad environment where stealing was one way to stay ahead, but they were no longer in that place. They were now in college, where people went to school to earn a degree with which they could make an honest living. I usually forgave the players who stole from me that first time. Once they knew it was a test, they rarely tried it again. If they did, they were gone. I didn't need permission from the chancellor to fire a player from my program. I could send him home at any time. I sent a few home that way, but not many. Most wanted the chance to make something of themselves, and I wanted to give them that chance.

Tim Autry, one of my players who became a college coach himself, said I knew how to deliver the hard hand to some players and the loving hand to others. I never treated all of my players the same way. Some of them I yelled at, getting right in their faces. Some of them I rarely said a word to, and when I did, it was soft and calm. Some of them, particularly in my early days, I would instruct with my foot. I literally kicked some butt—stuff that would get me fired or arrested in today's world of coaching.

The players noticed this difference in the way I treated them, but I think they understood it. I could motivate some players by forcing them to talk to me. I could motivate other players by leaving them alone.

Sometimes, I would be wrong. I remember yelling and yelling at one player until he held up his hand. He had had enough.

"Coach, if you just tell me what you want me to do, I will do it. Yelling at me isn't helping me," the player said.

I stopped. I realized he was right. In his case, I really had not told him what I wanted him to do. I was yelling at him when he didn't need it. When I instructed him on what I wanted him to do on the court, he did it. I didn't yell at him again.

I guess over time I also mellowed. Once I really learned what coaching was about, I discovered one of the most effective means of communication was simply putting a player in the front seat of my car and driving around. We were alone and away from his teammates. He could tell me how he was handling his schoolwork and his play on the court. I could tell him where he needed to improve. If he wanted to tell me about his home life, he did it in the car, far away from the prying and sometimes the teasing of his teammates. For many years, coaching young men by driving around worked very well for me. It got me and the player onto neutral ground, away from my office and the gym.

Most of the 400 or so players who came through my program went on to become accomplished young men. Only one, Earl Monroe, became a famous professional basketball player in the NBA. Counting the number of professional ballplayers is not how I measure the success I had at this game. I can look at any team photograph of my young men and point out the ones who became teachers, principals, college professors, medical doctors, and recreation directors. The list of young men who failed to become successes in life once they left Winston-Salem Teachers College is very short.

Let me be clear. I am not claiming credit for their success. All I did was provide the opportunity which allowed them to showcase their basketball talents. During the season, they were student-athletes. During the other nine months of the year, they were students. What they accomplished in life was due to the determination they had in college to learn how to "be somebody."

I used to pick up poems and inspirational pieces about coaching. One of them came from Converse, which was one of the first shoe companies to make contact with the small black colleges. The poem is too long to reproduce in its entirety, but it is called "Coaches Never Lose."

The poem says the job of a coach is over once the starting whistle blows because his job was to teach his boys the fundamentals of the game and then to teach them how to be men. Any coach's job is to teach boys to live up to their potential, to do their best, to never be satisfied with what they are but to strive to be as good as they can be. The poem says that a coach can never make a great player out of a kid who isn't potentially great, but that a coach can make a great competitor out of any child, and that he can make a man out of a boy.

I picked up that poem at some coaches' conference more than 30 years ago, and I've kept it stuffed in a box of memorabilia all this time. I think it describes what I tried to do my entire coaching career.

CHAPTER 13

Taking Stock
During the Golden Years
of the Early 1960s

By the beginning of the 1961-62 season, my Winston-Salem Teachers College teams had won 271 games and four CIAA championships
and had finished as runner-up in the CIAA tourney in several other
years. After starting at the bottom of the pile in 1945, behind schools
with larger male populations and diverse degree programs like Virginia
State, Virginia Union, North Carolina College, and West Virginia State,
our little teachers' college made up mostly of girls was on top of the
heap. My players were as skilled as any athletes at any similar-sized
college, black or white. We hadn't played many white colleges to prove
my assertion, but I think our CIAA championships against the best black
colleges in the Southeast were enough to prove my point.

By the early '60s, my network of recruiters who had been students
and players had expanded to Philadelphia. The best recruiter I had in
place was Leon Whitley, who had played on our 1953 CIAA championship team as a five-foot-ten guard.

Leon was one of the first guards I had used as a floor leader, a position that would become known as point guard in later days. I had recruited Leon when I went to the Penn Relays track meet in 1951. While I was up there, I heard about these two buddies, good high-school track runners who were also good basketball players. Both of them played in the backcourt on the first black high school to play for a Philadelphia city championship. I heard from other coaches that white colleges like LaSalle and Georgetown were talking to them and that black colleges like Cheyney State, Howard, and Morgan State were also in the running for their college playing services. I wasn't sure if I had a chance with these really talented kids who were being so heavily recruited, but I decided to try. Just as I had tried to recruit the 14-year-old Wilt Chamberlain, I pitched to all the outstanding players with whom I came in contact.

I found a gym near the Penn Relays and had these teammates shoot some basketballs. I didn't have them do anything too strenuous, as I didn't want to tire them out before their running events. The Penn Relays was their chance to showcase themselves, not my chance to recruit. I was sensitive enough not to be overbearing.

I liked both of them and talked to both of them about coming to Winston-Salem Teachers College. Leon liked the idea immediately, even though Georgetown had been talking to him about a track scholarship. That would have been a prestigious place and closer to home, but Leon also liked the idea of going to a small black college, where there would be more people like him, rather than being a lonely, poor black athlete among numerous wealthy white students. He figured he would fit in better in Winston-Salem.

Leon did fit. He had a fine four seasons with the school. He never called me anything but Mr. Gaines. He tells me that since I towered over his five-foot-ten frame, he was too frightened to call me anything but Mr. Gaines. He still calls me that today.

Leon's high-school teammate seemed to be interested in becoming a teacher, but he would slip through my fingers through no fault of my own. He decided on attending Bethune-Cookman College in Daytona Beach, Florida, because he had relatives in the city and in nearby Jacksonville, his hometown.

Personal connections to a town, school, or recruiter were one obstacle that I never overcame in recruiting, but which also frequently worked in my favor. If a prospective recruit had some sort of family member or friend who had gone to a school or who lived near the school, the athlete generally went to that school. This actually tracked with my recruiting method of developing close relationships with playground directors in the Northeast. These recreation directors were often the closest male figures in the kids' lives.

Leon Whitley's friend, the athlete I failed to recruit, was John Chaney. John would star at Bethune-Cookman and then move up through the coaching ranks from high school through NCAA Division II at the black Cheyney State University. He would move up to Division I in 1982 when he joined Temple University, which is where he is now. John is currently the most successful active black coach at a Division I university. In late January 2004, he surpassed the 700-win mark, with nearly 500 victories coming at Temple.

John Chaney and another of my big-time coaching buddies, John Thompson, the coach at Georgetown University from 1972 through 1999, removed any lingering doubts that blacks could coach in Division I. In 1984, Thompson became the first black coach to win the NCAA Division I title. Chaney has won six Atlantic 10 titles and has gone to the NCAA Division I tournament 17 times. Thompson joined me in the Hall of Fame in 1999 and Chaney in 2001.

I still regret not recruiting Chaney. Maybe if he had been playing beside his old teammate Whitley, we might have won some back-to-back CIAA championships in the mid-1950s.

The Teachers—the newspapers still were not regularly calling us by our proper nickname, the Rams—finished the 1961-62 regular season in February with an outstanding record of 21-3, the best record we had up to that point for lowest number of losses.

My team captain was George Foree, one of my Midwestern recruits, who I had found in Carbondale, Illinois. My leading scorer was Richard Glover, who had come from Newark, New Jersey. Richard stepped into the role of shooter once Cleo Hill graduated. Backing them up were Louis "Left-Hand" Parker from New York City, Willie Curry from

Fort Wayne, and freshman Teddy Blunt, who had been recruited for me out of Philadelphia by Whitley. We called Parker "Left-Hand" because that was in a time when most players were right-handed.

Leon had seen Teddy play in high school. When I was in town on business in the summer of 1961, Leon organized a pickup game as a tryout for several players. Leon sorted out the teams by strength and told them to play as hard as they could. Teddy stood out as a guard who could shoot and as a leader on the floor. That was one position I was always interested in filling—someone who could coach from the floor, rather than having me yelling instructions from the bench.

Teddy was recruited by several other CIAA teams, including Maryland Eastern Shore, North Carolina A&T, and Elizabeth City. There was another school that wanted him to play soccer.

Leon finally persuaded Teddy to come to Winston-Salem. His mother had just enough money to buy him a train ticket. He left Philadelphia with a footlocker of clothes, a sandwich, and a jar of water for him to drink on the train. When he arrived on campus, Teddy had absolutely no money. We had to spot him some money until his scholarship kicked in a few weeks later. He turned out to be great, one of the few freshmen I would start on a regular basis.

Because the Teachers were the regular-season champs for the 1961-62 season, we entered the 17th annual CIAA tournament in Greensboro as the favorites. We were poised to break a tie with Virginia Union for the total number of tournament championships (five) and the number of tournament championships in a row (three).

Because we were the top seed, the lowest seed in the tournament, the Saint Paul's Tigers, drew us as their opponent. As usual, I did not predict victory, even though the little college in Lawrenceville, Virginia, had never even qualified for the tournament before. I said something like, "Those players will be hungry, and that is the type of team that we have to watch." I had full confidence that my team was every bit as strong as they had been with Cleo Hill leading them in the 1960-61 championship, but I also knew that every so often, we got knocked off by an underdog team.

Well, as much as I worried about being upset, the Tigers were no match for my Teachers. At one time, we were ahead 41-8. We finally won 117-63 in the first-round game. I freely substituted to try to keep the score down, but it was no use. My team was too good.

I did see something in that early round of games that worried me. North Carolina A&T, the hometown team, beat Morgan State 130-62. A&T's coach, Cal Irvin, had not shown any mercy on his and my old alma mater.

Our next opponent was Virginia State of Richmond. We changed from a fast-break offense to a ball-control offense midway through the second half to win 88-74. I figured the switch would frustrate Virginia State, and it did. They tried to force us to give up the ball in the backcourt. When they did, they fouled us. They committed six fouls in the backcourt in five minutes, and we turned those fouls into 10 points. They never got the momentum going their way.

Oddly enough, A&T also had a lower-scoring game, winning their place in the final by beating Maryland State 68-60.

In the championship game, A&T played ball-control offense better than we did. They kept the ball away from us all night. They got ahead 14-6 in the first six minutes, and we never could get control. We also couldn't shoot. They hit 57 percent to our 43 percent. We went nearly six minutes without scoring a single basket. A&T won 80-66, spoiling our chance to break the CIAA record for winning consecutive tournaments.

It wasn't all bad. George Foree was named Most Valuable Player of the tournament. He and Teddy Blunt were named to the All-Tournament team.

Our season wasn't over. A&T would go on to play for the NCAA small-college championship, leaving us to go to Kansas City for the NAIA playoffs.

On March 12, we faced Indiana State of Terre Haute, a white college about which we knew nothing. I practiced every defense I could think of in order to be prepared for what they might try.

We started off slow and were down by eight points at the half, but we opened the second half with eight straight points to tie the score at 40 within two minutes. They came back, but we rallied again and sank another eight straight points. We won 83-71, earning us the right to go to the next round against Southeastern Oklahoma State College, another white college.

We could not buy a basket in the Southeastern Oklahoma State game, which did not start until 11:00 P.M. Maybe that was the problem. Just as the previous year, we started playing a NAIA playoff game at a time when most of my players would have been in bed back in Winston-Salem. I never did figure out why the NAIA would schedule playoff games so late at night, when the fans and the players would be sluggish.

I don't know if the late hour really did throw off the team's rhythm, but our shooting was terrible. We made only 17 of 64 shot attempts, a 27 percent shooting average, perhaps the worst any of my teams have ever shot in any game in my career. By contrast, Southeastern, nicknamed the "Savages," shot only 39 times but made 17 of them, for a 44 percent average.

I don't know what happened. The players missed easy layups and one-and-one foul shots. My top scorers got only 10 points each. I was quoted after the game that we deserved to lose for the poor play we exhibited. For the second year in a row, we had dominated the CIAA all year long, only to get bounced from the NAIA national championship. Once again, we missed our shot at garnering national attention because we did not play the kind of ball of which we were capable.

In the 1962-63 season, we virtually duplicated our 1961-62 season, winning more than 20 games and losing only six, good enough to win the regular-season CIAA championship for the second year in a row. But this was a very unusual season. We opened by winning five straight games at home. We then lost five straight games on the road. Don't ask me why. I don't know.

We went into the first round of the CIAA tournament against the Elizabeth City State Pirates, who we had beaten twice in the regular season. Our team scared me in the first half of that game. The Pirates stayed with us, even going ahead several times before we went into halftime with a one-point lead. After a little yelling at halftime, we opened the second half with 17 straight points. We won 101-81. Willie Curry

The 1962-63 team included (first row, left to right) Willie Curry,
Mickey Smith, Barney Hood, Lutheran Wiley, and Teddy Blunt.
Second row, left to right: Gilbert Smith, Richard Glover, Charlie
Simmons, Willis Bennett, and Willie Rozier. Third row, left to right:
Arthur Rucks, Willie Hussey, Mr. Jackson, Waldron Taborn, Ted
Ratchford, and Joe Cunningham

and Ted Ratchford from Charlotte, North Carolina, had 26 points each.
Mickey Smith from Washington, D.C., had 17.

The next night, we faced Johnson C. Smith, and we totally changed
the game plan. We slowed the game down and stalled much of the
time. We went into the half with a lead of 38-35 and did not even
score another point until 11:46 remained in the second half. We eventually won 54-49. It was a completely different game plan from what
we had played against Elizabeth City. That is the way you win games,
by always being willing to change the game plan.

The next night, March 3, 1963, we won the CIAA final against Virginia Union, 75-68. In this game, we mixed things up. We ran for a

191

while and then stalled for a while. Teddy Blunt was the floor leader as usual, directing Richard Glover as rebounder and scorer. We went into halftime with a 42-37 lead. We tried to stall for the second half, but Virginia Union kept creeping up on our lead. With 3:42 remaining, we led 62-60. At 2:28 remaining, Virginia Union tied the score. In overtime, our team sank their free throws, and we finally went ahead for good. Richard Glover and Teddy Blunt sank their shots and won the game for us. Teddy was named Most Valuable Player in the tournament for his foul-shooting skills, and he and Richard made the All-Tournament team. I was voted Outstanding Coach of the tournament.

The post-CIAA tournament opportunities were complicated. By winning both the regular season and the CIAA tournament, we technically earned the right to go to both the NCAA and the NAIA tournaments, but the CIAA commissioners had already voted that the CIAA tournament winner would go to the NCAA Division II (or small-college) championship. Complicating matters was the fact that I was the chairman of the NAIA's District 29.

To complicate matters even further, the NCAA switched the location of the regional tournaments on us. We were originally scheduled to play in Louisville, and then we were told we would be playing in Akron. In thinking back on it, I suspect it was because the Akron playoffs had Wittenburg, the number-one-rated small-college team in the nation. I still wonder if the decision was made to knock us off early.

When I couldn't get a good answer out of the NCAA as to why our regional game had been moved, I decided our team would play in the NAIA tournament. We had played in Kansas City for the last two years. We had lost in those two years, but I thought the players liked the idea of going back a third time to try and get that elusive win. We had lost in the second round in 1962 and in the quarterfinals in 1961.

We left Winston-Salem on March 10 with a motorcycle escort and a band playing for our good luck. We were seeded third, behind black Grambling State College and white Augsburg College from Minneapolis. We were going with an experienced team. Richard Glover, Willie Curry, and Barney Hood had all been to the NAIA twice. Ted Ratchford,

Teddy Blunt, Lutheran Wiley, and Mickey Smith had been once. All of my starters were experienced in playing for a national title.

I worried about facing Grambling State. They had a six-foot-ten player who seemed destined to go on to great things. He was Willis Reed, who would eventually be NBA Rookie of the Year in 1965 and to be named seven times to the NBA All-Star team. He would play on the same 1973 NBA championship New York Knicks team as my player Earl Monroe.

Our first opponent was Transylvania College of Lexington, Kentucky. On paper, we looked strong against them. They were 19-8 and unseeded. Most of their players were much smaller than our players. Their tallest man was only six-foot-four. Our field-goal percentage was 45 percent, compared to their 41 percent. They typically used a run-and-shoot offense, which we thought we could break.

For the third year in a row, however, our team just did not play well on a national stage. We were behind Transylvania 19-8 in the first 12 minutes. Instead of running and shooting, they slowed the game down and took only accurately thrown shots. We attempted only 26 shots in the first half, and we made only nine of those.

Willie Curry got in foul trouble early, and Richard Glover scored only two points in the first half. Only Teddy Blunt's steals kept us close, but he, too, threw the ball away several times.

We settled down in the second half, and Glover started hitting from inside, but our foul shooting never materialized. Our regular-season record was 69 percent, but in this game we shot only 40 percent. In total, Transylvania made 46 percent of their shots, while we made only 37 percent of ours.

Our shot at a national title would have to wait for another year.

Though we had yet to win a national title, all the publicity about how WSTC was dominating the CIAA was attracting some unwelcome attention from the professional ranks—not the National Basketball Association but the Harlem Globetrotters.

The Globetrotters had been around since the 1920s, founded by a man named Abe Saperstein, who was trying to duplicate the idea of a traveling black basketball team like the New York Rens. Saperstein and his players lived in Chicago, but he decided to use the name Harlem to play off of the Rens, who already had a strong national reputation. The Harlem Globetrotters didn't even play a game in Harlem until 1968.

Saperstein first envisioned the Globetrotters as a copy of the Rens, a professional team of black basketball players who barnstormed around the country playing local college teams as well as whatever passed for professional teams in the towns they were visiting.

In one town in the 1930s, the Globetrotters got so far ahead of a white team that Saperstein told his players to clown around on the court and show some fancy passes, so the locals would not get any angrier than they already were at how badly their team was being stomped. Saperstein was worried not only about not getting paid if he humiliated the local team, but also about getting involved in a racial incident. Though the game was played in a Northern city, where segregation of sports teams was not enforced as it was in the South, Saperstein knew that racial animosity could crop up at any time.

The crowd loved the on-court comedy and forgot how poorly their team was playing. Saperstein recognized that the crowd enjoyed the entertainment more than they did the competition. From that point on, he would have the team switch to their clowning mode once the game was under control. The Globetrotters still considered themselves professional ballplayers, and they wanted to win the games as much as they wanted to entertain.

By the 1950s, comedy had become the Globetrotters' trademark and the key to their success. They were still a real basketball team that defeated real opponents, but Saperstein had decided to market them as a squad of entertaining black ballplayers who had fancy passing and dribbling skills.

The Globetrotters were so successful that they had four different teams on the road playing seven days a week in an era when the NBA had only eight teams. The Globetrotters even signed Wilt Chamberlain for one year in 1958, when he played because he left the University of Kansas before graduation. At that time, the NBA had a rule that players had to have a college degree before they could turn professional.

It was this need for on-the-road players that sent Saperstein sniffing around the CIAA, which angered me.

The first black players were drafted into the NBA in 1950. One, Nat "Sweetwater" Clifton, was a Globetrotter whose contract was purchased by the New York Knicks. While the first experiment in integration on the professional court was under way, most of the NBA teams for the rest of the 1950s were careful about drafting black players. They did not want too many blacks, out of fear of what reaction the mostly white fans would have. Even a decade later, long after players like Oscar Robinson and Wilt Chamberlain had proven to be NBA stars, blacks still found it difficult to be accepted by white fans and teammates, as my player Cleo Hill discovered in 1961.

For the last three decades, Saperstein had been presenting the Globetrotters as a career opportunity for good black basketball players. With a limited number of blacks in the NBA, there literally was no other place for black ballplayers to play after college other than the Globetrotters. Saperstein thought he had first dibs on the careers of outstanding black ballplayers.

My first contact with him was in the 1940s, when he signed one of my first recruited players, Oris Hill, to a contract after Oris left Winston-Salem Teachers College. Oris did not exactly leave the college of his own free will. He cursed out the chancellor about something and was asked to leave. Another of my players, James Trice, would fill in for the Globetrotters on occasion. In the early 1950s, while they were still in high school and before they came down to Winston-Salem, Carl Green and Jack DeFares were approached by Saperstein and offered contracts to play for the Globetrotters.

I won't say anything more about Saperstein other than that whenever I saw a contract offer from the Globetrotters made out to one of my players, I would tear it up and then explain to the player why it was a bad idea to leave college for the Globetrotters. For one thing, the pay being offered in those days was usually less than my players would make as schoolteachers once they had that all-valuable college diploma. The pay of a schoolteacher wasn't much, but that bachelor's degree was their ticket to a professional life or to graduate school, where they could learn skills to earn more money.

I was also irritated that the Globetrotters were trying to lure athletes with the promise of on-the-road adventure. I knew there was no adventure in traveling with the team. The Globetrotters were playing a different city every night. Even if they did go overseas, there would be hardly any time to see any sights. In a few years, the players would grow tired of the road, or the organization would find someone else, and they would be released. There they would be—young, black, worn-out basketball players without the college degrees I had promised them.

Saperstein looked at black college basketball players as potential inexpensive employees for his team. He did not care if they graduated or not, while I had been telling them they were in college to prepare themselves for the rest of their lives. I had been drilling into their heads that playing college ball was a means to reaching the end of getting a college degree and starting a professional career. Saperstein was telling them they could play basketball for a living and didn't need any classes or a college degree.

I had nothing against the idea of any of my players trying out for professional basketball—the NBA or the Globetrotters—but I wanted those young men to finish college first. Cleo Hill had graduated and was prepared to be a teacher if his NBA career did not work out—which it didn't. He played in a regional professional league, but he had the good sense not to go to the Globetrotters. He went into teaching.

In all my years of coaching college basketball, I think I approved of only one player ever leaving school to join the Globetrotters. That was Carl Green. Carl was a great player, but he and college textbooks didn't get along. I wanted him to stay and tough it out, since he had been one of my best players in 1953-54, but he finally convinced me that he would be better off playing ball than he would be in a classroom. He left his buddy Jack DeFares in college.

Carl played for the Globetrotters for five years before going to work for a tailor, which was fitting, since he liked to wear nice clothes even while in college. Now that he is retired, Carl is still best buddies with Jack, who is also a clotheshorse. Carl tells me that they don't even pick up a ball to shoot anymore. All they do now is "dress and rest."

By the early 1960s, I had changed from a 1940s basketball coach who asked his best players how I could be a better coach into a coach who had a fairly wide range of methods of motivating my players.

Sometimes, I found ways to be nice and motivating at the same time. Other times, I was not nice and motivating. It was those times when I was not nice that I found that some players had changed my nickname from "Big House" to "Shit House" or "Out House" or "Big Nasty."

I will admit that I did some things to win those bad nicknames that I should not have done. Maybe I deserved some mumbling from players now and again. I never broke any league rules, but I really pushed some players hard.

For instance, Les Gaither, one my football players from 1946 to 1949, reminds me now that I never let the team drink water during practices because I thought that would make them "soft." That would get me fired today, maybe even arrested for assault. Les never held my tough training against me. He helped me assemble teams from New York City by going to his buddies and telling them that I was on the level with my offers of helping them get into college.

Carl Green reminds me that he played with a hernia during the CIAA tournament games of 1953. When we found out just before the tourney that he had the hernia, we went to a doctor over at North Carolina A&T. The doctor put a little piece of rubber over the hernia to hold in the intestines, and then we taped Carl up real tight. I gave him some aspirin for pain and told him to let me know if he hurt too bad to play. He played all three games of the tournament. I would probably get fired today for not taking a player directly to the hospital for that type of injury.

Bad names aside, the name I liked as much as "Big House" coming from my players was "Big Chief." If I heard that, I knew I was keeping a little bit of love as well as their respect. By contrast, my competing CIAA coaches called me "the Godfather" when it came to tournament time. I never liked that nickname very much.

Sometimes, my method of motivating players involved a little dose of humiliation. Once, I had three of my best players—Jack DeFares, Carl Green, and Don Bradley—go home for a long weekend without telling me or asking my permission, when the rest of the team was working out. When those players returned, they found I had confiscated their regular uniforms. All they had to play in were junior-varsity uniforms, which were a different color and which they described as "crappy." I remember making them practice in those uniforms. I don't guess the referees would have permitted me to play my team in two separate uniforms. At any rate, the guys got the message that if they were going to be on my team, they would earn the right to wear the uniform by showing up for all of the practices.

Sometimes, I would inject a dose of reality. I remember one game in the mid-1950s when Marshall Emery got into a fight with a Delaware State player when the other player intentionally tripped him after losing a jump ball. Marshall started wrestling with the other player on the floor. I ran out on the floor, snatched Marshall up in a bear hug, and brought him back to our bench. I was angry enough at him for getting into a fight that could have resulted in one or both players getting called for fouls or maybe getting tossed from the game. But I was more concerned that Marshall had broken the cardinal rule of basketball fighting: Don't ever get into a tussle in front of the opposing team's bench. Marshall could have gotten hurt long before anyone from our team could arrive to protect him.

Sometimes, I would try a little subterfuge. In 1964, we were in Atlanta playing in the Georgia Invitational Tournament. While our team was suiting up, I wandered onto the court to get a look at our first rival, Jackson State University from Mississippi. Those players were giants! And they were hot in practice. I walked over to the tournament director and told him that we would be skipping our warmup drill. Just as I had refused to let my 1950s teams see Earl Lloyd in person before they had to face him, I wasn't about to let my little Teachers see these monsters from Mississippi in practice.

That plan worked. The first time my Teachers saw Jackson State was when they walked onto the court to play them. My little Davids won against the Goliaths because my team did not have time to compare themselves to the height of the other players. It was purely a psychological game that worked. If you know the enemy is going to have

The 1963-64 team won the early season Georgia Invitational Tournament, although we were banned from post-season CIAA championship play because of our selection of tournaments the previous season. Kneeling, left to right: Ted Ratchford, Joe Cunningham, Charlie Simmons, Teddy Blunt, Willis Bennett, Earl Monroe, and ball boy John X. Miller Standing, left to right: Louis Parker, Richard Glover, an unidentified tournament official, Willie Curry, Richard Smith, James Reid, and Gilbert Smith

(WINSTON-SALEM STATE UNIVERSITY ARCHIVES)

the advantage, then don't allow your side to study them too long before they have to face them. Let the players' adrenaline peak on the court, rather than letting them stew in that adrenaline 20 minutes before the game.

Sometimes, I would inject a little dose of humility and humanity into the coach-player relationship. Some coaches never fraternize with their players. I remember reading stories about how thrilled football players would get when University of Alabama football coach Paul "Bear" Bryant would personally speak to them.

I would sometimes stop off at the players' dorms and play a few hands of cards with them. Some coaches don't want to be "one of the guys" with their team, but I found that it helped build a bond. The kids knew that I cared as much for them as they cared for each other. By staying close to them, I was not only the coach but also part of the team.

Sometimes, I would use just plain hard work to impress upon them what they were supposed to do. My old teams agree that they used to hate holidays—and they are not being sour on family. I would not let them stay with their families for the entire holiday break. I would make them come back and practice for the upcoming holiday tournament. During the holidays, they didn't have to go to class. That meant they could spend most of the holidays practicing how to win games.

Sometimes, I would use some psychology on my team.

As I mentioned earlier, I actually gave my players few real rules that they were supposed to follow as members of the team. I just demanded that they act responsibly. I kept telling them that basketball is a simple game. Any small child can play it. But life is much more complicated, and it takes some degree of sophistication to get through it unscathed. Now that we were winning ball games and being declared champions, or at least were predicted to be champions on a regular basis, I wanted my players to know that they were not going to get any advantages that were not there for other students. Yes, they were heroes on campus, but I insisted that they remain grounded. They were merely students at Winston-Salem Teachers College who engaged in a sport that the other students did not play.

But while I insisted to them that they were mere students, I also warned my players that they could get into legal trouble much easier than any other students. I warned them that girls would be chasing them, but that they had better not force themselves on any girls. That was a sure ticket to jail—and I wasn't going to be there to get them out of that kind of scrape.

I didn't expect any gamblers to pay attention to basketball at small black colleges, but I warned my players that penny-ante poker had better be the only gambling I ever saw them doing. I told them about the great black college and playground players I had known in New York

City who had lost their entire futures for the instant reward of a few hundred dollars.

Sometimes, I would show the players how to use some psychology on the other team. From the beginning, I discouraged the trash talking between players that runs through the college and professional game today. I never understood what verbally insulting another player was supposed to do, other than get him angry enough that he would make a mistake and foul you. That did not seem to be the best way to win ball games. Why not beat them by being better players?

Instead of allowing my team members to insult the other players or to respond to insults coming from their opponents, I told them to keep their mouths shut but to make it obvious to their trash-talking opponents when the game was going our way. If their opponent was trash talking, the way to shut him up was to go over his head and make a basket, then point to the scoreboard or the basket and smile. I told my players to not say a word, but just to smile and maybe wink. I told them to make their point by performing on the court without saying a word. When my players followed those instructions, they found that the other players would either get frustrated and stop the trash talking or would get even more frustrated and start making mistakes that would result in our team getting more foul shots.

I never let up on teaching and practicing the fundamentals of basketball. One of my favorite practice drills was to use a no-bounce basketball. This was a ball that was regulation size and weight but which literally did not bounce, so it could not be dribbled by the players. All you could do with this ball was pass it from player to player until one got in range of the basket. My showboaters who thought they could do everything themselves did not like the no-bounce balls, but a basketball team simply cannot rely on one or two stars.

Another fundamental drill was picking out places on the floor and having players shoot shot after shot after shot, until they knew where that basket was with their eyes closed. By his ability to shoot in a darkened gym, Cleo Hill had proven to the players on his teams that this type of drill worked. Some of my New Yorkers looked down their noses at slow, well-aimed set shots, claiming that was the only kind of shot my Midwesterners could sink, and that most baskets would come from the fast break. I ignored those players. I was the coach.

In the early fall of 1963, Leon Whitley was about to do a big favor for me, Winston-Salem Teachers College, and one certain high-school graduate who had decided to pass on higher education. He was about to suggest to Vernon Earl Monroe that he give college a try.

CHAPTER 14

I Stumble onto
Earl Monroe

In the early fall of 1963, after recruiting Teddy Blunt for me in 1962, Leon Whitley in Philadelphia shifted his attention to an athlete who had played against Teddy in high school. What caught Leon's eye was that, under this kid's leadership, his high school had beaten Teddy's high-school team when it was at its very best.

I usually trusted Leon's judgment without question because he was not that far removed from his own playing days. He knew about the rigors of balancing college coursework, basketball practice, and being on the road for several months. These playground ballplayers may have had the skills, but they did not have a sense of the environment into which they would be going if they were selected for a college team.

Leon was only 10 years older than Teddy's generation, so the kids he was talking to on the playground seemed to relate to him. He was not some old-man recreation director employed by the city to pass out basketballs and restring hoop nets. Leon would get out on the playground and play basketball with these guys, so he could judge their skills himself. And since he had served as a point guard on the 1953 CIAA championship team, they respected his skills as well. The CIAA, even though it was a conference of small black colleges in the South, was well known among the black teenagers in the Northeast.

This athlete that Leon was watching now had amazing basketball skills and was well mannered to adults, but he was also somewhat shy. The biggest negative in Leon's eyes was that he was indifferent—or, in Leon's words, "lackadaisical"—in his attitude toward school and his future. Like too many of the kids Leon saw from the inner city, the kid did not have a sense of what he could do to shape his own future. He was growing out of his teenage years, and he had no idea what he was going to do with his life.

Leon called me several times as he watched the teenager play summertime ball to tell me how good he was. While Leon was surprised at how good the kid was, he was also honest with me that the young man seemed uninterested in preparing for much of anything in his future.

What troubled me most about this prospect was that he had already graduated from high school and had come home from a college preparatory school, apparently deciding that he either could not or would not do college-level coursework. That was in the front of my mind whenever Leon called to push him. The kid had already turned his back on one college, so what would stop him from doing the same with Winston-Salem Teachers College? I didn't want to waste my time on a quitter.

Instead of going on to college, the kid had gone to work as a shipping clerk in a paper-plate factory. For fun, he played pickup playground ball at Leon's recreation center, just as he had done during his high-school years. That was all basketball seemed to be to him—something to do for fun, rather than something to get him to a higher level of education and a professional career that would come only with a college degree.

All that was true, Leon admitted in his phone calls. But Leon said this kid could play basketball like no one he had ever seen. When Leon first contacted me, he had a hard time describing the player's talents, other than saying they were amazing to see. He seemed to be able to adjust to his opponents' body language and to exploit any slight mistake into a major advantage. It was as if the teenager was anticipating what the defending player was going to do in response to his attack—before he even attacked. By the time the defending player had figured out what the kid was going to do, he had already done it. The basket had been made, and the kid was on his way back to set up his defense, while the defenders were still standing around trying to figure out what had just happened to them.

The teenager's athletic background made me curious and also a little concerned. When Leon had asked the kid how long he had been playing, he was shocked to hear how he had not even picked up a basketball until he was 14 years old. He had grown up more interested in baseball and soccer. He had gone out for basketball only when a junior-high coach demanded that any 14-year-old who was already six-foot-three had to play junior-high ball.

By the time he reached high school, the kid had grown only to six-foot-four, a common size among ballplayers, and certainly not a size that would make coaches take notice. Because he had started playing so late in his youth, his high-school coaches had not even picked him to start on the varsity team until midway through his junior year. That was far too late for any of those coaches to have a chance to develop his skills beyond what he already brought to the team. Most of the skills he was showing now on Leon's playground had been developed on that same playground. He polished those skills by playing in the Baker League, a playground league in South Philadelphia similar to the Rucker tournaments in New York City. While he had a good, if short, high-school career, most of the kid's reputation among other players had been made on the playground.

It was during one phone call from Leon that I laughed out loud when he made a statement that I did not think could ever possibly work out to be true.

"Mr. Gaines, this kid could turn out to be your next Cleo Hill," Leon said.

I remember that his tone of voice was very serious, and stayed serious even when I laughed back into his ear.

I did not see how it was possible that I could luck into finding another player who was as blessed with talent as Cleo had been. I had coached scores of basketball players since 1946, when I started, and more than a dozen since Cleo had graduated in 1961. Many of them had been great, wonderful players who had helped Winston-Salem Teachers College win CIAA championships.

But only one of them had been a Cleo Hill.

Cleo had been able to shoot any kind of shot from any place on the court. He had proven to be easy to coach and easy for the other kids to like and follow. He had been a superstar on a team that was not jealous that he got that kind of superstar attention from me, the newspapers, the referees, and eventually NBA scouts. And Cleo made sure his teammates got their share of the credit. He might have been my superstar, but he never took the label seriously, and he never let me take it seriously either. I did not see how finding such a player again just two years after Cleo had graduated was possible.

Once again, I was wrong. Once again, I stumbled onto a great player. Once again, my bumper-car philosophy of moving along in the direction in which I was bumped would prove to be a benefit to me and Winston-Salem Teachers College, which would change its name to Winston-Salem State College this year.

The promising athlete's name was Vernon Earl Monroe. The newspapers would call him Vernon for the first year, but they would start using Earl in his second. By his senior year, the name the newspaper and fans would call him was "the Pearl."

I finally gave in to Leon's phone calls and told him to go ahead and send Earl down in the fall of 1963. I might have guessed that there would be a catch, and there was. Leon said Earl had a friend named Steve Smith (Sahib Abdul Kharir), who would have to come along, too. As best buddies, they wanted to go to the same college.

I had heard this demand once before. It was the same one Cleo had demanded with his best buddy, Artie Johnson. I could take both of them or neither of them.

When Leon told me Steve was only five-foot-ten, I cringed. He was bigger than five-foot-seven Artie Johnson, but smallish players were not what I needed.

Leon Whitley kept calling to tell me how good this player from Philadelphia was. That player turned out to be Earl Monroe, consequently it's a good thing I listened to Leon. In this photo, Earl drives to the basket against the University of Akron.

207

Maybe it was my imagination, but I thought I could hear Leon whispering over the phone, "Cleo, Cleo."

Finally, I agreed to take both Earl and Steve, sight unseen, and unsure what I would do with both of them. Just as with most players I recruited, I had never met either recruit in person, had never seen either of them play, had never seen a scouting report on them, and had never met their parents. I just trusted Leon Whitley that these kids could be college basketball players and, more importantly to them, that they could become college graduates on their way to professional careers in education.

It would be nearly 25 years before I would finally admit to Leon that he was right, that the player he had found was a match for Cleo Hill.

Actually, Earl was not raring to become a teacher. The college preparatory school he had attended was affiliated with Temple University, but I don't think he ever got an idea of what he might major in before he quit school. Instead of thinking about trying another college, he contemplated skipping college completely and entering the American Basketball League.

The ABL was a league that Harlem Globetrotters owner Abe Saperstein had created in 1961, when he thought he had been cheated out of the NBA franchise for Los Angeles. Saperstein's Globetrotters used to open for NBA games in order to attract crowds. When he was passed over for the franchise, which was given to the owner of the Minneapolis Lakers, an angry Saperstein jumped into financing the ABL. He apparently jumped too fast before realizing how expensive it was to create a league from scratch. The ABL lasted only two years, just long enough to attract the attention of players like Earl—who knew that the NBA would not take anyone who did not have a college degree—but not long enough that Earl could actually play for any of the teams.

With the folding of the ABL, Earl was left with the choices of staying at his dead-end job, playing for the Globetrotters, or coming to Winston-Salem. After some more urging from Leon, Earl decided to try college once more.

Before Earl could change his mind, Leon loaded him and Steve on the train and sent them south. I don't think either one of them had been more than 100 miles from home.

Between the two of them, Steve and Earl had one overcoat. When I climbed up in the train car late at night to find my new recruits, I found them huddled together under that one coat. As I gathered up their meager belongings and we headed for the car to take them to their dorm, one of them asked why the "local" trains were not running. These Philadelphia natives assumed that every town had a subway. Just like my kids from New York City, these Philadelphians would be in for culture shock when they discovered what living in a small Southern city really meant.

When I had Earl and Steve try out, I was pleased at what I saw. Both of them could play basketball, just as Leon had promised. I don't remember sensing any greatness in Earl during those practices, but I could see that he could play. Teddy Blunt, Earl's old high-school rival, assured me that Earl would be cool as a cucumber on the floor when we faced opponents.

Teddy also told me about the nicknames that Earl had back on the playgrounds of Philadelphia: "Black Jesus" and "Magic." I guess the "Black Jesus" nickname came from his performing miracles on the court. "Magic" must have referred to the same thing.

That Earl did not immediately shine in college and live up to his teenage nicknames—and that I did not recognize his "magical" skills right away—may surprise some people. I saw those spinning moves he had perfected on the playgrounds, but I had seen similar moves from my New York playground players. I was more interested in seeing if Earl fit in well with the team, or if he would be a showboater who I would have to control.

Earl did fit in with the team, but he was just another freshman to me. Freshmen did not normally start on my teams unless my older, experienced players got into foul trouble. Even though Earl was obviously talented, I still had better players on the team who had already proven to me that they could play well under pressure during big games. I was not about to pull them out of the starting lineup just to make space for an unproven freshman, even if Earl had undeniable potential.

In most of the games in Earl's freshman year, I simply did not need his services because not many of my players got in foul trouble. That

Earl Monroe sat on the bench during most of his freshman year may sound surprising for a man who is on the list of the NBA's all-time top 50 players, but it is true. I played him only enough in his freshman year that he averaged around seven points a game. He made only 163 points that year.

But I knew what I had and who I had. There were several times during his freshman year that I put Earl in during tightly contested games, just to see how he would perform under pressure. He always did well, always surprised the opposition, and always pleased his coach and his teammates. I just did not need him in the games all of the time.

At one point in Earl's freshman year, he decided that he wanted more playing time. He demanded that he get more minutes or he would go home. I knew how to handle that kind of talk from a freshman. I called his mother and his sister, perhaps the only two people in the world who Earl trusted to help him make decisions. They called him and convinced him that I recognized his value and that his time would come.

It was during his sophomore year that Earl had enough playing time to begin to incorporate his playground skills into his college game. He would spin; he would move in and out; he would dribble with his back to the basket, then spin around to send the ball sailing toward the rim that had been out of his sight just moments earlier. It was as if he could see the goal from the back of his head and could make any necessary adjustments once he had spun around and was in the air taking his shot.

Whenever anyone would ask him how he developed the moves, Earl would shrug and say, "I don't know what I am going to do next, so how can a defender know what I am going to do next? I only know what I am going to do when I do it, so it is hard to defend me."

Some of his explanations of his "shake-and-bake" moves, as he called them, made no sense to anyone who was not a playground player. In one article, he was quoted as saying, "I had to develop flukey-dukey shots, hesitating in the air as long as possible before shooting."

And that is all the answer that Earl has ever given anyone about the way he played the game, both as a college student and as a professional star.

While Cleo Hill was scientific and seemed to have studied the game in great detail, Earl has always maintained that his moves and shot selection were more trial and error. If something worked, he used it. When it didn't, he discarded it. As Earl once said, "This is not rocket science. I just roll with the game, and when I make a basket, I make a basket."

Earl was not perfect, and his teammates knew it. I remember Teddy Blunt being able to figure out the spin move during practice and steal the ball from Earl. Once he had the ball in his hands and was smiling at Earl, Teddy explained what he had seen in Earl's movements that allowed him to grab the ball. While Teddy may have been able to do it in practice, stealing the ball from Earl didn't happen often during college games.

There was something Earl was lacking. That was an athlete's body. To look at him, he was nothing special, loping onto the court from the sidelines. At six-foot-four, he wasn't all that tall. He weighed less than 190 pounds, so he looked skinny. His knees knocked together. His legs were not all that muscular. His arms were not muscular at all. I don't remember asking him to work out with free weights to make himself any stronger, but he seemed to do okay with what he had.

The ending of the 1963-64 season, Earl's first, was kind of strange. We finished the year 22-4 for the season and 17-3 in CIAA competition, the best record in the league, but we were banned by the CIAA from participating in the tournament that year. The previous year had been the one where we won the right to participate in both the NAIA and NCAA tournaments. The CIAA ordered us to represent them in the NCAA, but I chose to go to the NAIA, so the CIAA banned us from all postseason play for one year. There we were, the best team in the CIAA, and we were banned from participating in the conference tournament.

We did get some satisfaction from the CIAA tournament. The winning team that year was North Carolina A&T. A&T had beaten us by only one point early in the year, and we beat them in one of the last games of the season, just days before the tournament. Though we did not get a chance to prove it, I think our players came away with a sense that they could have won the tournament if they had been given the chance.

In 1964-65, Earl's sophomore year, he came into his own—or maybe I let him come into his own. He made 697 points, for an average of 23 points per game. That was five times as many points as he had scored in his freshman year, when I left him on the bench.

It was during this second year of Earl's college career that the white people of Winston-Salem began to hear about him. The stories by Luix Overbea, the black sports reporter for the *Winston-Salem Journal*, started focusing on Earl. Those stories started to rise to the top of the newspaper. But Earl was not yet "the Pearl."

The season had not gone well for the team, even with Earl's blossoming. We had started with a national ranking but lost it over the course of the season, as we could not put together a long winning streak to capture the attention of the sportswriters and coaches. I think most of our problems can be attributed to our players suffering injuries through the season.

We were 11-6 in CIAA play and 18-6 for the season going into the final game with Livingstone College in Salisbury, North Carolina. It seemed like every other CIAA team was also having a strong year, at least against us, as every one of our losses had come against a conference opponent. Even Livingstone, a small private school, had upset us by one point earlier in the year.

We got our revenge in the final game of the season, whipping Livingstone 99-58, but that was not enough for us to take the CIAA regular-season championship. We were third in the rankings, behind North Carolina A&T and Norfolk State. Still, Teddy Blunt and Earl Monroe were named All-CIAA.

By the luck of the pairings, we faced Livingstone again in the first round of the tournament. We beat them 84-59 this time. That put us up against Norfolk State for the next game.

That was a thrilling game, but thanks only to our sloppy play. We had a 12-point lead at one point, but that had shrunk to just four by the half. Two baskets by Norfolk State tied the game. We eventually lost in overtime. Though Earl scored 30 points, we took too many bad shots and made too many errors. We ended the season with a 20-7 record. Norfolk State went on to win the tourney.

Earl scores again against Akron.

(PHOTO BY FRANK JONES PHOTO, COURTESY OF WINSTON-SALEM STATE UNIVERSITY ARCHIVES)

Even though we did not win the CIAA tournament, we still got an invitation to go to the NAIA for the fourth time in five years, representing District 29. I hoped that my players could redeem themselves after playing so poorly against Norfolk State.

This is a photo of the 1964-65 team. Front row, left to right: *James Reid, Ted Ratchford, Sonny Ridgill, Joe Cunningham, and Gilbert Smith.* Back row, left to right: *Robert Brannon, Kennon Thomas, Teddy Blunt, Steven Smith (Sahib Abdul Kharir), and Earl Monroe*

(WINSTON-SALEM STATE UNIVERSITY ARCHIVES)

We left for Kansas City on March 8, 1965, with the good news that a local black-owned radio station, WAAA, would be broadcasting our games from Kansas City. Finally, our fans in Winston-Salem would be able to follow our progress, rather than having to wait for the results in the paper the next day.

Some of the members of the team I was taking were experienced in national championships. This would be the third NAIA trip for Teddy Blunt and Ted Ratchford and the second for Joe Cunningham. The rest had never even been on an airplane.

Our first opponent was a small Catholic liberal-arts college, Saint Norbert of De Pere, Wisconsin. Just like every other time the players got on a national stage, they froze up in the first half. We trailed by as much as nine points and went into the locker room behind 32-27. We were playing their slow game, not our fast-break game. Our shots were falling short of the basket and bouncing off the rim.

After a good dose of yelling at halftime, the team loosened up. With about nine minutes left in the game, we went ahead and stayed ahead. We won going away, 87-69, with Howard "Sonny" Ridgill and Earl Monroe both getting 23 points and Ted Ratchford coming in with 19. James Reid was the real hero of the game, coming off the bench to score 16 points, including the points to put us ahead.

In the next game, we faced High Point College, our neighboring liberal-arts school just 20 miles away from Winston-Salem. We went ahead near the end of the first half and kept the lead for the entire second half. High Point went cold like we sometimes did in national games. They didn't sink a single shot for the first four minutes of the second half. Earl led us again, scoring 22 points. We beat High Point 78-62.

We faced Oklahoma Baptist College the next day, and the boys went cold on me again. We lost the game 71-62. Sonny and Earl both could not sink their shots. Earl still got 20 points, but if he had hit everything he threw from the floor and the foul line, he would have made 50. Sonny, who had 23 points in the first game of the tourney, had just two points in this game.

We tried to keep Oklahoma Baptist on a slow game, but their two tall men started hitting in the second half, and that allowed them to start pulling away after we had tied the score at 39 at halftime. James Reid, who had been the hero just one day earlier, did not sink a single basket. Nowhere was there any good news. We sank only eight of 18 free throws, while Oklahoma Baptist sank 19 of 31. Teddy Blunt, one of our most dependable players, fouled out with plenty of time on the clock.

I still look back on those free throws and wonder. They seem a bit out of balance. I am just not sure if we were treated fairly by the referees on the called fouls.

Our record for playing in the NAIA tournament was now 5-4. We had reached the quarterfinals twice, lost in the second round once, and lost in the first round once. Even if the referees were favoring the other teams, that still did not explain why we always fell apart at the NAIA. It just seemed that every time my team got into an unfamiliar gym, they could not figure out how to find the basket. It was as if the floor were longer or wider than they were accustomed to, or the basket was higher than it should have been. Something was wrong with our national play, but at that point I could not figure it out.

The next year, 1965-66, we closed the regular season with a win over Livingstone again, ending the year at 17-4, but three of those losses were against one CIAA team, Norfolk State. We finished second in the regular-season rankings.

We beat Johnson C. Smith 96-86 in the opening round of the tournament, but it was another sloppy performance. Most of my stars fouled out, including Earl, though he did score 32 points. One of my steady performers in this game, as he had been much of the season, was Sonny Ridgill of Winston-Salem, who had gone to nearby Atkins High School. He would be named All-CIAA, as would Earl.

Our second game was against Howard University. In a bout described by *Winston-Salem Journal* reporter Overbea as "spine-tingling," we were behind 47-42 at the half and fought back. The game was tied at 79 at the end of regular time when an official called goaltending on my new freshman, William English of Salem, Virginia. The biggest problem with that was that the other official had called Howard for a personal foul with just seconds left on the clock. The fouls negated each other. We did not get our foul shot, so the game went into overtime. We eventually won 85-84 to send us into the finals.

In the finals, we faced Virginia Union, who had beaten us the previous year for the championship, and to whom we had since lost once in an invitational tournament and twice in the regular season. Earl scored 42 points and showed what Overbea described as "dazzling ball handling." Stealing the ball to set him and the rest of the team up was Willis Bennett from Boston, who I found at Laurinburg Academy. Earl was named Most Valuable Player of the tournament and All-CIAA. Willis was named to the second team, in part for grabbing 13 rebounds and getting numerous steals.

We had won yet another CIAA tournament, and it was obvious who the star was. Earl had set a scoring record for a single game in the tourney. My next-highest scorer was Joe Cunningham with 15. Joe had served as team captain for the year. He would finish school and go on to a short career with the Harlem Globetrotters.

By winning the CIAA, we qualified for the NCAA Division II championship, the first time we would play in NCAA competition. Every other time, we had gone to the NAIA.

Our opponent in the first round was Oglethorpe College, a little white school in Atlanta that used the "shuffle offense," something we had not encountered since Oklahoma Baptist in the NAIA last year. We led 32-27 at halftime, but we made errors in the second half. At one point, we did not score for five minutes, and Oglethorpe went ahead 61-52. Everyone but Sonny Ridgill had an off night. Earl scored only 15 points, while Sonny had 20. The NAIA curse had followed us over to the NCAA.

It was just a few days after our defeat in the NCAA Division II championship that I was in the stands for the final game of the NCAA Division I championship. I was there on March 19, 1966, when college basketball history was made.

Looking back on it, that night did not seem historic at all as it was happening. For all the hoopla the press makes of "March Madness" and the Final Four today, the final game of the 1965-66 NCAA Division I championship seemed like just another game at the University of Maryland's Cole Field House. I don't even think it was a sellout. Anyone who wanted could have walked up and bought tickets the night of the game.

What was historic was what happened at the beginning of the game. From one direction came the starting five of Coach Adolph Rupp's University of Kentucky team, nicknamed "Rupp's Runts" because none of them was taller than six-foot-five. From another direction came the starting five of Coach Don Haskins's Texas Western College, now the University of Texas at El Paso, better known as UTEP.

Kentucky's starting five were all white. Texas Western's starting five were all black.

Ever since the major white colleges, primarily in the North, had slowly started to integrate their basketball teams over the past decade, there had been some unwritten rules followed by the white schools' coaches. You could recruit an excellent black player, and you could recruit a second good black player to be his roommate in the dorm and on the road. But if you started to recruit any more than two, you ran some risks.

The biggest risk was angering the alumni because most of them were white. The administration and coaches believed the alumni would not identify with black athletes on the floor. If you angered the alumni, you ran the risk of losing their financial support. If you lost their financial support, you lost your coaching job. This was true of all white colleges, not just those in the South. In fact, no major white Deep South college had recruited their first blacks in 1966.

This was not just an issue of Southern racism because Kentucky was a Southern team. Texas Western was also Southern. This was an issue of racism in general because even the coaches of the most liberal-minded Northern colleges knew that putting black players on the floor was a social experiment that many students and alumni might not be ready to accept.

It was true, however, that the social norms had been slowly changing to favor blacks over the last several years. The last several NCAA championship teams had started three or four blacks, but no predominantly white school had dared to start all five. I have read that the University of San Francisco coach put five blacks on the court at once during a game in the middle 1950s, when Bill Russell was his star, but an outcry from the alumni had been enough to warn off any other white coaches from trying the same thing. I think in that game, the rotation eventually put five black players on the court, but the coach had not started the five. Tonight, history was being made.

Another reason for not starting five black players was more insulting. The standard thinking among the white coaches of the day was that the fifth man on the court, usually the playmaking point guard, had to be a white athlete. Even if the four black players were all higher-scoring players and better rebounders, the white player was there on the floor to do the thinking for the team.

What Texas Western coach Don Haskins did was ignore all of those risks and put five black players on the court at one time during the national championship game. He had white players on his bench, but they were not as good as the five black players. I knew that to be true because Texas Western had several black players who had been recruited by CIAA schools. The team's six-foot-eight center, Nevil Shed, had played for North Carolina A&T before transferring to Texas Western.

Coach Haskins did one thing that surprised me that night, other than starting all black players. He pulled his center, Shed, and replaced him with a boy who was only five-foot-six! What that did was shake up the Kentucky players, none of whom were very tall themselves. One of those Kentucky players was Pat Riley, who would later coach in the NBA and who is currently with the Miami Heat.

The Texas Western Miners went ahead and stayed ahead of Kentucky's Wildcats all night long. It was not even an interesting game. It was a boring game! But what was interesting was that the black players played a slow, passing game.

In other words, Haskins's all-black starting NCAA Division I team played nothing like the all-black CIAA teams had been playing for 15 years. The black players for Texas Western played more like a white team than they did a black team! I think my players' playground-based fast-break game would have been able to beat the by-the-book Miners—if Division II had been allowed to play Division I.

Once the game was over, all of the black coaches in the stands left the gym. I imagine we went to play cards. I really don't think that we realized the significance of what we had witnessed and what was about to happen to our recruiting programs. What was about to happen had really started at least a decade earlier, but from that night onward it was going to be growing at a rapid pace.

We were going to start losing our best recruits to the white colleges. Once word got around to the black high schools that a major white college in a large Southern state had started five black players and had won a national championship without putting a single white player on the court, recruiting would change.

I've read of one study that showed the change came even more rapidly than I and other black coaches could have imagined. This study showed that the percentage of black players on teams at white colleges went from 10 percent in 1962 to 34 percent by 1975. Between 1966 and 1985, the average number of black players on teams increased from three to six.

I don't think I can overemphasize what was happening in our society while this was happening on the basketball courts. At the same time that my black teams were playing in the NAIA against white teams, white cops in Alabama were beating civil-rights protesters. President Lyndon Johnson was calling for federal enforcement of voting laws that would ensure that poor blacks in Mississippi could vote. The governor of Mississippi was still trying to keep his state's white teams from playing black teams.

Now, here was a white college coach who had already decided that his black players were his best ballplayers.

I was disappointed to hear that Coach Haskins received hate mail for his decision to put five black players on the court. But I had to think that the hate mail he got was generated by only a small portion of the fans of his program.

I still believe in the basic premise of crossing over. Sports fans want to see good sports, and they don't really care about the color of the player on the court, the football field, or the baseball diamond.

Still, I was not surprised when I heard Rupp try to explain away Kentucky's loss by saying that the Texas Western team were hired guns brought in just to play basketball. He claimed they were not real students. Some stories said Rupp used racial epithets in describing the Miners. I would not be surprised. Rupp was well known to be a racist, but the sports press of that day pretty much ignored it when he used words that he shouldn't.

Rupp was wrong, of course. I later learned that almost all of the Miners graduated from Texas Western, just as almost all of my kids graduated during my career.

There was a downside for the black players who were finally admitted to the white colleges. When the rush to recruit black kids for white colleges came about, I don't think the white coaches really paid much attention to making sure that their athletes graduated.

CHAPTER 15

Our Championship Season

Before the 1966-67 season got under way, I watched some remarkable scrimmages between my team and Wake Forest.

Billy Packer, the guard who had been so impressed with the play of Cleo Hill that he brought his teammates over to scrimmage against our team, had graduated from Wake in 1962 after making All-ACC three years in a row. Billy returned to campus as an assistant coach in 1965. He started those scrimmage games again, this time hoping that his Demon Deacons would learn something from Earl Monroe.

I watched Earl and Wake Forest's Paul Long have some great battles with each other, almost as if they were playing real games. Billy was watching, too. He asked Earl if he would come over to Wake to teach his players how he did the spin move. Earl went, but he had a difficult time explaining it to the Wake players. Billy helped him slow down his movements enough so the players could at least see what he was doing. Earl's moves were so instinctive that he could not explain them.

The 1966-67 season started off as it usually did, with my expressing worry to the newspaper about how prepared our team was for the upcoming games.

I remember that just before our first game, with neighboring High Point College, I said, "We have had plenty of practice, but that is not like playing a real game. High Point already has two games under its belt and has won both. We still have to work out our kinks."

We actually lost that game to High Point, 89-84, thanks to the fine team they fielded, including Gene Littles, the first black player for the college. Gene would go on to a short playing career in the American Basketball Association and a short coaching career in the NBA. He was another one of those players I missed convincing that he should come to Winston-Salem. Every time I see him now, I tell him how much I "hate" him because he would have made me a better coach.

We were not off to a good start, but things would get much better after losing that opening game.

Earl Monroe, now entering his senior year, was proving to be everything that Leon Whitley had promised me he would be—another Cleo Hill. Because I used him as a substitute his freshman year, Earl had scored only 163 points for the season, averaging seven points per game. In his sophomore year, he scored 697, raising his average to 23 points per game. In his junior year, he scored 746, taking his average up to 30 points per game.

After that season-opening loss, Earl started cooking. I am not sure what sparked his production. Maybe it was the knowledge that he was good enough to be drafted into the NBA, or maybe it was just a sense that he was in his last year, and he wanted to go out with a bang.

Somewhere along the way during his college career, Earl had shed that lackadaisical attitude he had as a teenager. He had become more focused, more purpose-driven. I don't know if I instilled that in him as his coach, or if he just naturally matured while taking his college courses and coming to basketball practice, where he knew his team depended on his leadership. Whatever it was, the "shake-and-bake," "flukey-dukey," back-to-the-basket spinning moves Earl had been perfecting since he was 14 began to click on the court.

It was sometime early in the 1966-67 season that Luix Overbea, the black sportswriter for the *Winston-Salem Journal*, made some remark in print about Earl's scoring totals. He called the scores "Earl's pearls."

Overbea did not call Earl "the Pearl" in that article, but the mention of "pearls" sparked something in our fans. Not long after that column ran in the newspaper, the fans at our home games started chanting, "Earl, Earl, the Super Pearl." Whenever we would fall behind in a game, the fans would start chanting, "Give the ball to Earl."

The demand to watch Earl, particularly when we played rivals like North Carolina A&T, grew so much that I moved almost all of our home games out of Whitaker Gym on campus and over to Winston-Salem's Memorial Coliseum.

During those early home games, I noticed some white fans in the seats—not many, but some. White people in the city had not been coming to Winston-Salem State College games since Cleo Hill's era six years earlier.

As the season stretched out and news of Earl's playing abilities began to make the television news, I began to see more white fans. Eventually, I estimate that as many as a third to maybe half of the coliseum's seats were occupied by white fans. As it had been with Cleo, the tickets were general admission. There was no reserved "colored seating," as there had been at some sporting events in the not-so-distant past. While integration was struggling in other Southern cities, a skinny black ballplayer from Philadelphia was making it work in Winston-Salem.

Word of mouth about Earl's exploits helped the nervous process of integrating the city's schools. The city's largest high school, R. J. Reynolds High School, had been effectively integrated in the fall of 1966. As the white boys heard from their new black classmates about Earl's spinning moves to get away from defenders, some barriers came down, and real conversation started between the two races. The common ground was a love of sports in general and basketball in particular, and a shared interest in how one player could be so good. Eventually, some of those white high-school boys and their parents started coming out to see the games. They might have come in handfuls of four or five at a time to allay their discomfort, but they started coming.

At first, it must have been uncomfortable for the whites. Black people and white people simply did not sit next to each other in public settings in the South. The sit-ins that had forcibly desegregated the downtown lunch counters had occurred just a few years earlier. Some of the schools in the state still had not desegregated.

Now, here were white people coming to a black basketball game where all of the concessions would be served by black people. I think the whites overcame their discomfort because at halftime you could see those white fans standing in line with black fans talking about the fantastic game they had seen already and wondering what tricks Earl had for them in the second half.

What brought blacks and whites together—what made the whites cross over to experience black basketball—was Earl Monroe. White fans who would be nervously eyeing the sea of black faces surrounding them at the start of the game would be cheering with those same black fans by the end of the game. Everyone there was cheering for the same things—a victory by the Teachers and a good show by Earl.

I remember at the end of one game, Earl was coming out of the locker room when he ran into an elderly white man who was waiting with a basketball.

"Young man," the old man said, "I have driven 700 miles one way just to see you play, and it has been worth it. Would you sign this so I can prove to my friends that I met you?"

The racial barriers may have still been up in Mississippi, Alabama, and other places around North Carolina, but it was obvious to me that my theory of sports bringing the races together was working.

On February 21, 1967, Earl passed the 1,000-point mark for the season in a game against Livingstone that we won 115-77. Earl scored 53 points. That night was the 22nd straight game we had won after the opening loss against High Point. In the crowd that night was at least one professional basketball scout and a *Sports Illustrated* reporter. Though we easily won the game, I had three key players get banged up a bit—Eugene Smiley, Johnny Watkins, and Earl.

The next day brought a surprise letter from the NAIA. One of High Point College's players had once enrolled at North Carolina A&T before leaving for the army. When he returned, he went to High Point instead of A&T, which was against a recruiting rule. The NAIA ruled that all of the games played by High Point under the NAIA jurisdiction would be forfeited and counted as wins for the opposing teams. Our loss against High Point was being declared a win. Suddenly, we were an undefeated team at 23-0 and the 1966-67 CIAA regular-season champion.

Our last game of the season was against the nationally ranked Akron Zips, a team we had never played but which we knew was averaging 85 points a game while giving up only 67 points.

The national ranking of Akron was a puzzler. We had Earl Monroe, who was averaging 44 points per game, but we were unranked by both the Associated Press and United Press International. At the same time, we were ranked fourth by the NAIA. Akron was ranked number four by both the AP and UPI. They had finished among the top 10 small colleges for the last five years.

On paper, Akron looked hard to beat—tall, good rebounding skills, and stingy on defense. Another worrisome note was that their bench was full of seniors who played regularly. I was used to playing the same five players. I had Vaughn Kimbrough and Steve Smith as reserves, but my other players had seen limited action during the year. My bruised players from the night before seemed to be ready, but I would still say that they were not at 100 percent. I might have to play someone else against more experienced players.

I need not have worried. The newspaper article the next morning started with this: "The unbelievable, fantastic Earl Monroe scored 53 points last night as the Winston-Salem State Rams upset the nationally ranked University of Akron Zips 92-84."

Finally, the newspaper was calling the team by its proper nickname. Instead of the Teachers, a nickname we never officially had, we were now the Rams, which had been our official nickname since the mid-1940s. I had a love-hate affair with "the Teachers." It was hard to recruit a kid who had no interest in pursuing a college degree in education when all of the newspaper clippings he found mentioned "the Teachers." On the other hand, the nickname made us sound mild, so we could sometimes sneak up on more powerful teams.

Akron was not an easy game, as my players were nervous. Earl was fouled early and missed both his first free throws. He then steadied his

This poster was used to promote our final game of the 1966-67 season against top-ranked University of Akron. We would face them again in an early round of the NCAA Division II tournament.

(WINSTON-SALEM STATE UNIVERSITY ARCHIVES)

226

nerves and scored the first seven points of the game for our team. Akron got an eight-point lead on us before all of our players finally woke up and started playing. At halftime, we led 47-42. When the second half began, we ran up a 15-point margin and then tried freezing the game.

In the end, we finally got a good balance out of the team. I was particularly proud of my sophomore William English. He led both teams with 11 rebounds, and he scored 19 points.

We opened the 1967 CIAA tournament with a 114-73 rout over Hampton Institute. Monroe scored 42 points, and English got 28.

Our next opponent in the tournament was our old nemesis North Carolina A&T. We had beaten them 87-85 in Greensboro and 104-93 in Winston-Salem during regular-season play. But on that night, March 3, 1967, A&T had our number. There we were sitting with a 25-0 record, and we got blown out 105-82 by a team coached by my old friend Cal Irvin.

By every measure, we were the best team in the conference, and we got beat! It proved that no basketball team is so strong that it cannot be beaten on any given night. Part of the problem was Monroe, who scored only 20 points, his lowest total for the whole year. He made only seven of 26 shots from the floor. English hit for 13, James Reid 18, and Eugene Smiley 15, which were not bad totals for them. What was amazing to me was that A&T scored many of their baskets on fast-break layups. We got beat at the fast-break game!

We won back a little of our pride by beating Johnson C. Smith 100-93 in the consolation game.

There was some good news that came out of that CIAA tournament. Howard University made the finals for the first time in its history. Its coach was Marshall Emery, who had played for me from 1950 to 1954. He barely lost to A&T in the finals, 76-73. It would have been fun to coach against my old student in the finals, but that did not happen that year. I was also named CIAA Coach of the Year for leading the Rams to our best season ever, but I think I was more proud of watching Marshall coach in the finals.

Still, our season was not over. It was obvious that we would be invited to postseason play for the NCAA Division II championship. That meant that Earl had a chance—a small chance—to beat the small-college single-season scoring record, 1,255 points by Bevo Francis of a small school called Rio Grande in Ohio. At that point, after his poor showing in the A&T game, Earl had 1,064 points. I was not sure he would make it.

On the day we left for the first round of the NCAA Division II playoffs in Akron, Ohio, I noted something interesting on the front page of the *Winston-Salem Journal*. It was a photograph of a United States Army corpsman. Lawrence Joel was being awarded the Congressional Medal of Honor for his bravery in tending to wounded soldiers in Vietnam. The person giving him the honor would be President Lyndon Johnson.

Lawrence Joel was black and from the slums of Winston-Salem. After having to search for news about black people in the 1940s and 1950s, here was a photograph of a black man on the front page of the newspaper with a lengthy story describing his bravery. The times were changing for the better.

On the day we were to play in the first round of the NCAA tournament against Baldwin-Wallace College of Berea, Ohio, Earl got word that he had been selected a small-college All-American by United Press International, to match his selection as an All-American by the Associated Press, which had come the prior week. The article noted how Earl was just 102 points away from breaking Bevo Francis's small-college scoring record. Also selected by UPI at the same time was Phil Jackson of North Dakota, who would go on to play in the NBA and to coach the Chicago Bulls and Los Angeles Lakers.

Earl got a third of the way toward the season scoring record that night when he scored 34 against Baldwin-Wallace. That was just five short of the tournament record for a player. The game was never in doubt, as we led 50-41 at the half. We won 91-76. Bill English was second in scoring with 20 points.

The day after that game, the *Sporting News* named Earl an All-American. Joining him in that honor were Lew Alcindor, Elvin Hayes, and Walt Frazier. This was perhaps more important than the other two All-American honors because the selection panel was made up of general managers and professional scouts of the NBA. Earl was described by the magazine as having "tremendous ability with the ball. He is a great shooter with a remarkable percentage from the field."

It was obvious then that Earl was not going to be a schoolteacher, at least for a few years. We still had no idea which professional team would want him. I knew one thing. He was not going to go to the Globetrotters. I would tear up any contract offer from them, if they had the nerve to mail him one.

Our game in Akron against the host team, the Akron Zips, was a shocker for the hometown fans. What shocked them was the ending of a 54-game home winning streak. The team had not lost to an opponent at home since February 1964, more than three years earlier. We beat them 88-80.

For the first time in print, Luix Overbea used the nickname "the Pearl" in referring to Earl. Overbea wrote that it was the Akron fans who started calling him "the Pearl," on March 12, 1967.

I wonder if it was some fans from Winston-Salem who had made the trip to Akron who really started calling him "the Pearl," after hearing the cheer back home. It just does not make sense that Akron fans would be cheering on an opponent by calling out to him as "the Pearl," but the newspaper story makes it clear the nickname started in Akron.

Earl scored another 49 points, breaking the tournament single-game record by 10 points and going a long way toward closing in on the small-college single-season scoring record. I think the real hero of the game was Steve Smith, Monroe's friend from Philadelphia. Steve had sat on the bench as a sub for most of his career, but when both Earl and James Reid got into foul trouble in the second half, Smitty stepped in to take over the team. He did not score any points in the game, but he steadied everyone and was able to get control of the game, so the shooters could go back to work.

The game stayed exciting all the way through, with Akron closing to within two points, 74-72, with more than six minutes to play. Earl then made eight straight points to put us ahead again.

Our next stop was Evansville, Indiana, for the first game of the final round of eight regional champions. We had a devil of a time even getting out of town. The airport in Winston-Salem was socked in by fog, so we had to leave from Greensboro. What should have been a four-hour trip turned out to be an 11-hour ordeal.

Our first opponent was the Long Island University Blackbirds.

I am not sure if the irony of the pairing of Long Island and Winston-Salem was caught by anyone else but me. Our opponent was one of the New York colleges which had been caught in the point-shaving scandal of 1951. As part of the solution to get rid of the gambling taint, Long Island and other Northern schools like City College of New York had stopped recruiting black kids from around New York City. In the early 1950s, those kids from the playgrounds of Harlem, the Bronx, and Newark had nowhere else to go but to small black colleges in the South. Long Island University had inadvertently helped me build the reputation of Winston-Salem Teachers College.

I had one other connection to Long Island University. Clair Bee, the legendary coach who built the university into a basketball powerhouse in the late 1940s, had been the featured speaker at that Murray State College coaching clinic I attended as the only black coach in 1946. I suppose Coach Bee could have barred me from the clinic had he wanted, but he did not, so my first lesson on coaching came from one of the masters of the craft. Coach Bee had left the school after the point-shaving scandal and was not affiliated with them at all in 1967.

All Earl had to do was score 20 points and he would break the single-season scoring record for small colleges. He got his record in the Long Island game, when he got 29 points in our 62-54 victory.

This was not an easy win. We were behind at several points in the game, and the outcome was never secure until the last few minutes. William English and James Reid pulled their weight again, Bill scoring 15 points and James 10. Steve Smith had to come in again. Once again, he did not score any points, but he kept the game under control. Smith rescued us again!

Our opponent in the semifinals was Kentucky Wesleyan, the defending national small-college champion. With the scoring record safely in hand, Earl helped out his teammates by feeding them the ball. Eugene Smiley led all scorers with 27 points. Earl ended up with 24 points and Bill English with 22. This was a close game, the lead changing hands five times. The score was tied seven times.

Finally, we had advanced to the finals of a national championship. Four other times, we had been invited to play for the national championship of either the NAIA or the NCAA, and we had always gone cold on the floor. The team had frozen up each time and played as if they had never seen a basketball.

Not this time. On Friday, March 17, 1967, the Winston-Salem State College Rams beat the Southwest Missouri State Bears 77-74. The winning margin was provided by two free throws sunk by Earl with 25 seconds left. That gave us the three-point margin that we kept for the rest of the game.

History was made in several ways. It was Winston-Salem State College's first national championship. It was the first time that a Southern college had won the small-college championship. We were the first CIAA school to win the small-college championship. Most important of all, it was the first time a "Negro college"—as Overbea described us in the newspaper—had won the small-college championship. In 1966, a white college with five black starters had won the NCAA Division I championship. Now, in 1967, a small black college had won the NCAA Division II championship.

The night belonged to Earl again. He scored 40 points—another tournament record, the second he had secured on the way to the national title. He was named the Outstanding Player of the tournament and was selected to the All-Tournament team. He ended his college career with 1,329 points for the season and 2,935 points over four years.

But we almost lost this game. We were ahead 37-34 at the half, but during the second half we fell behind as far as four points. We were behind 73-70 with less than four minutes to play when English sank one free throw and Earl sank a three-point basket to send us ahead.

When we returned to Winston-Salem, there were 1,500 people waiting at the airport to greet us, and hundreds more were in their cars lined up on the street outside the airport because there was no

Pictured here are the 1967 NCAA Division II Champions with their trophies: First row, left to right: *Brent Cromwell, Earl Monroe, Steve Smith (Sahib Abdul Kharir), John Watkins, and Eugene Smiley.* Second row, left to right: *Ernest Brown, John Michael, John Latham, William English, David Green, and Vaughn Kimbrough*

(WINSTON-SALEM STATE UNIVERSITY ARCHIVES)

room for them. The mayor of the city welcomed us home, as did the chairman of the city's chamber of commerce. As we had been delayed by several hours getting to Evansville, we were delayed by several hours trying to get back home.

Only one person on the team was missing from the celebration. That was Earl Monroe. He stayed behind in Evansville in order to take the national teaching exam. He was scheduled to graduate in May, and every teaching-college graduate had to take that exam. My father stayed with him to keep him company.

I've always thought that this example of Earl's desire to finish his college education was overlooked at the time by the news media. Earl was certainly going to be drafted by a NBA team, but he had gone to college to learn to be a teacher. He had promised his mother, his sister,

*The city of Winston-Salem hosted a dinner party for the team
when we returned with the championship.*

(PHOTO COURTESY OF FORSYTH COUNTY PUBLIC LIBRARY PHOTOGRAPH COLLECTION)

and me that he would take—and pass—that national teaching exam.
And he did. In a few days, Earl Monroe, one of the best college basketball
players in the history of the game and a promising future professional
athlete, got word that he was qualified to become an elementary-school
teacher.

I still look back on Earl's decision to take that exam—even though
he was going to be playing professional basketball—as the mark of a
mature young man. The kid who had once decided that college was
not for him was now the national scoring champion on the national-
championship college team. He was going to be a professional basketball player, but he still wanted to prove to himself and everyone else
that he could be a teacher.

Earl would be drafted that year by the Baltimore Bullets. He didn't
have an agent, as agents were not that big in the business in those days.

When Earl Monroe was named to the Naismith Memorial Basketball Hall of Fame he asked me to attend.

(CLARENCE E. GAINES PERSONAL COLLECTION)

I told him not to sign anything until I had a chance to look over the contract. I still remembered the contracts the Globetrotters had been sending to my players, and I wanted to protect him.

The Bullets' management sat at Earl's house one night until he came in at 4:00 A.M. after spending the evening partying with friends. Exhausted and not paying much attention to the details of the contract, he signed for one year at a salary of $19,000—much less than he was worth, and much less than he could have gotten if only he or an agent had reminded the team what he had just accomplished on the college court.

I arrived before the Bullets' management could leave the house. When I read the contract, I hit the roof and yelled at Earl as if he were still one of my college players. I had told him not to sign anything, and he had done it anyway! His excuse was that he was tired and he just wanted to prove to the country that he could play basketball in the NBA. I was able to talk the management into at least extending the contract to two years and upping it to $20,000. It was not what he was worth, but it was the best I could do under the circumstances.

Earl "the Pearl" Monroe went on to be the NBA Rookie of the Year in 1968 for the Bullets. He was named an NBA All-Star four times. He scored 17,454 points in 926 professional games, scoring more than 1,000 points in nine different seasons. His career average was nearly 19 points a game. He played four years with the Bullets before joining the New York Knicks in 1971. For a while, the critics thought that he and Walt Frazier, another guard playing for the Knicks, would not get along. They found a way. Earl the Pearl helped the Knicks get their last NBA championship in 1973. He retired from the game and the team after the 1980 season. He is now the president of the Earl Monroe Group of Kenilworth, New Jersey, where he is an industrial-painting contractor.

Earl has never forgotten his old coach. For many years when he was a professional player, Earl would sometimes pop in on my practices to shoot a few rounds with my players. The team members were amazed. Here was one of the best professional players in the NBA dropping by to practice with a small-college team.

Earl still comes by Winston-Salem to look in on his old coach to make sure I am still moving. Just about all of the players I have coached do that on a regular basis. That is one of the great joys I have received from coaching. I built teams through the years who still consider themselves teams and who still consider their college coach their friend, mentor, and teacher.

CHAPTER 16

The 1970s—
Black Players Cross Over
to White Universities

As I might have expected following a team that had such a super-star for the previous three years, the two years after the departure of Earl Monroe were pretty bleak. The first was even a losing year for us.

We started 1967-68 with high hopes. We were ranked seventh in the AP poll and 10th in the UPI poll. We lost by only one point to the number-one-ranked team in the nation, Kentucky Wesleyan. Then un-focused play set in, and I never could correct it. We ended the year with a record of 10-14. We were the seventh-seeded team in the CIAA tourney and got knocked off in the first game.

We came back somewhat in the 1968-69 year with a 14-14 record, but I was unhappy with the play of the team. Still, we lost in the CIAA tournament by only one point as a sixth-seeded team to the second-seeded Norfolk State.

It was in 1969 that the state officially designated the school

Winston-Salem State University. In 1972, it became part of the University of North Carolina system.

Things were not all bad on the basketball court in those years. Once Earl left, I had another kid who turned out to be a strong member of the team. He even went on to outshine Earl on one night.

William English was one of my few recruits out of the state of Virginia, from Salem, a little town in the Shenandoah Valley just west of Roanoke. Since he lived so close, I did something with Bill that I rarely did with any of my other recruits. I saw him play before I recruited him.

A call had come in to me from his coach, Roland Malone, who suggested that I come up and see this kid who was being recruited by several other colleges in the CIAA. I visited a game and liked what I saw. I gave him my best pitch, but William still decided on Fayetteville State Teachers College, our competitor about 150 miles to the east.

On the day that he was scheduled to leave for Fayetteville State, William had a change of heart. He called me and said, "Can you come up and get me?" I jumped in the car with two other coaches, and we drove the 100 miles to Salem as fast as we could, before all six feet, six inches and 220 pounds of him could change his mind.

William turned out to be a fine recruit, someone I sensed would be able to help take up the slack once Earl left. One of the things I remember about William's playing days was that he and Earl were among the few players who started off my rope drills with jump shots. While every other player on their team was content to shoot easy layups in order to avoid missing and climbing ropes to the top of Whitaker Gym, William and Earl would shoot jump shots until they tired. Then they would switch off for the easy layups.

I liked that about those players. They had confidence in themselves and their shooting ability. And they knew when to switch to something less exacting than jump shots. That was what I always needed on the court—thinking team members who planned ahead, rather than just reacting to what they saw in front of them.

Like any freshman, Bill—we got tired of calling him William after a couple of years—did not get a lot of playing time, but he always made sure that he was physically ready to go into the game. Conditioning was important to me, and the players realized it. When you were a substitute on my team, you were not a benchwarmer by definition. You were expected to go into the game if one of the starters got hurt or in foul trouble and to pick up that player's intensity. You might not be a starting-five star, but you had better be prepared to become one if I called on you. Bill understood that, and he helped convince the other subs. He helped the other players stay in condition even if they did not expect to play.

Bill English set a record for the school that still stands, a record that Earl Monroe had previously set.

In February 1968, Bill was secretly married on a Saturday night. He told me about it, but he did not tell his teammates. What irritated me at the time was that one of my top players could not wait until the end of the season to get married, but I had no say in the matter. I don't remember trying to talk him out of it, but I did demand one thing of him—that he come in from his honeymoon to play that coming Monday night.

I don't know what he told his bride about why they couldn't leave town on a real honeymoon, but Bill told her something. They never left Winston-Salem, which is not exactly a garden spot for newlyweds. On the evening of the game—February 19, 1968—Bill showed up for the pregame warmup just two hours before the game was to start. The other players looked at him with puzzled looks. He had not been around all weekend. It was as if he had disappeared from the face of the earth, and now he was suited up for the game.

The game was against Fayetteville State, the team Bill had almost joined. That night was magical in some way. Bill was hot, and the other players sensed it. They kept feeding him the ball. At the end of the game, Bill had scored 77 points, breaking Earl's record of 68 points in a game. The record still stands as the highest score by a player in a single game in school history.

There is something else much more important that Bill English contributed to his school other than a good scoring night. After he graduated, he tried out for the pros but returned to join the city of

Winston-Salem's Recreation Department. He would eventually run a recreation center in one of the city's poorer neighborhoods. When he would get home from his day at work, he would come over to the campus, where he would coach basketball with me.

For more than 20 years, Bill English served as a volunteer coach for the Rams. He did not receive any pay from the college in exchange for his services. All he got was the chance to help young men develop their basketball skills. I knew I had developed a sense of loyalty among my players, but to have one of them serve me as a coach without pay went beyond all my expectations.

The Rams got back on track in 1969-70, though we did not win the regular-season championship. Even though we had a winning record of 17-8, we finished third in the conference.

In the opening game of the 1970 CIAA tourney, played in Greensboro that year, we squeaked out an upset win over Norfolk State, which was seeded second in the tourney. Allen McManus of Charlotte was the hero of the night when he stole the ball and then sank two free throws to put us ahead 97-94. Allen made 12 of 15 foul shots and 12 of 23 baskets. This was a tough game against a better opponent. They were ahead by as much as 15 points at one time during the game, but my players showed a lot of spirit and slowly but surely made their way back into the game.

Our next opponent was Elizabeth City. Once again, it was a close game. We finally won 86-83. My players lost their concentration in this game, losing leads of 15 points in the first half and eight points in the second half. Still, I had four players in double digits, including Vaughn Kimbrough, who was the sole person left from the 1967 championship team.

The next night, Allen McManus again proved to be the hero when we won a thrilling game 79-77 over Maryland State. Allen made 11 of our last 14 points. We played sloppily for much of the game, hitting only 14 of 44 shots in the first half. Luckily, our defense kept Maryland State away from their goal.

The game ended on a curious note. In the excitement of trying to catch up, Maryland State called for a time-out when they had none

Allen McManus was an All-CIAA star for WSSU in basketball and football.

(WINSTON-SALEM STATE UNIVERSITY ARCHIVES)

left. That resulted in a technical foul, which Allen shot and made. Those were the last and the winning points scored in the game. I was named the Outstanding Coach after the game, and McManus and Kimbrough were named to the All-Tournament team.

Though we were the 1970 CIAA tourney champions, we did not go to NAIA or NCAA postseason play. I was the District 29 chairman that year, and we had created a rule that bypassed tournament winners in favor of sending teams with the best records. We did not have the best record in District 29 that year, so we did not go. I did not feel it was right for me as an NAIA chairman to try to play in the NCAA, so I did not send in an application.

I felt good about the year. We did not have a single superstar, but the whole team pulled together. When it was needed, someone stepped forward to help us win the games. The team spirit was there, and that was almost as good as going on to try for a national championship.

I can remember that one of the first people to congratulate me on that 1969-70 season was Dr. LeRoy Walker, a man I describe as being someone who always knew what to do and when to do it. I first met him in 1950, and we have been friends for the last 54 years. Along with John McLendon, LeRoy worked behind the scenes to help black athletes cross over into mainstream sports. He was one of the people working with Al Duer in the 1950s to integrate the NAIA.

One of the ways to characterize LeRoy is to note that he played football in college—all 155 pounds of him. That demonstrates what a tenacious man he really was. He was so small in college that the trainer at Benedict College in Columbia, South Carolina, had to alter the smallest set of shoulder pads that he could find. When the starting quarterback was injured, LeRoy stepped in and led the team to victory. He led Benedict to a conference championship in his junior year and was voted an All-American. He graduated from Benedict and went on to New York University, where he was the first black person to get a doctoral degree in exercise physiology.

I first met LeRoy when he was the track coach at North Carolina Central University. It was during his tenure that I learned the most about fielding track teams, knowledge that I was able to pass along to my track coaches in my role as athletic director for Winston-Salem State. While he was coach, he produced 111 All-Americans and 12 Olympians in track and field. He later served as CIAA president and, even more importantly, as NAIA president in the years after they finally allowed black athletes into the NAIA tournaments. He would be the first black man in history to coach a United States Olympic team, the 1976 team that participated in the Montreal Olympics. In 1996, he served as president of the United States Olympic Committee and was instrumental in bringing the games to Atlanta that year. He helped me make contacts within the Olympic Committee that allowed me to conduct basketball clinics and coach teams in several other countries.

While I am mentioning people who played roles in my career but who were not my football or basketball players, I need to mention Mary Garber.

On Thanksgiving Day in 1947, when Winston-Salem Teachers

Here Clara, me, and my old newspaper reporter friend, Mary Garber, celebrate my receiving an honorary degree from Wake Forest University.

(CLARENCE E. GAINES PERSONAL COLLECTION)

College was playing a football game, I looked up and saw this tiny white woman clutching a notebook and looking around the sidelines. When I asked her what she wanted, she surprised me by informing me that she was a reporter assigned to cover the football game. She asked for a program so she could identify the players. We didn't have any programs. We were too poor of a school to print programs. I got her a trainer, and with his help she noted the names of the Teachers and even the names of the players of the other team.

I had my doubts that this petite woman knew much about sports in general and football in particular, but if she was all that the newspaper was going to send, I would have to deal with her.

That day began a professional relationship that has lasted nearly 60 years. I don't know if Mary knew much about football then, but she sure learned how to cover it, as well as all other sports. She became a fixture at black sporting events, covering black high schools and Winston-Salem Teachers College for the *Twin City Sentinel*, the city's afternoon newspaper, which she had joined in 1940. She started covering black sports when all of the white sports reporters and editors returned from World War II. They reclaimed their regular beats, so she shifted to something they did not want to cover.

Through the years, Mary Garber got better at recognizing the skills of young black athletes, and there is proof that she helped make some careers. When Carl Eller, the defensive end for the Minnesota Vikings in the 1960s and 1970s, was inducted into the Pro Football Hall of Fame in 2004, he made a point of thanking Mary for writing about him while he was in high school in Winston-Salem. That exposure helped him to get noticed by college scouts such as those at the University of Minnesota, where he played.

Mary would often hang around my office looking for a story angle. I remember talking to her one day when one of my athletes came in to ask some question. This was in the later years, when sloppy clothes and habits had invaded the campus. The male student was wearing a hat that he did not take off in my office. The student asked me something, and I replied without looking at him, saying, "I cannot hear you." The kid kept asking the same question louder and louder until he was shouting, and I kept telling him, "I cannot hear you."

Mary was looking at me as if I had lost either my mind or my hearing. The student's question was spoken in plain English, and she understood every word he was saying.

Finally, I realized the young man was never going to catch on to the lesson I was trying to teach him. I finally told him that as long as he was showing me disrespect by wearing that cap in my office, I could not hear him. He removed it, and I immediately answered his question.

That student, who was not a bad kid at all, never wore that cap again in my office, and Mary never forgot the story of how I taught one person a lesson in respect that he never forgot. She wrote about that incident for the newspaper, as she did another incident that occurred at the coliseum.

We were playing our game when a kid who had obviously been drinking started making a spectacle of himself. He was a big kid, so the other spectators were afraid of him as he grew more belligerent. I went up into the stands, threw my arm around him, and just whispered in his ear that he was ruining the game for everyone and was not setting a good example for the students in the audience. I suggested he go home.

By that time, the police had arrived, but I waved them off. I made sure the young man got out of the stands without being arrested.

Whenever the newspaper wanted an update on my status over the last few years of my career, they would always ask Mary Garber to write it because she knew me so well. She knew my likes and dislikes, my quirks, and my motivational tools. If I had buried any bodies, she would have known where they were buried.

There was one story she knew that I don't think she ever wrote about because it could have gotten me in trouble. It was a day she witnessed the power a head coach can have. That day, the junior-varsity game was running long. That game threatened to interfere with the start of the varsity game. She commented that the varsity game would start late. I shook my head, said it would start on time, and pointed to who was running the game clock. It was my son, Clarence Jr. Clarence Jr. let the game clock run through time-outs and during free throws. The second half of the game lasted about half the time it should have, but the two coaches never noticed or never objected. They must have thought time was flying.

Mary kept right on working into the mid-1990s, as I did. She and I consider ourselves brother and sister, thanks to our decades of working in sports.

By the late 1960s and early 1970s, the effect brought about by Texas Western having an all-black starting five in the 1966 NCAA Division I championship hit home for small black colleges. Top black players who would have normally chosen from among the black colleges were now being courted by the white universities.

Actually, in North Carolina, it started a little sooner than that. Among the first black players at the small-college level was Mike Malloy, who joined Davidson College. Henry Logan was recruited by Western Carolina College in 1965. Logan did not disappoint the white coaches who took a chance on him. He averaged 30 points a game and once scored 60 points in a game.

The story was much the same over in Chapel Hill, home to the University of North Carolina. Charlie Scott was recruited as their first black player in 1967. Charlie was born in New York City and attended Laurinburg Institute in North Carolina, a black prep school which had graduated several good ballplayers who starred at CIAA schools.

Charlie made an immediate impact when he joined the Tar Heels. In 1968 and 1969, he helped lead the team to its second and third Final Four appearances, as well as Atlantic Coast Conference regular-season and tournament wins in each of those years. He averaged 22 points a game and is still the fifth-leading career scorer at the university. If he had come of age just a few years earlier, I might have had a shot at him because in his final years of high school, the most famous black player of the day was Earl Monroe of Winston-Salem State. If Charlie had been looking for a hero, he would have found him on our team.

In Winston-Salem, the first black player at Wake Forest was Charlie Davis, who came to the school in 1968. He came from Harlem and the very playgrounds where I recruited in the 1950s and early 1960s. He made All-ACC for three years and in 1971 became the first black player to be named ACC Player of the Year. He averaged about 25 points a game and finished with 1,970 points. He still holds the ACC career record for free-throw percentage, with more than 87 percent accuracy.

It was as if the white universities had discovered some great secret—that black athletes could play basketball. Once they discovered that secret, the white coaches told all of their white coaching friends, and the gold rush to recruit talented black athletes was on. That gold rush has never ended.

Recruiting black players started slowly, with most colleges recruiting only one or two. Once the old worries that alumni would not accept a black starting five disappeared, the recruiting pace picked up quickly. College coaches and administrators discovered that the alumni wanted winning programs more than they wanted to keep a white starting lineup.

While this was good news on the surface for the black athletes who had been shut out of these colleges for decades, there was a darker side.

Marshall Emery, a player of mine in the 1950s who went on to coach at Howard University and Delaware State, two black colleges, told me he, too, was experiencing difficulty in recruiting the top players. What he was hearing from the recruits and their parents was disheartening. Top black prospects were no longer willing to talk to top black colleges.

When I recruited a player in the 1940s, 1950s, or early 1960s, all I promised him and his parents—if I ever talked to his parents—was a college education. When Marshall came along 15 years later and tried to make the same pitch, he got questions back from black parents. How much television time would their son get? How often would he be seen by the professional scouts? Sometimes, he was even asked what kind of a car and how big of an apartment their son would be getting from the school.

"The white man's ice is colder than our ice" was Marshall's colorful answer to a reporter who asked him about the sudden difficulties in recruiting black players for black colleges.

Recruiting top white players to the top white schools had sometimes involved illegally paying the players in some fashion. Recruiting violations had never been much of a problem with the black colleges. Even if any CIAA coaches had wanted to entice prospects, I don't think many of our programs could have afforded cars, apartments, make-work jobs, and other enticements white schools could offer. All the black schools had were scholarships. But for increasing numbers of black athletes and their parents, that was not enough.

I won't say that the quality of players I was recruiting started to deteriorate once the white schools started competing with me, but I will say that many of the star players I used to reach were no longer interested in talking to me. The big white schools were now onto the tricks the black colleges had been using for years. Paid scouts for big universities were now hanging out at the same playgrounds my unpaid scouts used to watch for talent. Once those scouts found a promising kid and tipped off the coach, recruiting visits would be made at the drop of a hat from faraway cities, trips that were not in the budget for my little athletic program.

Within a few years, my network of unpaid scouts and college boosters was damaged because it was unable to compete with university publicity machines that were well oiled with cash to promote their schools to impressionable kids and their parents. I was still hearing about prospects, but not the top candidates I used to see.

The handwriting for basketball coaches at black colleges was not quite on the wall, but let's say the scrawls were beginning to form.

At the same time that the teams were integrating on the court, so were the referees.

Two men, James Burch of Raleigh and John Russell of High Point, were among the first black officials to work Atlantic Coast Conference games in North Carolina.

Burch applied to referee in the Southern Conference in 1967 and was assigned to freshman games. When the ratings came out, he found he had been rated highly by the coaches. That led to him refereeing ACC freshman games. Just like Jackie Robinson, he heard a few catcalls, but not as many as he thought he might have caught.

He discovered that looks could be important. James tells me that there was one ACC official who seemed not to like him because in those days he wore a large bush haircut and muttonchops. Years later, he learned that the official who had been against him thought the haircut was some sort of black protest, but after watching James officiate he realized that his haircut did not make any difference in his officiating.

I helped James break into officiating a Southern Conference tournament by going to our CIAA committee and getting him released from working our conflicting tournament. It was his chance to break into a Division I tournament, and none of us black coaches wanted him to miss his opportunity.

John Russell was one of those John McLendon players from North Carolina College who gave me trouble back in the late 1940s. After officiating in the army as a hobby, he taught in the public schools and started officiating in the high-school ranks. When the high schools integrated, he was among the first black officials called. He applied to the ACC in 1970, just one year after James Burch.

As with Burch, the league officials warned Russell that he would be booed and insulted, but John's take was that referees are always booed and insulted, so he had already heard those catcalls from black fans.

In a North Carolina State game, the fans yelled that they had some watermelon they would give him if the calls went their way. Russell ignored them—or maybe he stuck it to the North Carolina State team a little. That is always the way a referee can get back at disruptive fans, by looking very close at all plays for calls against the offending team.

When Russell officiated CIAA games, which he did for at least 15 years, the coaches called him "General John." We coaches could try to bluff him, try to yell to get the call changed, but he would ignore all of us. I rarely lost my cool with him because he could always throw a technical foul on an angry coach. When so many games were decided by single digits, you did not want to lose a game by arguing with a referee.

I remember one game when General John drew an imaginary line on the floor between me and the Norfolk State coach. In front of 8,000 fans, he drew a line with his foot on the floor—this was in the days before the real lines of the coaches' boxes were drawn—and warned us both to stay on our side of the line. It worked.

It was during this time of racial change that I got an offer myself to move to a white university.

The contact came from the University of Wisconsin at Milwaukee to interview for a position as their athletic director. The invitation came out of the blue in 1972. I may have been to Milwaukee a few times, but I had no ties to the school and had not been courting the position. I was quite happy being athletic director and basketball coach in Winston-Salem, but you can never be sure about something until you investigate it in person.

I was interviewed by a black vice chancellor, which helped explain how they had heard of me. During the interview process, it was made pretty clear that the job was mine if I wanted it, but I wondered what kind of job it really would be. The baseball field was torn up for the construction of a new building. It was obvious that the school did not care that much about baseball. I thought I could expand their track program, but the coach of that program made it clear that he wasn't interested in doing that. The basketball gym was below the standard for a Division I school.

The outgoing athletic director did not tell me anything specifically, but by reading between the lines of what he was saying, I could tell he was not happy. He implied that I would not be any happier than he had been in the position.

I got the feeling that the university's officers were looking for a black face to put in the position, and that my success in Division II had brought me to their attention. They were not quite sure who I was, but I was a successful black person in athletics, and that was enough for them.

I drove around Milwaukee and noticed that the city was as segregated as Winston-Salem ever was. Then I looked at the houses that the administration was hinting I should buy. They were much more expensive than the houses in Winston-Salem. And then I calculated that the property taxes I would pay on a new house would be about 10 times what I was paying on my house in Winston-Salem! I would be getting a big raise, but not enough to cover the city's property taxes.

Finally, I met with some black student leaders, and they were angry about something or other—as all student leaders, black or white, were in the early 1970s. One of them started telling me about the teachings of Louis Farrakhan. She stopped talking when I told her I knew him personally from his days of running track at Winston-Salem Teachers College.

When I returned home to Winston-Salem and reviewed the poor social situation in Milwaukee, the expense of living there, and the lack of commitment from the university to expand their athletic programs, I decided that there was no place like home. Just as quickly as the offer to move had come, I sent them my polite regrets.

We had an off year in 1970-71 with a record of 14-11 and did not go to the CIAA tournament. In 1971-72, we bounced back to a record of 18-9 but lost 80-79 to Virginia Union in the first round. In 1972-73, we finished the regular season with a nice 22-7 record and won our first-round game 77-74 over Virginia State but lost the next game 88-70 to Fayetteville State. The following season, 1973-74, was another off year in the regular season. We finished 14-12 but qualified for the CIAA tourney. We lost 85-81 to Virginia Union in overtime.

In 1974-75, we had a much better year, finishing first in the

250

Southern Division. This was particularly good since I had not been able to recruit any really big men. My tallest player was just six-foot-five. My stars were Tom Paulin of Newark, New Jersey, and a freshman named Carlos Terry of Lexington, North Carolina. I rarely started freshmen on my teams, but Carlos was an exceptional player, one of the strongest I had ever recruited. Tom was a transfer from Essex Community College in Newark. His coach was my old star Cleo Hill, who knew a thing or two about recognizing basketball talent. After more than 20 years, my network of unpaid scouts was still finding players for my team. Cleo would eventually send me six players from his junior college.

We opened the CIAA tournament with a win over Virginia State, 100-75. Our next opponent was Coach Bobby Vaughn's Elizabeth City team. He and I had been playing each other for 24 years and were used to playing tricks on each other. Just before this game, Bobby told a reporter a story that our teams were once playing each other and he was ahead. The game was winding down, and one of Bobby's assistants poked him in the side to call time. He hastily called time, then realized that he didn't have any assistants. Then he looked up into my smiling face.

Now, I don't remember that story, but I do remember at least one game where I had run out of time-outs and the other team luckily called one for me.

Another story that I don't remember that Bobby insists happened was a game played in Winston-Salem. Bobby says he noticed that one of the nets was new and was tight enough that it allowed the ball to hang for a second before dropping to the floor. We were attacking that net, so its tightness gave my players just a second or so longer to get back on defense. Bobby noticed that the net his team had to attack was older. The ball went right through to the floor, so his team had no delay to get back on defense.

"Don't worry about it," Bobby told his team at halftime. "We'll switch sides at halftime, and we will get the slow net."

I swear that I don't remember that game and don't know what he is talking about, but Bobby insists that the slow net somehow switched sides at halftime. He says my team got the second or so lag time once we made a basket in the second half, just as we had it in the first half.

Carlos Terry was one of the stars for us in the late 1970s.

(Winston-Salem State University Archives)

Now, how could I have done anything to that net? I was in the locker room with my players the whole time. Bobby insists that a clued-in custodian must have switched the nets, but if that had happened, wouldn't some Elizabeth City fan have noticed?

Bobby got back at me for that game. The next time we went down to Elizabeth City, Bobby had his custodian crank up the furnace, which made the gym extremely hot. It was like playing in Arizona in that gym. His team had practiced in the heat, but my team had not. My team was dying, while Bobby's looked like it was enjoying a sauna. Every time I tried to open a door to let in some fresh air, the custodian would come around and close it.

Old coaching stories aside, Elizabeth City was ahead most of the way in that CIAA tourney game. My team was just plain cold, while their star player, Thomas Blue, was hot. Blue had made 20 rebounds and 24 points when he went for a simple layup with 35 seconds remaining. He missed it. One of my players made a basket in the closing seconds that won the game for us, 75-74. My team shot 31 percent from the field, a percentage that should have lost us the game. We were lucky, and Elizabeth City was not.

The next night, we faced Norfolk State. We blew a 12-point lead to lose 80-76. I couldn't believe it. Had we kept that lead, we would have been in the CIAA finals for the first time since 1970. Norfolk State certainly knew how to get there. They had been there nine of the last 11 years.

Our playing wasn't over. We were selected to play for the NAIA District 26 championship. In the first round, we drew Barber-Scotia of Concord, North Carolina, a small school that had some hot shooters. They had scored more than 100 points in 10 games that year. I was more than a little worried because Tom Paulin, one of my star players, was out with a leg injury. In fact, several of my players were hurt. We edged Barber-Scotia 90-88.

That win put us in the District 26 final against Guilford College in Greensboro. One of my reserves, Horace Johnson, who had not played more than 10 minutes combined all season long, came off of the bench to help us upset Guilford 89-82. One of the players we beat on Guilford's team was Lloyd "World" B. Free, who would go on to a professional career with the Philadelphia 76ers and other teams.

This upset sent the team to Kansas City once again. It was the first time I had been back to the tournament since 1965. We had been three straight years in 1961, 1962, and 1963 but had never managed to capture the NAIA.

One of the reasons we never captured the NAIA reared its head yet again in our first game, against Eastern Montana. Our players just went cold when they got into a national tournament. We blew an eight-point lead near the end of the game but still managed to win 82-75.

We played better in the next game, upsetting Central Washington 57-56. George Gibson became the hero of this game by knocking a jump ball back to midcourt, far enough that Central Washington could not take a last-second shot. I could not control my freshman Carlos Terry, who confidently told a reporter, "I'm ready to meet Kareem." I did not like trash talkers and told Carlos to watch his mouth.

The basketball gods struck Carlos for his overconfidence by giving him and another of my players, Melvin Garrett, a case of the flu that very night. We lost 67-59 to Saint Mary's of Texas one night later. Our star of the game again was George Gibson, who substituted for the injured Tom Paulin. Once again, cold shooting on our part had ended our NAIA hopes. Maybe there was just a Kansas City curse against me and my team that I did not know about.

The next season, 1975-76, was a very good year for us, with only four losses. Our CIAA Southern Division record was a perfect 16-0.

One reporter for the *Winston-Salem Journal* was speculating that because I had 574 wins to my credit, I must be shooting for 600 wins as a retirement goal and looking for one more CIAA tourney win to go out on top.

In the first game of the tournament, against Elizabeth City, it looked like it was raining basketballs. The reporter totaled 193 shots at the goal in 40 minutes of play. Of course, neither team was making many of those baskets. We barely won the game, 77-74. Once again, one of my ballplayers was talking out of turn. Mike Brown said, "We outclass the rest of the teams in this thing." That statement could only lead to a downfall.

In our next game, we lost 91-89 to Norfolk State in two overtimes. I am not sure there should have been an overtime. Tom Paulin took a jumper at the buzzer when the game was tied at 75. He collided with a Norfolk State player, but no foul was called, and Tom's shot went wide. That created the need for overtime.

We almost won in the first overtime, but Norfolk State sank a shot from 25 feet at the buzzer to tie the game.

*George Gibson, another player from the late 1970s, was an
evangelist in college and remains one today. Here he drives
against the Norfolk State Spartans.*

(Winston-Salem State University Archives)

In the second overtime, Norfolk State went ahead 91-87 with 41 seconds to play. Carlos Terry made one basket with 20 seconds remaining, but we never got a chance to tie.

We played Guilford College again for the NAIA District 26 championship just a day after I learned I had been named NAIA Coach of the Year, along with Sam Moir of Catawba College. We had played Guilford three times in recent years and won twice, but they evened the score this time. We were beaten 108-107 in overtime. Once again, the game came down to the end. As time ran out in overtime, Carlos Terry fouled a Guilford player. The referee sent that player to the foul line with no time showing on the clock. He missed the first shot and made the second. The game was over, as was our chance to go to Kansas City. What a game this was! We took 102 shots from the floor, and Guilford took 90. Carlos hit a season-high 36 points. We were down as much as 12 points in the first half and then fought our way back in the second half.

The 1976-77 regular season was an off year for us, as we finished with only a 14-9 record. But it also turned out to be a CIAA championship season. That season, in which we lost three straight games at the end of the year, could be categorized as a Cinderella season for us, as we turned a bad record into a face-saving CIAA tourney championship.

We started the roll with a 75-68 victory over Virginia State that was carried on NBC television. Our heroes were George Gibson and Carlos Terry, who complained, "I don't get the credit that is due me." Gibson got 32 points. Carlos got 29 and a chance to show off his reverse dunking style.

We followed that with a win over Virginia Union.

We won the championship game 80-73 over Saint Augustine's. One of the stars of the game was Marco Dillard of Trenton, New Jersey, who had been a substitute for most of his career.

With a record of 17-9, we headed to Towson, Maryland, for the first round of the NCAA small-college playoffs. Our first opponent was the number-one seed, Towson State, a team we had never played. My star, Carlos Terry, was distracted by reports that he was thinking of becoming a professional player. We were no match for Towson State. We lost 102-83 against a team that I described as "a buzz saw." We kept the game close in the first half, but they blew us out of the water in the second half. Still, Carlos got 30 points in the game.

We finished hot during the 1977-78 season, going into the CIAA tournament in Hampton at 22-2. We were the tournament favorite and were ranked second in the nation by the NAIA.

We won our game against Virginia Union, 79-72. It was closer than the numbers indicate. Carlos Terry was the hottest shooter. Too many of my players were cold.

We were upset in our second game by Norfolk State by a score of 60-57. Once Norfolk State got their momentum going, there was no stopping them. Our team sank only 25 percent of its shots in the first half and only 30 percent for the entire game. It was our third straight CIAA tournament loss to Norfolk State. The three games were decided by a total of seven points. My teams from those years never could figure out Norfolk State.

The season was not over. We started competition in District 26 to go to Kansas City again for the NAIA. We beat neighboring Guilford for the second straight year, 65-61. The game was a thriller, two of our players slapping down Guilford shots that would have won the game in the last seconds. The game went into overtime, and we got a few breaks.

In Kansas City, guard David Harold was the hero with 22 points in our first game, a 77-60 victory over Bethany Nazarene. We were cold through much of the game and were leading only 38-34 through the first 24 minutes. Finally, we hit a long shot, and the momentum shifted.

Right in the middle of this tournament, Mike Mulhern, a reporter for the *Winston-Salem Journal*, speculated on the front page of the sports section that I would be leaving after the tournament. It was my own fault. In December, I had openly, idly mused that, at age 54, I might be ready to retire from my state-government job at the university and find something else to do, so I could collect a pension plus a separate paycheck. I had some contacts in Mexico who wanted me to organize their national team for the 1980 Moscow Olympics. And my old rival Charlie Christian had resigned from Norfolk State, and there was some speculation that I wanted his job.

Needless to say, nothing came from either of those job offers. Just as I had realized that I did not want to leave Winston-Salem for Milwaukee, I did not want to leave for Norfolk or Mexico.

Our next game was a controversial win over Briar Cliff of Iowa. We were ahead 64-63 with one second remaining when Briar Cliff threw in the ball. Carlos and a Briar Cliff player went up for it and collided. No foul was called on Carlos, and the game was declared over. It was as tough a game as I had ever seen played, the Rams fighting back from being down by 12 points. Our heroes were David Harold and Reggie Gaines, who in that game violated my rule of not taunting the other players. The curious thing about Briar Cliff was that most of their top players were from Panama.

That hard-fought game, which one of my players compared to what it must be like to play in the NBA, sapped our strength. In the quarterfinals, we fell apart and lost 89-76 to Kearney State. At one point, we did not score for a full 10 minutes, while our opponents slowly built a lead. We simply ran out of gas. Our players did not hit their shots, and they made simple mistakes like traveling with the ball. At one point, we were ahead 66-65. One minute later, we were allowing the game to slip away.

Once again, the Kansas City curse had hit. Something about that city and the NAIA tournament always adversely affected my teams. In some games, the players could do no wrong and looked like a championship team. Then, in the next game, they would look like junior-high kids practicing to make the varsity. I never could figure it out, and I never could coach them past it. It did not matter how talented the entire team was or who the individual players were, they still froze up in Kansas City.

That was the last season for senior Carlos Terry, who had shown some sparks of being like my superior players of the '50s and '60s. Carlos started out toward an NBA career, but he just never made it. He came from a very supportive, intact family, but he allowed himself to be

Reggie Gaines was All-CIAA in 1980. Here he shoots against Howard University.

(PHOTO BY ROLAND S. WATTS, COURTESY OF WINSTON-SALEM STATE UNIVERSITY ARCHIVES)

influenced by people he should have never met. I never could get through to him that if he looked to his parents' example to run his personal life and used his talent to develop his professional life, he could go far. His life was cut short in a traffic accident outside of Washington, D.C.

The 1978-79 and 1979-80 seasons were virtually identical, with records of 19-9 and 19-7. In 1979, we were seeded first in the Southern Division of the CIAA and won our first tournament game 84-78, but we lost our second game 85-66 to Norfolk State. In 1980, we were again seeded first in the Southern Conference but lost 76-75, again getting beat by Norfolk State.

It was in the late 1970s that I helped out in a reverse "crossing over" situation by supporting Virginia Union's hiring of David Robbins as head coach. Dave was white but had coached for years at a black inner-city school in Richmond. The local press called him "the White Shadow," after a TV show about a white coach inspiring black basketball players.

When he started out, Dave was not all that popular among the other coaches and CIAA fans because some thought he was taking up space that belonged to a black assistant coach moving up to head-coaching status. I rejected that idea and told everyone I did. Just as black coaches deserved the right to compete for coaching positions at white schools, Dave deserved the right to compete for the coaching position at a black school. Crossing over could—and should—go both ways.

I did not make a mistake with Dave, but I lived to regret supporting him. His school whipped up on mine more often than I whipped up on his in the 1980s. In 2004, he won his 600th basketball game in 26 years of coaching.

The '70s had produced only two championships for the Rams, compared to five in the '60s. I had a few job offers that would have taken me out of Winston-Salem, but I still had not seen anything that would have allowed me to reach as many young men as what I was doing.

Though the handwriting on the wall was becoming a little clearer as I entered the 1980s, my fourth decade in coaching, I still saw no reason to retire from the only job I had ever had.

CHAPTER 17

The 1980s and 1990s— The End of My Era

As the 1980s dawned, it was time for me to take stock of my career. The Winston-Salem State University Rams had won more than 640 games, nine CIAA tournament championships, and one national small-college championship. I was 58 years old in 1981, still young enough to coach, of course, but closing in on the years when most people start to think of backing off.

Newspaper reporters were starting to ask me about the goal of winning 700 games, since we were still winning 15 games a season. I told reporter Mary Garber, now a reporter for the *Winston-Salem Journal*, that if I reached 750 wins sometime in the 1980s, I would retire. If I didn't reach 750, I told her, then I would continue coaching and going after that goal in a wheelchair.

I was joshing her, and she knew it, but she still printed what I said. Newspaper reporters know a good quote when they hear one, and I knew they wanted good quotes. I remember another one I told Mary that fit with the irascible reputation I tried to groom: "The meek will inherit the earth. They will inherit it just as soon as the strong get through stomping all over it."

Actually, I never set a goal of winning any number of games at any time in my career. I had been a football coach whose first season had resulted in no wins, but I remember being optimistic about that 1946 season, thinking that we would win some games, if not all of them. I went into every basketball and football season I coached believing we would win our share of games, if not all of them.

Reaching the milestones of 500, 600, 700, and 800 wins—which I achieved in the 1989 season—really just meant that the athletes who played for my teams had risen to the expectations that I had for them as individuals and as teammates. The milestones themselves really did not mean anything to me as a person.

To prove that, I only have to point out that the strongest, most dominating teams I ever fielded were in the mid-1960s, when we captured wins 300 and 400 within a few years of each other. In fact, number 400 came in 1967, when we were on our way to a national championship. The newspapers did not make that big a deal out of win 400 because many coaches had either won that many or were within range of it. My players of that era don't even recall much of the details of winning games 300 and 400 because I had told them that those games were just like any others they would play those seasons.

I don't think any coach sets out to make a name for himself. That is because I knew—every coach always knows—that the Peanut Gallery was hiding just around the corner, waiting for a misstep or two. It is almost as if a pack of detractors is issued with the awarding of the coaching job. Every coach knows when he is hired that he has already been fired, but the exact date just has not been decided by the current or future university chancellor.

So if you already know you are going to be fired, how in the world can you set out to win a certain number of games, or even get excited about reaching certain milestones?

Through the years, I had been given numerous awards, mostly related to my teams' winning CIAA championships. I was selected CIAA Basketball Coach of the Year in 1953, 1957, 1960, 1961, 1963,

1966, 1970, and 1977. I was inducted into the CIAA Hall of Fame in 1968 and served in the CIAA Coaches Association from 1972 to 1976. I was inducted into the North Carolina Sports Hall of Fame in 1978.

From 1966 to 1972, I was the NAIA's District 26 chairman, which demonstrated how much the sport had changed. It was just over two decades earlier, in the mid-1950s, that the NAIA and the NCAA had been for whites-only college sports teams. Now, here I was helping form policy for the association.

In Winston-Salem, I was active with the Rotary Club, the Heart Association, the YMCA, and Experiment in Self-Reliance. I even served on the local board for the American Automobile Association.

Then, in 1982, I received a humbling honor that confirmed I really had made an impact on the game. I was inducted into the Naismith Memorial Basketball Hall of Fame in Springfield, Massachusetts. I joined my old friend John McLendon, who had been inducted in 1979. We were the first two black coaches to be so honored. The other inductees in 1982 were Coach Everett Case of North Carolina State University, Al Duer, who helped integrate the NAIA, and players Harold Greer, Slater Martin, Frank Ramsey, and Willis Reed.

The other black coaches now in the Hall of Fame are John Thompson of Georgetown, John Chaney of Temple, and Lenny Wilkins, who has coached several professional teams. Lenny is actually doubly honored by the Hall of Fame for both his playing ability and his coaching. I somehow missed recruiting Lenny, even though he was from Brooklyn. Maybe he never played in the Rucker tournaments in Harlem, where I did most of my scouting. If he did play, I just didn't recognize his talent when I saw it.

The 1980s did not start off well for the team. In 1981, we had our first losing year since 1968, finishing with a 10-15 record. The next few years, we seemed to coast along.

In 1984, we won 20 games and lost 10. We won the tournament opener 67-48 against Bowie State, though we started out so slow I had to call a time-out to remind the boys that if we lost that 9:00 A.M. game, we would be back in Winston-Salem by 5:00 P.M.

The next game, we beat Virginia State 88-86 by going ahead in the final 14 seconds.

Then we drew Norfolk State. The newspaper described us as "sacrificial lambs" for our play in the first half, when we were down 18 points, but we fought back. We just did not fight back hard enough. We lost 64-60.

In 1984, I got a pleasant surprise when John Thompson's Georgetown University team won the NCAA Division I championship. That made John the first black coach to win the title. During his interviews with reporters, John complimented me by saying that I could have been the first black coach to win that tournament, if I had only been given the opportunity to coach Division I ball.

Things started to change for me in 1985, when a new chancellor, Dr. Cleon Thompson, came to Winston-Salem State University. Though he had graduated from North Carolina Central University, a CIAA school, we had never met, as he had spent most of his career at the administrative level of the University of North Carolina system. At that level, he did not deal with athletics at all.

As I had been a part of the campus for 40 years under several chancellors, I had no reason to believe anything would change under Dr. Thompson. I was about to be surprised.

At his first speech to the faculty and staff of the university, Dr. Thompson said something like this: "I have to show Coach Gaines that he does not run Winston-Salem State University."

My assistant coach, Tim Grant, had been one of my players. We turned to each other with the same thought: "Uh-oh." Actually, our first thought was "Oh (something else)," but decorum prevents me from writing what I really thought of Dr. Thompson's mention of me in his speech.

Just as Tim and I looked at each other, I could see several other faculty and staff members turning to each other with puzzled looks on their faces. The comment I had just heard was hardly a statement about how Winston-Salem State University was at a crossroads, and that if everyone worked together, the school would move onward and upward to greater challenges and accomplishments. Whatever chancellors usually say in their first speeches, I don't think most of them go out of their way to insult one their staff in front of the rest of the staff. If the statement had been intended as a joke, I did not find it funny, and I did not laugh.

Nothing about Dr. Thompson's first impression of me was true.

Never in my 40 years of service to Winston-Salem Teachers College and then Winston-Salem State University had I tried to influence the operations of the school. Never had I tried to push my athletes through the school. Never had I asked to have them treated as special cases because they were athletes. In fact, that was one of the cardinal rules I taught my players: You are a student first and an athlete second. You are in college to get an education first and then to play sports, not the other way around.

When my players failed to make their grades, I had them sit out games. If they couldn't overcome their problems with books or discipline, I fired them—sent them home—without batting an eye. I did not care how high they could jump toward the backboard or how straight they could throw to a teammate or from how far away they could sink a basket. If I made a mistake in recruiting someone who really did not belong in our school, I got rid of them.

An example of that had occurred shortly before Dr. Thompson arrived. In 1983, one of my athletes was arrested on suspicion of sexual assault. I did not wait for his case to be tried. I removed him from the team. Other coaches may have blindly defended such a player until he went to trial, but I fired him. I did not want anyone or anything to distract from the idea that school was school, sports were sports, and morals were morals.

If the new chancellor was worried about my prominence on campus and in the community, there was nothing I could do about that. While I did not relish the role, there was no denying that I was the "face" of Winston-Salem State University, particularly in Winston-Salem.

I am not being conceited or making an idle claim.

Honestly, I doubt most residents of the city in those days could have named the chancellor of Winston-Salem State University. At the same time, those same people could not have named the president of Wake Forest University. Shoot, most of the residents of any city probably cannot name their city councilman.

But just about everyone in Winston-Salem knew who Big House was. I hadn't gotten any shorter, and the combination of Clara's good cooking and away-game food had ensured that I was as big as I ever was. I still looked like my nickname suggested I should. Because I was on television and my photo was in the newspaper during the season, whenever I walked down the street, people of all colors would look me in the eye, smile, wave, and speak to me. I would return the greeting as if they were my friends, though I may have never seen them before that very moment. It did not cost me a penny or a moment out of my day to be nice to folks.

Call it a combination of the success of integration and the success of my basketball teams. I would get into elevators with groups of little old white ladies who normally would have been afraid to be in a closed space with a big black man. Those ladies would smile, hold out their hands, and say, "Hello, coach." They would ask me how the team was doing. Sometimes, they really would know what they were talking about.

Sometimes, even I was surprised at who knew me. I once went over to Wake Forest and was walking down the hall when an Oriental student who could not have possibly been to any of my games pointed at me and asked in accented English, "Big House?"

What if I were the most famous person representing Winston-Salem State University? What if I were only a basketball coach instead of the chancellor of the university?

At little or no cost to the school, I had traveled around the world telling everyone I met about this high-quality university in Winston-Salem, North Carolina, where a young person of any color and any financial means could get a worthwhile college degree. In the early days, I had recruited teachers. As the school expanded its educational programs, I recruited for all kinds of degrees. I had met thousands of people and had left each of them with a positive thought about the school where I coached and taught.

When I traveled abroad, all of my expenses were paid by some sponsoring body. The university was never out of pocket for any of my trips. In 1973, I participated in the first World Basketball Tournament in Lima, Peru. In 1977, I took a CIAA all-star team to the Ivory Coast in Africa to show them what an American-style education could do for them. From 1973 to 1976, I served on the United States Olympic Committee. In the 1980s, I was invited by the United States Air Force to conduct coaching clinics for its base coaches in Germany, Italy, and Turkey. That had been a great trip that put me in contact with hundreds of young men who might be getting out of the service one day and looking for a college where they could spend their government education dollars.

In the 1980s, long before the nation's financial ties were so strong with China, I was there for the Jones Cup, teaching the residents of the world's largest nation about basketball. I took Dave Robbins of Virginia Union with me. He still laughs that there was no Chinese phrase for "Big House," so they called me "the Mansion."

I mention these trips not to flaunt them but just to point out that I saw my role as an ambassador of the college. My motto in dealing with every chancellor since 1946 had been, "Let me coach, and I will leave the administration to you." It was an arrangement that I had not broken in my career.

Under no circumstances did I want an up-front or behind-the-scenes role in running the school. I had always believed my job was a lot more interesting and productive than any administrative job could ever be. Each year, I got to see several young men I had coached over four years graduate and then go off into the professional world to seek their own way. I had played a role in preparing them for those careers by teaching them confidence in themselves, how to work as a team, and how to deal with glorious victory and devastating defeat with the same level of grace. All any college administrator had to show for those same four years was the same columns of numbers he had been staring at four years earlier. I had no desire to be that person.

I think the die was cast between me and Dr. Thompson from that first public meeting. The future of Rams basketball was going to be different, whether I was there or not.

In the 1980s I traveled to many countries conducting clinics. In China they called me "The Mansion." I like to think we laid the groundwork for future athletes such as Yao Ming to learn the sport.

(CLARENCE E. GAINES PERSONAL COLLECTION)

When it came university budget-cutting time, my basketball budget came under scrutiny. I did not lose my assistant coach, but my recruiting budget for scholarships was slashed in half. At a time when out-of-state tuition was $9,200 a year, I was told to run my scholarship program on $35,000 a year. I am guessing that was about the same amount of money the major university athletic programs spent on telephone calls.

At the same time my program was being cut, I learned that the recruiting budgets at some of our traditional CIAA rivals were over $100,000. Unless a wellspring of alumni-donated money suddenly bubbled up so I could create more scholarships, my ability to compete for the top out-of-state players was about to disappear.

This lack of ability to give scholarships to talented players kept some good players from coming here. My first star, Cleo Hill, sent his sons to other CIAA schools because he could not afford to send them to Winston-Salem State. Cleo Jr. helped beat the Rams while he was attending North Carolina Central.

There was a lot of irony in what had happened with Cleo. I had been able to get him into Winston-Salem Teachers College because he was so poor he qualified for student aid. But because Cleo had graduated from college and become financially successful, his sons could not go to their father's alma mater 20 years later.

I felt I had come full circle in 40 years. After building a basketball program that was at least competitive with the best schools in the CIAA, I was going to be forced to rely on in-state students. Instead of looking for the best players who could be persuaded to come to Winston-Salem, I now had to hope that they came on their own and walked on, as the returning veterans after World War II did.

In the fall of 1985, the same year Chancellor Thompson arrived, the newspaper described our upcoming year as one "without a superstar, with a glaring weakness or two, and with untested players who have to play important roles."

There was one good piece of news from my competitors. Dave Robbins had lost his star player. Charles Oakley, all six feet, eight inches and 240 pounds of him, had moved on to the Cleveland Cavaliers. I had always liked Charles. When I was chosen to coach an all-star team,

I fought tooth and nail to get Charles onto that team at a time when organizers were dismissing him as being from a small school.

We finished the 1985-86 season with a 16-12 record.

The next year, 1986-87, was about the same. The torch of dominance had passed to Dave Robbins at Virginia Union and Charlie Christian at Norfolk State. We had been picked to finish sixth in the Southern Division of the CIAA the previous year but ended up winning it, so I had grown used to this underdog role.

Actually, the critics were right this time. We finished 15-12 for the year.

The basketball news in the mid-1980s was that the white universities which had been recruiting black athletes for 20 years had suddenly noticed that many of those black kids were not leaving their schools with college degrees. Just as I and my fellow coaches at black colleges had predicted, the white schools which had recruited the kids we used to get had been neglecting the education of those same kids while exploiting their athletic talents.

The way the white schools decided to address the problem started at the wrong end of the horse. The NCAA created Proposition 48, a rule that set 700 as a minimum score on the Scholastic Aptitude Test for admission into college, with some allowance if the student had good high-school grades. One of Winston-Salem State's professors, Dr. Brady Hauser, had helped develop a grid matching SAT scores with grade-point averages to help qualify athletes so they could play sports.

Coaches and presidents at black colleges did not support Proposition 48 in general because it was designed to keep prospective students out of college. It did not address the issue of the level of education the kids got in college once they were admitted. That was where the problem was. Black kids in college were going to sports practice, but no one was making sure that they learned anything in their classes.

Grambling State's president, the most vocal critic of Proposition 48, said, "Black athletes at white colleges have never been educational entities. They have been industrial commodities."

One effect of Proposition 48 was that some freshmen would be admitted into college but would not be allowed to play until they proved they could make good grades. That was detrimental to Division II schools because we could not afford to support an athlete for a year who was not playing the sport for which he had been recruited.

I frankly don't remember the SAT scores of any of my players, but I do know what happened to them once they got into college. They learned. Nearly every one of my athletes came from a poor, broken-home background. Once I got them into school, I told them that they had been given the golden opportunity of a free college education. They could make their own futures, but only if they applied themselves.

I can't speak for any other Division II schools or black colleges, but most of my players did take advantage of that opportunity to learn once they entered college. What Proposition 48 seemed designed to do was keep an unknown number of students from even being allowed to try to succeed in college.

The accumulated effects of running a shoestring program began to take a toll within a few years after my scholarship budget was cut. The high-school players and their parents who had decided to cast their lot with black colleges could tell the difference between the better-financed programs and mine. In 1989, we won only six games, the absolute worst year in my coaching career. In 1990, we won only nine. We won 10 in 1991 and six again in 1992. After suffering through only two losing seasons from 1946 through 1988, my teams now had posted four losing years in a row.

In 1990, I got caught up in a new state rule that had nothing to do with me. The state university system ruled that no one could hold both the head-coach and the athletic-director positions. The rule was put into effect after North Carolina State University head coach and athletic director Jim Valvano had been accused of helping his basketball players skate through their classes. I reluctantly resigned from my athletic-director position and chose to keep my role as head basketball coach.

When I gave up a large part of the duties I had held for more than 40 years, I thought I could hear the current members of the Peanut Gallery cracking their shells.

The financial crippling of my program can be seen in the last team

I fielded. In the 1992-93 season, 13 of the 15 players on the basketball team were from North Carolina. There was nothing inherently wrong with using North Carolinians, but in years past I had always tried to find the best players no matter where they lived. Five of the 15 were walk-ons, young men who wanted to play college basketball but who had not been recruited by me for that purpose. There is nothing wrong with walk-ons, but I think even they would admit that if they had been outstanding ballplayers, some college would have offered them a scholarship. In years past, I had enjoyed the luxury of recruiting tall players and athletes who had natural leadership skills on the court. I had gone to New York City, Newark, Philadelphia, and the Midwest to find the best black ballplayers coming out of high school. Now, I was reduced to acting like a P.E. teacher in a high school, choosing my starting players from the students who had come out for the team.

In 1993, another rule was going to affect me. The state university system had a rule requiring that professors who reached their 70th birthdays had to retire. The rule was in place so the university could get rid of old, tenured professors who had lost their edge.

The rule was not hard and fast. It allowed the granting of waivers on a year-to-year basis, so a school could keep popular or good professors if they were still contributing despite their age. The chancellor at the university could grant the waiver.

I applied for a waiver, asking to be allowed to keep my coaching and teaching status past my 70th birthday. My immediate supervisor and the faculty senate both voted in support of my staying on at the school. To my surprise, the vice president for academic affairs recommended that the chancellor deny my request for a waiver. The chancellor told me that he would go along with the vice president's recommendation and deny my request.

In effect, I would be forced to retire on my 70th birthday.

I never found out the circumstances behind why the chancellor refused to consider my waiver. If some alumni—the Peanut Gallery—were behind the plan to force me into retirement, I wonder why the chancellor did not ask those same alumni why they did not donate enough money to finance a first-rate scholarship program. There was never anything wrong with my basketball program that the funding of athletic scholarships could not have fixed.

If I had grown too old at age 70 to relate to young men aged 18 to 22, I would have thought that my assistant coaches, Tim Grant and Bill English, would have found some way to tell me. And if I had grown too old, I would have had mass defections from team members rebelling against "the old man." Most of them were playing for fun anyway. They had no great expectations that they would be discovered by NBA scouts. If they didn't like it, they could have always left the team.

That did not happen. Even in the darkest days of my last five years, I still had kids wanting to play basketball. Maybe I didn't scare them like I used to in the 1950s and 1960s, but I think they still respected me.

I had winning seasons from 1983 to 1988, when I was 60 to 65, so I still knew how to win basketball games.

I could have made a fuss about my "retirement" by publicly appealing the chancellor's decision to deny my waiver, but that would have only attracted undue attention to the university itself. I had given 47 years of my life to this school, so it made no sense to me to hurt Winston-Salem State University in any way. Instead, I sat at the table during the hastily called press conference while the chancellor announced my retirement. Anyone at that press conference could see I was unhappy, but I was not going to admit I was. It was obvious that the chancellor was firing me, but we stuck with the charade to make it look proper.

Looking back after talking with friends, there was a far less embarrassing way the university could have asked me to leave that I would have agreed to. I could have coached the 1993-94 season as a farewell tour. At the very least, that would have given the scores of players I had coached over the years time to pick out a game to come see me on the court one last time. It would have given Winston-Salem Teachers College and Winston-Salem State University alumni who had followed the Teachers and the Rams from 1946 through 1993 one more time to come out and see the old coach.

The university could have promoted my retirement tour and maybe even pocketed a reasonable sum of money that could have gone into the underfunded coffers of the athletic department.

Whoever planned my retirement never thought of that strategy.

Instead of giving me and 47 years' worth of former players and fans a chance to become accustomed to the idea that I would be retiring, the administration dropped the word with just one home game and the 1993 CIAA tournament left on the schedule.

Before my last home game, I didn't try to sell my team on any "Hip, hip, hooray!" theatrics on my part. I think that would have insulted the kids' intelligence. I just told them to play their best.

It would have made a nice Hollywood ending for my players to win one for the House, like in that old Ronald Reagan movie, but that was not going to happen. In the final home game of my career, on February 20, 1993, my old nemesis North Carolina Central, the college that inspired me to start recruiting basketball players, defeated my Rams 90-82.

What I did think was special was that nearly 100 members of my past teams came to watch that last game, including 10 of my 1967 championship team. Those fellows had heard about what was happening. Using their network, they called everyone, and people made arrangements to come back and be with old Big House one last time.

Friday, February 24, 1993, was the opening round of the CIAA tourney. There was no Cinderella story there either. Elizabeth City whipped us 105-64. We actually led by five points in the beginning, but the stronger team won. We couldn't control their players on either end of the court.

My career ended at 828 wins and 445 losses, a winning percentage of .652. At the time, it placed me second on the all-time wins list behind Adolph Rupp. Of those 445 losses, 120 occurred after my recruiting budget had been slashed in half.

Could I have surpassed Rupp's record of 875 wins? Not that it was ever a goal of mine, and not that it matters now, but it was possible. My last winning year was 1988, when we won 16 and lost 12. If our team had averaged 16 wins a year over the last five years of my career, instead of the 7.4 we did average, Winston-Salem State University would

These WSSU players who came back for a reunion game can still play!
First row, left to right: *Charles Riley, Harold Kitt, Teddy Blunt, Don Helton, Eugene Smiley.* Middle row, left to right: *David Blizzard, Stenson Conley.* Back row, left to right: *Ed Sherrill, Tim Autry, Earl Monroe, Johnny Latham, Ralph Jones, Carlos Terry, and Eddie Gregg*

(CLARENCE E. GAINES PERSONAL COLLECTION)

have won 80 games. My career wins would have been 871, just four behind Coach Rupp.

The numbers game of who had the most wins always meant a lot more to sportswriters than it did to me. I enjoyed every win. I was irritated by every loss. That is the nature of coaches.

But I want to make it clear that I did not continue coaching because I was chasing Adolph Rupp's record. I had started thinking about retiring more than a decade and at least 300 victories earlier, long before even getting close to Rupp. The reason I kept coaching was that I enjoyed working with those kids whom I was helping to mold into young men.

My point is that youth leaders in church, Scout leaders, 4-H leaders—people who work with young men and women—know how I felt about coaching. I got a thrill out of seeing a new crop of young men walk onto my court each fall. Each basketball season brought me one or two or three or four new faces who were there at Winston-Salem State University to learn a career and to help their school defend its reputation on the hardwood.

The faces I saw in 1993 were just as fresh, just as enthusiastic, just as hopeful about their future as the faces I saw in 1946, when I took over the job of head coach. Each new athlete who walked onto my court made me just a little bit younger because some of his enthusiasm for the coming season rubbed off on me.

I guess that was the great unpaid reward I got from my job. Those kids kept me young.

Momma? Daddy? Grandmother? Uncle Manuel? Uncle Lawrence? I know you thought I would become a dentist, but you really just wanted me to be somebody. I think I kept my promise to you by coaching all those young men to be winners on the football field, on the basketball court, in the classroom, and in their chosen professions. I am satisfied with the career I had and the service I rendered to Winston-Salem State University.

CHAPTER 18

What I Learned from Coaching

I have never run my own business, so I can't give any sports analogies as business advice to help business owners and managers become healthy, wealthy, and wise.

What I have done is spend 47 years working with young, impressionable men, showing them how to work together in teams to achieve goals that individually they could not reach. I have shown mostly poor boys how they could overcome the lack of a stable home life to become successful and financially secure. I have demonstrated that if a coach stays around long enough in one job and recruits enough top players, he will win enough games to attract attention to his college.

The most important thing I learned from coaching is what Jackie Robinson proved in 1947. By hanging tough and ignoring the catcalls, Jackie proved that the barriers put up between races and social classes can be taken down when the people on both sides work at understanding each other. I now know that when that happens, both sides are better off because they both have increased their understanding of the other side.

I did not come by this enlightenment easily. When I started coaching in 1945, I had no real idea what I was supposed to do to motivate players to win ball games. My job as an assistant coach was to pick up the practice footballs and wash the uniforms. That hardly called for any coaching philosophy.

But I guess I had the basics already and did not know it at the time. Back in Paducah, I had been the kid who knew who owned what sports equipment and which kids were better at some sports than others. It was my job to get the kid who owned the two bats and the hardest softball out to play, even though I knew he could not catch an easy fly ball. I knew we couldn't insult him or ignore him because he was the kid we most depended on to have a good time. He had the equipment! Learning persuasion is an essential part of coaching.

When I got to college, I learned a little more about coaching by absorbing knowledge of every position on the football team. I found it fun to learn what the quarterback was expected to know, even though as a lineman I would never play that position. Other players just wanted to know how to catch the ball or block a rusher. I wanted to know everything there was to know about the game. Curiosity about the sport is another trait of a coach.

I guess possessing those two elements—being a good organizer and being curious—was why Coach Hurt at Morgan State asked me to come in and talk with Coach Brutus Wilson of Winston-Salem Teachers College about his assistant-coach position.

Here is what I learned from all those years of coaching and teaching.

Never judge a young person's ability based on the circumstances of his surroundings.

I did not pluck my players out of white middle-class homes with a father going to an office every day while the mother stayed home baking cookies so the neighborhood boys would have something to eat after they got through shooting hoops in the driveway. I took most of my players out of tenements and slums that no one would categorize as a "home." Many came from broken homes and never mentioned to me even having a father. Their clothes were secondhand. Sometimes, the food they ate was provided by the government. The spending money they had—if they had any at all—was won by pitching pennies against a crumbling brick wall.

My players were poor—the type of kids that society tells us will always be poor because they have always been poor. When I found them, they were in a welfare and educational system that treated them as hopeless victims. Though they were not yet 18 years old, many people had already evaluated their future as dismal.

I saw those poor kids differently than the welfare administrators saw them. While some might have dismissed them as playground players, I saw them as athletic young men whose minds had never been challenged.

Their athletic skills were obvious to anyone who watched them wheeling and spinning around the playground. What was less obvious was how well they could think. I trusted my scouts to get inside the heads of those young men by asking them what they wanted out of life and how they would get there.

Sometimes, we did not like what we heard. My scouts and I discarded the fast-buck hustlers who did not want to put in the time in college to learn the life skills to achieve their goals.

More often, we heard kids talk of dreams they were willing to work to fulfill. We selected those students to come to Winston-Salem. Even if their grades were questionable, we gave those young men their shot. We stuck by the kids who were slow but determined learners.

I learned from coaching that young men and women can accomplish just about anything, if given the chance and the knowledge that their elders and teachers expect them to succeed. I know this sounds simplistic, but my teams proved it time and time again on the football field, on the basketball court, and in the classroom.

I don't think most of the coaches in the major white universities picked up on these facts when they first started recruiting black ballplayers. They allowed the impression that black ballplayers were not really students to become their first and lasting impression.

The result of this laziness on the part of coaches could be startling. I remember seeing an account of how one college basketball player had to read aloud the story of the death of Maryland player Len Bias because the player's roommate could not read the newspaper. This incident took

*North Carolina governor Jim Hunt came to dedicate the C.E.Gaines
Center in 1976, which made my mother (pictured here with Governor
Hunt and me) proud. I had become "somebody" important enough to
attract the attention of the state's chief executive.*

place in one of the nation's premier state universities, a school known
for turning out engineers.

This sort of gross negligence of the educational process never occurred in my program, and I doubt it happened in any CIAA school.

There is only one explanation for why that player was in that university. He was functionally illiterate and unable to learn when he was
recruited from high school. Once recruited, the university did nothing
to help him. They just let him play basketball. The university intentionally ignored the clear evidence that the young man could not read
or properly function in society. Both the coach who recruited him and
the university professors who saw him in class openly and repeatedly
failed that young man.

I sincerely believe that kids, assuming there is nothing mentally wrong with them that interferes with their brain power, can learn college-level professions. I do not think it matters how disruptive or poor an environment they came from. Every kid can learn.

I am not saying every kid can master every course. What I am saying is that, in college, most kids can discover something they can do. All it takes are adults—parents, guardians, friends, and elementary, junior-high and high-school teachers and counselors—to tell those kids that they can achieve whatever they want to achieve. In my coaching career, it was my network of scouts—former players and graduates of Winston-Salem Teachers College—who recognized the thinking abilities of the athletes they were seeing. They investigated those prospects and convinced me that those young men could handle college-level work.

My scouts and I expected academic achievement from our players as much as we expected athletic achievement. Usually, we got both. The number of students who have come to this school at the recommendation of graduates is amazing. Harold Clawson, a retired school administrator from Charlotte, estimates that he sent more than 60 kids to Winston-Salem State University who participated in some sort of sports program. He figures that more than 500 went to the college on his recommendation that it was a school that could offer black students a strong future.

I think Winston-Salem State University's athletic program has proven that dumb jocks are not the norm. I am guessing that 80 to 90 percent of my players graduated and had viable careers. Only a few of my players went on to professional basketball. Most became teachers, coaches, recreation directors, doctors, and lawyers. They pursued other types of professional careers that lasted long after their knees would have given out on the professional basketball court.

To prove my point that colleges today are not demanding enough academically of their players, as I did, one only has to listen to pre- and post-game interviews of college ballplayers on television or radio. Those players—white or black—can barely communicate with the person interviewing them. If the phrase "you know" were ever banned from the vocabulary of today's college sports stars, there would be no interviews at all.

I find the slurring of speech and the use of street slang to be beneath the level of what I would expect of young men taking college-level courses. All of my players went to English and vocabulary classes in college, and they passed them. They had to pass them because they were planning to be teachers, not professional basketball players.

It was just that simple in their day, and it is just that simple today. I do not understand why the same standards we expected in the 1940s, 1950s, and 1960s do not apply in today's colleges.

It is not completely the fault of the players that they cannot string sentences together. I blame the public-school systems that did not force those young men to learn proper English at an early age. Those college kids sound the way they do because their elementary, junior-high, and high-school teachers, plus their college professors and college coaches, did not believe they could be taught to speak proper English. That is ridiculous. If the kids I plucked from the inner cities could learn proper English, there is no reason why college kids cannot learn it today.

I learned from coaching that there is—and should be—a difference between "wannabe" and "gonna be."

Several years ago, Nike had a TV campaign where kids proclaimed that they wanted to be like Mike—Michael Jordan, who starred at the University of North Carolina and then with the Chicago Bulls. The campaign centered on the kids' imitating Jordan on the basketball court. The campaign insinuated that all the kids had to do to "be like Mike" was buy his $100 shoes.

What was missing from that advertising campaign was any mention that to be like Mike, the kids had to learn what Michael Jordan learned in college—how to read complicated contracts, how to handle money, how to evaluate business enterprises outside of sports, and how to be a successful person off the basketball court. The ad campaign never even mentioned that Mike was an intelligent, well-educated, thinking man. According to the Nike commercials, Michael Jordan was just a basketball player who could hang in the air while he dunked the basketball.

I started my sports career as a wannabe. I wanted to be the best high-school lineman in Kentucky—and I was. I wanted to be the best lineman in college—and I was.

But my life was also filled with role models who taught me what my life was "gonna be" after college, if I applied myself. "Gonna be" was much more realistic than "wannabe." I had parents, grandparents, aunts, uncles, neighbors, schoolteachers, Sunday-school teachers, Boy Scout leaders, high-school football coaches, and family doctors who pointed out to me at an early age that my physical prowess would start to fade once I got out of college. Once my "wannabe" goal of being a good lineman was over, I would have to be ready to move into the "gonna be" part of my life.

I learned from coaching that I had to get through to my team members that they were "gonna be" teachers or some other type of professional once they graduated from college. Even if they were lucky and good enough to try out for professional basketball, they may not make it past training camp. Most of them didn't. But when they didn't, they had a profession that would take them as far as they wanted to go.

In only a few instances did I reluctantly agree that a kid should chase his "wannabe" dream over the "gonna be" reality of getting a college education. I keep going back to the example of Carl Green. Carl followed his dream of playing with the Harlem Globetrotters, but he had retained enough of the "gonna be" talks I had with him while he was in college that he became a successful businessman once he left the Globetrotters.

I learned from coaching that disappointment can come suddenly, but that it also quickly fades away. Once that disappointment is forgotten, one can concentrate on the much bigger goal of ultimate success. Here is one example.

On February 28, 1987, my Rams were playing our old foe Virginia Union in the second-round game of the CIAA tourney. We had played a fair season to that point—our record was 19-9—but we had not won a CIAA championship since 1977.

We were ahead 70-69 and on the verge of an upset. The seconds were winding down when Virginia Union called a time-out to try for a final run at the basket. When time started again, Virginia Union's center got close enough to throw two shots at the basket. He missed both times, but he also committed a traveling violation in the process of shooting the second time. The ball then bounced into the arms of another Virginia Union player. That player thought he heard a whistle announcing the travel. The player almost threw the ball into the stands in frustration. My players also thought they heard a whistle and stopped going for the ball. For a moment, everyone on the court froze in place, but one Virginia Union player grabbed the ball from his teammate and threw it up at the buzzer. The ball went into the goal, and the score changed to 71-70 in favor of Virginia Union. The game was over. We had lost.

All of the referees denied blowing a whistle to call the travel, but most of the players and people at courtside swore they heard a whistle that froze the players on both sides. We had lost on an uncalled travel and a phantom whistle that had allowed an opposing player to make an uncontested basket.

"I don't think I've ever felt so badly about losing a game," I said at the time. We were knocked out of what would have been a shot at the finals of the CIAA tournament. Coach Dave Robbins apologized to me for having to win like that. Though his team had won and had advanced to the finals, he felt badly for me.

I don't remember the details, but I think it was the next season when a refereeing error occurred in our favor and we beat Virginia Union. I had to apologize to Dave for our winning the game.

I learned from coaching that you should never stop preparing. Whenever I realized that my team was not going to be as strong as I would have liked, I would begin preparing for the coming season by going out and recruiting new players. If I already had all of my slots filled, I would begin practicing the team. I never coasted at the beginning of a season.

I don't think anyone should ever say "I've prepared enough" for a meeting, a game, or a profession. I found that the more I learned and the more I prepared, the better I was as a coach and as a person.

One thing I learned from coaching is so simple that my grandsons say it is the most important piece of advice that I have given them.

Don't be a dummy.

There are so many ways that piece of advice can be used.

It can be literally applied to the use of one's brain. Stay in school. Get the best education you possibly can and then use that education to make your life better. So many people are given the opportunity to go to high school and then college, and they throw away that opportunity by not going to classes regularly or even dropping out entirely. Once they are out of school, they ask society and the government for help in making a living. They portray themselves as victims of a poor education, when they consciously chose to ignore the educational opportunities given them.

It can be figuratively applied to how people conduct themselves. People who drink too much or who use illegal drugs remove themselves from the reality of life and fit the definition of dummies. If their drug abuse becomes harmful to themselves or others, they might even find themselves removed from society by being put in jail. I saw that happen to one of my best players. I never could understand how he allowed himself to be used by an inanimate substance like alcohol or drugs. He was the strongest player I ever had, but he gave in to his weakness.

I learned from coaching—and from being a parent—never to set too many rules.

Some coaches had lights-out rules. Some had bed checks. Some demanded this or that. And if you did not live by the coach's law, you were out.

I never did that. The only real rules I imposed on my players were to conduct themselves civilly to everyone they met on campus, to report to class, to report to practice, and to report to the games. Other than that, I expected them to use their own judgment as to how to conduct themselves as young men. In one sense, I was not giving them any limits at all, which theoretically would have allowed them to run wild. But in reality, they kept themselves in check because they knew I expected more of them.

If I had one hard-and-fast rule, it was that they treat everyone they met on campus with respect. My players knew from me that the lady

After my 800th win, this photograph was taken. It appears on my page at the Naismith Memorial Basketball Hall of Fame website.

in the lunchroom was just as important to me as the chancellor of the university. They had better not give her any "athlete attitude."

I don't understand why coaches tolerate "athlete attitude." Just because an athlete can play a child's game a little bit better than others on campus is no reason to let that kid think he has any more privileges than any other student on campus.

I am not saying that athletes should not have egos. That is part of being good. What I am saying is that athletes should keep those egos under control until they get on the court or the field. When they are not playing the game, they are no better than anyone else on campus.

In reality, by keeping my rules to a minimum, I was being more restrictive on my players. I was making them think how they should comport themselves. Part of the way I did that was to give them every opportunity to see how my family acted. Many of them had never experienced an intact family with a father, mother, and children sitting down to eat at the same table. Many of them had never had a mother asking them about homework and a father imposing discipline when it was necessary. For most of those kids, this simple exposure to family life was instructive in how they should raise their own families.

I learned from coaching that every student is motivated by something different, and that all kids will not respond to the same stimulus.

Some kids came to my teams already finished players. I never had to tell them a word as to how to play their position. Some kids were like clay and had to be molded into the kind of players I needed at that particular time.

Some kids wanted me to talk softly to them. Others wanted me to yell at them—they just didn't know they wanted me to yell at them.

Some wanted to fear me. Some wanted to love me. I think all of them wanted to respect me. They all knew I wanted to help them get through college and to become better basketball players along the way.

I think all my work with those players helped me to be a better parent.

Clarence Jr. remembers that one of his most important early jobs was being a ball boy for the Rams. Whenever anyone fell on the court, Clarence was out there in a flash, wiping up the sweat with a towel. He knew that sweat on the court could make another player fall in the same place, possibly hurting himself. Clarence took great pride in drying off that spot. I had given him a job of great responsibility. He knew it and appreciated it as the ball boy and as my trusted son. Today, Clarence Jr. laughs when he sees the sometimes casual way sweat is mopped up from a court. He swears no one was as efficient as making that court dry again as he was.

That may sound funny coming from an adult, but Clarence Jr. knew I depended on him for that job. That job was important to me and critical to the safety of all the players on the court. I think my trusting him with that job made him respect me just a little bit more as a dad.

Clarence Jr. sometimes reminds me that both Clara and I demonstrated to him and Lisa and all of my players how much we valued a college education by displaying our diplomas on the walls of our home. He has a point. We were teachers trying to convince young men that they should also be teachers. What better way to show our pride than to display the diplomas from our universities?

CHAPTER 19

What College Basketball Needs to Do

When I started recruiting players in the 1950s, I was always in search of a big man to play center, someone six-foot-seven or more. Finding that big man was difficult. Someone like Wilt Chamberlain at seven-foot-one was an aberration.

Now, when you look at the heights and weights of the players playing today, six-foot-seven is the average height. Players over seven feet tall are almost common. This increase in the height of the players has led to some calls to change the rules of basketball to fit the size of today's players.

Some people believe that with seven-foot players, the basket should be raised above the 10 feet it has been for more than 100 years in order to make dunking obsolete, or at least harder to achieve. I don't know about that. How far would you raise it—six inches? a foot? two feet? How high would the rim have to be before it got out of dunking range?

If you did raise the rim, that would mean that the tallest players—who are not necessarily the best players—would have an even greater advantage over the shorter players. By raising the basket, you would limit the type of play on the court by favoring the taller players. I don't think that is a good idea. It might also affect the vision of the fans sitting in some of the seats. Today's arenas were designed for 10-foot rims.

Another option might be to change the distance to the goal. In January of 2004, the NCAA rejected changing the three-point line from its current 19 feet, 9 inches to 22 feet. They also ruled that the free-throw line would stay 15 feet from the basket.

Personally, I think increasing the distance to the goal would increase the value of the three-point shot.

I've also wondered if widening the court from its current 50 feet might be a good idea. Widening the court would give the offensive players more room in which to operate and require the defensive players to cover more space. That could open up the game more and take away some of the height advantage of tall players who stay close to the goal. If the better shooters had more space from which to launch shots, that would increase their advantage over the taller players.

The problem with widening the floor, of course, is that it would require redesigning every college gym in the nation. Several rows of bleachers would have to be removed. At schools where the sport is already sold out, my idea would not be met with much enthusiasm by the bean counters, who are always looking for more ways to make money.

I doubt that anyone is going to listen to a retired coach suggesting changes to the basic rules of the game—changes that would cost them money. But I will offer a few ideas I think would improve college basketball.

I know the top prospects are always going to be lured to the professional ranks, sometimes right out of high school, like LeBron James, Kobe Bryant, and a handful of other players. Legally, I guess the question of barring those players from skipping or quitting college to head to the pro ranks has been dealt with years ago.

Still, high-school and college athletics are not supposed to be the minor leagues for the NBA. School is supposed to be where young people prepare themselves for entering the adult world, not where they practice their talents while waiting for the Nike film crew to arrive.

Isn't there some way for the professional owners and college coaches to work on a joint, massive educational plan aimed at high-school students that would emphasize the idea that a college education should be the ultimate goal of every talented sports star? Can't the NBA and the NCAA agree that a career in the professional ranks is icing on the cake for some college graduates, rather than a realistic dream for every high-school kid?

I am not talking about some agreement to force high-school and college players to stay in school before trying the professional ranks. That cat is out the bag, and such an agreement would probably be against antitrust laws.

I am talking about having professional athletes who have built real careers beyond their playing days convince high-school kids that their future could be assured if they combined a real, long-lasting career with a short-lasting athletic career. I want kids to know it is smarter to develop a real career in the real world than to gamble they will have a long professional sports career.

Would it not be impressive for a high-school student to hear from a man who is a football player in the fall and a lawyer during the other nine months? Would it not be inspiring to learn that a top college athlete is applying to medical school at the same time he is going into the professional draft? Maybe those dreams are reserved for the smartest of the smart. But would not a kid look up to a man playing professional basketball who spends his off-season working as a recreational director or as a sports coach for a club team?

Here is just one example that jumps to mind. Look at Alan Page, one of the "Purple People Eaters" on the defensive line of the Minnesota Vikings. He played professional football from 1967 to 1981. He got his law degree in 1978. He is now an associate justice on the Minnesota State Supreme Court. Every off-season, Page went to law school because he knew he would not be a football player nearly as long as he would be some other type of professional.

To accomplish results like this, of course, coaches and college administrators would have to make sure their recruits signed up for real majors. If those boys are really wrapped up in sports, let them major in education and learn how to be basketball or football coaches at the junior-high and high-school levels. Don't put them in "basketball theory" classes. I read one sports exposé book where a test question in one of those classes asked, "How many halves are in a basketball game?" I totally reject the label of "dumb athlete," and every coach and college president should, too.

Besides putting the education back into college athletics, I would also like for high-school recruits to reevaluate where they play. I want them to think about that old saying, "It's better to be a big fish in a small pond than a small fish in a big pond."

This is an unabashed attempt to suggest that good players look at the idea of bypassing Division I schools to play at Division II and even Division III schools. Good—but not fantastic—players have to face the reality that if they sign with a leading Division I university, they may be on the bench for at least their freshman year, if not their entire college career.

Good coaches often have more talent on their team than they can play at any one time. When Earl Monroe played for me in his freshman year, he sat on the bench. I did not need him. I had other talented players.

Sports have not changed that much in 40 years. Extremely talented freshmen may start at some Division I schools, but most can expect to ride the wood. On the other hand, Division II schools are more open to playing freshmen. The reason, of course, is that the talent pool is only so deep. If a Division II school is able to grab a top-notch player out of high school, that coach would be foolish not to play him as much as he can. The top Division I schools, however, have sophomores, juniors, and seniors they have to keep happy and have to keep from trying to make the jump to the NBA.

What I am suggesting is that, in addition to evaluating the academic offerings of schools, talented high-school players should also evaluate how much playing time they will really get if they join a particular school. The prospect should ask the coach how he expects to find an open slot if the starting positions are already filled. I am willing to bet top Division I coaches will have a hard time answering that question, while Division II and III coaches will have an easier time.

Then the recruited high-school player should ask himself the question, "Is it better to be seen on regional and national television sitting on the bench in Division I, or is it better to have the newspapers writing about how I came through in the clutch and won the Division II championship?"

My point is that moderately talented players are more valuable to Division II and III teams than they are to Division I schools that normally recruit top-of-the-line players. If a small college has a strong academic program in a major that interests the player, then that player could be noticed faster—and get more credit for—advancing the smaller school's athletic program. Another way for the player and his parents to look at this suggestion is that if the player is really good, the press and the professional scouts will find him quicker at a smaller school where he stands out than at a larger school where he blends into the rest of the roster.

As an extension of that point, I would rather Division II colleges strengthen their programs than succumb to the lure of moving up to Division IAA and then Division IA. When they move up to a higher division, schools have to invest hundreds of thousands of dollars, even millions, to expand and sometimes create more sports teams for both men and women. What happens if a Division II school simply does not have that many students interested in women's bowling or volleyball?

I will admit that some of my feeling is personal. In 1970, seven colleges that used to be CIAA schools formed the Mid-Eastern Athletic Conference. Jumping to the new conference were former CIAA foes such as North Carolina A&T, North Carolina Central, Howard, Morgan State, and the University of Maryland Eastern Shore. Later, other CIAA schools like Norfolk State and Hampton joined. North Carolina Central came back to Division II in the CIAA.

When the MEAC was formed and some CIAA schools left to join it, Winston-Salem State University was left without its most natural rival, North Carolina A&T, located less than 30 miles away. In the '50s and '60s, the games between these two schools were natural sellouts. Now, we cannot play each other as conference rivals, but Division I schools can play us in exhibition games. That way, we can play North Carolina A & T, and in the fall of 2004, we play Wake Forest for the first official time.

The MEAC's membership is too spread out to be as fan-friendly as the CIAA. Bethune-Cookman is in Florida. Delaware State is in Delaware. How can fans be expected to cover the long distances between the games? By contrast, the CIAA schools are in North Carolina, Virginia, and Maryland. CIAA games are much closer, allowing fans to support their teams.

Of course, as I say this, Winston-Salem State University is also thinking of moving up to Division IAA. As I said before, I never talked school policy for the administration, but I personally believe in a strong small school over a weak large school.

And that, my friends, is where I guess I will leave it. I am not in a position to give much advice and have anyone take it, but it sure is fun offering it anyway.

Some of you may be wondering what Big House is doing today.

Clara and I still live in Winston-Salem, where we stay active in St. Paul United Methodist Church and a number of social and civic activities. Once a week, she and I deliver Meals on Wheels to shut-ins. I go to Rotary once a week, where they still tell the story of how I invited the whole club to attend one of our Rams home games. I sat them right behind me on the bench, so they could see the action up close. At the next Rotary meeting, they complained that I blocked their vision of the court because I was always standing up and yelling at the officials or my team. Well, you can't please everyone all the time.

I participate in several medical research studies at Wake Forest University Baptist Medical Center. It is nothing serious. I just like to entertain doctors who wonder how an 81-year-old man who once weighed 295 pounds is still around to taunt them.

I still go to every Rams home basketball game. I have to go to those games. My name is on the outside of the building, the C. E. Gaines

As I've said before, in this book and always to friends and family, Clara has always been with me in the good times and the bad. This picture was taken after my 800th win.

*Hey! I can even win at riding lawn mowers! This was taken
sometime in the 1970s, judging from the clothes I'm wearing.
This was a "celebrity" race at Bowman Gray Stadium, where
WSSU played its football games.*

(Photo by Frank Jones, courtesy of Clarence E. Gaines personal collection)

Center. I even go see Wake Forest games on occasion. I even go see the
Wake Forest women's team. That is how much I still enjoy the sport of
basketball.

Clara and I go to the CIAA tournament each year to see my old
players and old rivals and to spread stories about both. Even if you do
not particularly like basketball, going to the CIAA tournament is a must.
It is part tourney, part show, part family gathering. It is one of the few
tournaments where many of the fans of teams defeated early hang
around for all of the games. There is so much to do and there are so
many old friends to see that no one wants to go home, even if their
favorite basketball team has.

I keep up with what is happening in college basketball at all division levels. As I write this, I am hoping that my old Philadelphia prospect John Chaney of Temple University will make a good run for the NCAA Division I championship next year. Our mutual buddy John Thompson went all the way in 1984, and there is no reason why John can't do it also.

I also hope that one of my former players, 1992 graduate Monte Ross, an assistant coach with Saint Joseph's University, will have the thrill of making it to the Final Four one day. His team was 27-1 just before the 2004 NCAA playoffs began. If they go all the way and win the Division I championship one day, it will be a Cinderella story that I will enjoy. Saint Joseph's got knocked off in 2004, but there is always next year. I had 47 years of waiting until next year. Better yet, maybe some Division I school will pick up Monte as a head coach.

I am part of a committee that nominates old veterans to the Naismith Memorial Basketball Hall of Fame in Springfield, Massachusetts. I come in handy on the committee because I am old enough to remember firsthand the contributions of many of the old-timers. My other committee members don't always take my advice, but at least I am a voice for those who are up for the honor.

When given the chance, I urge young boys to join the Boy Scouts of America, the organization with which I have my longest association, going back more than 75 years. I still count my first Scout leader, Tommy Withrow, as one of the big influences on my life outside of my loving parents, grandparents, uncles, and aunts. I was rewarded by the Boy Scouts with the Order of the Silver Buffalo several years ago for my volunteer service through the decades.

Clara and I visit our children, grandchildren, and godchildren so we can offer them advice, whether they want it or not. Offering advice is what old people are supposed to do and what coaches were specifically trained to do.

When I am not doing anything else, I take phone calls from my former players. I enjoy hearing from all of them and learning what they and their kids and now their grandkids are doing today. When we talk, we might touch on the championships won on the football field and the basketball court, or the times I made them practice when they did not feel like it, or the racism they had to overcome in the days of segregation.

But rather than dwelling on their old days as players, we are more likely to talk about what they did as students and how they became adults pursuing their chosen professions. When I hear that I helped a young boy become a responsible man, I know that I did the right thing by skipping dental school to become a coach in 1945.

When these boys, most growing into old men themselves, continue to call their old coach to thank him for helping them get a college degree, it makes me proud to answer to the nickname of Big House.

Acknowledgments

Carter Cue, the archivist at the Winston-Salem State University Archives at the O'Kelly Library on campus, was invaluable in tracking down historical articles and photographs and in identifying players. He has an amazing memory and a sense of organization that helped assemble all this material into a history.

Billy Rich of Winston-Salem helped guide the writing of the manuscript by offering ideas and insights into my career.

Shera L. White, director of public relations for the CIAA, provided some photographs from their archives. The CIAA remains the most exciting conference in all of basketball.

Claudette Weston of Weston & Associates contributed background material and provided me with support during my coaching years. Whenever anything needs to get done in Winston-Salem, people turn to Claudette.

The staff of the *Winston-Salem Journal* Archives allowed access to old newspaper clippings about my career and the college careers of my players.

Bill Patterson and all the staff of the Public Information Office at Winston-Salem State University are going to be invaluable in promoting this book to alumni and friends of the university.

Molly G. Rawls, the photo archivist at the Forsyth County Public Library, and the rest of the staff at the library helped in finding photos and working with the microfilm machines to refresh memories about old basketball games.

I could not have won all those games without the help of men like Harold Clawson, Waltin Young, Leon Whitley, Les Gaither, Cleo Hill, and all those other Winston-Salem Teachers College graduates too numerous to name who scouted players for me. While they are mentioned in the text, they need just one more thanks from me. Scores of "kids" who are now productive members of society came to Winston-Salem at the recommendation of these men. Those kids became teachers, school administrators, recreation directors, college professors, doctors, and lawyers—participants in every career that one could imagine.

I want to thank a couple of people not mentioned in the text who took me under their wing—Coach Norm Sloan of North Carolina State University, who recommended me for teaching overseas basketball clinics, and Charlie Harville, who showed me how TV sportscasting works.

I also want to thank Vivienne Conley, who spent more than thirty years at WSSU leading the dance and cheerleading programs; Marcellene Scales, who handled many other aspects of WSSU's women's athletic programs; Albert Roseboro, who performed many jobs at WSSU, including succeeding me as athletic director; Harold Bell a former football player at WSSU and now a sports writer in Washington, D.C., who always stuck with the school's fortunes in good times and bad; and Ernie Pitt, publisher of *The Winston-Salem Chronicle,* who always supported the school.

I need to thank the staff of John F. Blair, Publisher, for believing the autobiography of an old coach is worth reading.

Finally, I want to thank all the folks who threw their arms around the black coaches who finally broke into NCAA Division I. Men like John Thompson, John Chaney, Tubby Smith, George Raveling, and Nolan Richardson were able to demonstrate their skills thanks to dozens of people who believed in them. The crossing over of blacks into formerly all-white sports was finally accomplished when these capable men were given their chance.

Index

Vines, Theodore, 64, 67 (photos)

Virginia State University, 76, 88, 92, 103, 130, 157, 185, 251, 256, 264

Virginia Union University: and CIAA, 76, 153; and Earl Lloyd, 103; and Dave Robbins, 260, 270; 1940s Morgan State opponent, 52, 53; 1940s CIAA championships, 130; 1950s CIAA championships, 136; 1960s CIAA championships, 153, 157, 185, 188, 191, 192, 216; 1970s CIAA championships, 250, 257; 1980s CIAA championships, 283, 284

WAAA Radio, 214

Wachovia Bank, 15

Wake Forest Baptist Medical Center, 294

Wake Forest University, ix, x, 147, 148, 149, 151, 158, 167, 221, 246, 294

Walcott, Eugene. *See* Farrakhan, Louis

Walker, LeRoy, 242

Wallace, Cleo, 99

Wallace, Kevin, 99

Warner, Ed, 116

Washington, D.C., 43, 45, 125

Watkins, Johnny, 224, 232 (photo)

Wellman, Charles, 64, 67, 73 (photos)

West Virginia State University, 77, 103, 104, 130, 185

Westminster College (Pa.), 159

Westminster College (Utah), 159

Whitaker Gym, 126, 147, 148 (photo), 158, 167, 172, 179, 223

White, Sherman, 116, 155

Whitley, Leon: as player, 133, 186, 187; as recruiter, 185, 188, 202, 203, 204, 205, 208, 222; photo of, 106

Wilberforce College, 75, 142, 144

Wiley, Lutheran, 191 (photo), 193

Wilkins, Lenny, 263

Williams, Bobby, 153, 154 (photo), 157, 174

Williams, Kenneth, 143 (photo)

Wilson, Jodie, 131 (photo)

Wilson, Howard "Brutus": as head coach, 63, 65, 66, 67, 68, 69, 71; photos of, 60, 64; recruits Big House as assistant coach, 59, 61, 64, 278

Wilson, Jodie, 131,

Winston-Salem Coliseum. *See* Memorial Coliseum

Winston-Salem Journal, 134, 147, 158, 167, 170, 212, 222, 228, 254, 257

Winston-Salem, N.C.: as home, 250, 258, 266; description of, 61-62, fan support in, 214, 231, 233; recruiting players to, 105, 109, 173, 180; using sports to integrate, 146, 150, 167, 168, 223, 230

Winston-Salem State University: as Slater Industrial and State Normal School, 62; basketball scrimmages with Wake Forest, 149-50, 221; general references as Winston-Salem Teachers College and Winston-Salem State University, 171, 174, 184, 223, 273, 276; recruitment to, 186, 195, 202, 206, 230; responsibilities to, 74, 76, 97; team nicknames, 65; track team, 128, 129; 1940s basketball teams, 9, 63, 72, 73, 79, 8, 90; 1940s football team, 9, 64, 65, 68, 71, 72, 79, 80, 243; 1940s history of, 59, 63, 64, 278; 1950s basketball teams, 119, 105, 106, 130, 131, 136, 146, 148, 150, 154, 166, 196; 1950s history of, 124, 126, 136, 144, 250; 1960s basketball teams, ix, 154, 157, 158, 173, 185, 188, 190, 193, 211, 216, 221-37; 1960s history of, 231; 1970s basketball teams, 240, 250, 256, 257, 259, 260; 1980s basketball teams, 261, 263, 270; 1990s basketball teams, 271, 272, 274, 281

Winston-Salem Teachers College. *See* Winston-Salem State University

Wiseman, Nathaniel, 162

Withrow, Tommy, 36, 297

Witttenburg, 192

Wooden, John, 92

World Basketball Tournament, 267

Wright, Johnny, 10

YMCA, 83, 107, 123, 125, 129, 168, 263

Young, Waltin, 140, 142, 144